CW01072439

This book presents the proceedings of the Ada-Europe International Conference held in Dublin, June 1990. These meetings constitute the most significant events in this field within Europe, and attract delegates from around the world.

This year's conference takes as its theme the impact of technical and management issues in the software engineering economics of Ada, as well as technology transfer and training. With the start of a new decade in which Ada comes of age both in terms of use and acceptability, papers also assess the impact of Ada through descriptions of projects in which Ada has been used throughout their life cycle. Discussion of topical issues affecting the development of Ada 9X is also presented.

The papers will make informed and essential reading for all involved in the use of Ada in industry and research.

Ada®: Experience and Prospects

The Ada Companion Series

There are currently no better candidates for a co-ordinated, low risk, and synergetic approach to software development than the Ada programming language. Integrated into a support environment, Ada promises to give a solid standards-orientated foundation for higher professionalism in software engineering.

This definitive series aims to be the guide to the Ada software industry for managers, implementors, software producers and users. It will deal with all aspects of the emerging industry: adopting an Ada strategy, conversion issues, style and portability issues, and management. To assist the organised development of an Ada-oriented software components industry, equal emphasis will be placed on all phases of life cycle support.

Some current titles:

Ada: Languages, compilers and bibliography
Edited by M.W. Rogers

Proceedings of the 1985 Ada International Conference
Edited by J.G.P. Barnes and G.A. Fisher

Ada for specification: possibilities and limitations
Edited by S.J. Goldsack

Concurrent programming in Ada
A. Burns

Selecting an Ada environment
Edited by T.G.L. Lyons and J.C.D. Nissen

Ada components: Libraries and tools
Proceedings of the 1987 Ada-Europe International Conference
Edited by S. Tafvelin

Ada: the design choice
Proceedings of the 1989 Ada-Europe International Conference
Edited by A. Alvarez

Distibuted Ada: developments and experiences
Proceedings of the Distributed Ada '89 Symposium, Southampton
Edited by J.M. Bishop

Ada: Experiences and prospects

Proceedings of the Ada-Europe International Conference
Dublin 12-14 June 1990

Edited by

BARRY LYNCH

Generics Software Ltd,
Dublin, Ireland

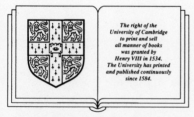

The right of the
University of Cambridge
to print and sell
all manner of books
was granted by
Henry VIII in 1534.
The University has printed
and published continuously
since 1584.

CAMBRIDGE UNIVERSITY PRESS

Cambridge
New York   Port Chester   Melbourne   Sydney

Published by the Press Syndicate of the University of Cambridge
The Pitt Building, Trumpington Street, Cambridge CB2 1RP
40 West 20th Street, New York, NY 10011, USA
10 Stamford Road, Oakleigh, Melbourne 3166, Australia

First published 1990

Printed in Great Britain at the University Press, Cambridge

Library of Congress Cataloguing in Publication data available

British Library Cataloguing in Publication data available

ISBN 0 521 39522 4

"The spectacles of experience;
through them you will see clearly a second time"

CONTENTS

PREFACE

The annual Ada Europe Conference is now in its ninth year. 1990 heralds the beginning of a new decade and the end of one in which Ada came of age in terms of use and acceptability. Now is the time to reflect on the past and to look to the future in the light of our experiences. Hence the theme of the conference: *"Experiences and Prospects"*. Papers were sought describing experiences of using Ada throughout the project life-cycle.

Additionally, Ada is going through a crucial phase of assessment and enhancement: the standard is under examination and changes can be proposed through the 9X process. The outcome of this will determine the shape of Ada through to the next century. This conference falls mid way through this activity and is thus an ideal forum for discussion of topical issues.

Over 60 extended abstracts were submitted and thanks to a distinguished panel of over 30 referees, each paper was separately refereed by 5 individuals. I thank each of the referees (listed at the end of this book) for their professionalism, attention to detail and promptness in returning the papers. Because of the quality and number of submissions, 30 papers have been accepted for presentation. The papers were chosen by the Programme Committee based on the evaluations of the referees. For their dedication in performing this difficult task, I extend my gratitude to the members of the P.C.:

Angel Alvarez
John Avramopoulos
Toomas Käer
Hans-Jürgen Kugler

I specially mention the local organisation of the conference and exhibition by Ada Ireland. Without the help of my colleagues Avril Tobin and Hans-Jürgen Kugler of Generics Software, Dudley Dolan of BIS Beecom and Andrew Fleming of A.M.S., none of this would have been possible.

My thanks also to Alan Harvey and Cambridge University Press for their cooperation in arranging the publication of these proceedings in the Ada Companion Series.

Barry Lynch

Programme Committee Chairman

PART I: Ada Application Experience I - Commerical Systems

MARC: A Telecom System in Ada

Ingemar Häggström

TELESOFT, Telelogic AB, 149 80 Nynäshamn, Sweden

ABSTRACT

This paper presents our experiences of using Ada in the MARC project. MARC is Swedish Telecom's system for supervision of PABX's. (Private Automatic Branch eXchange, i.e. program-controlled private telephone switches). The development of MARC started in the fall of 1983, making it one of the first Ada applications in Sweden. Since then, four major releases of the system have been delivered. In this paper, Ada's influence on software development and life-cycle costs are discussed. Furthermore, a comparision is made between the average CoCoMo-project and MARC.

1. INTRODUCTION

Ada was used as early as autumn 1983, during the first development stage of MARC, making MARC one of the first Ada applications in Sweden (if not the first). The suppliers of Ada technology had only just started up, and the earlier products were characterized by long delays whilst the compiler translated the Ada code to machine code, and also by slow program execution. But since then, development has been rapid, and now six years later, Ada is beginning to live up to its high expectations.

During the same period, new functions have continuously been added to the MARC system. MARC is a centralized system which monitors the operation of PABX's. When certain alarms are detected, MARC automatically repairs the fault.

The present software release of MARC, MARC 2.1, runs on the Micro-VAX computer at four locations in Sweden. Approximately 1500 PABX's are supervised by the system. The software is 90% written in Ada and the total volume of software is 32500 lines of code (semicolons).

Five major software releases of MARC have been delivered since 1984:

1. MARC 1a

In 1984, MARC 1a was developed for the retrieving and analysis of the error message buffer from the SL1-PABX. The system was run on a Motorola 68000 based computer.

2. MARC 1bc

In 1986, MARC 1bc was delivered. This system handles a number of different types of PABX and is run on a Micro-VAX computer.

3. MARC 2

In the summer of 1988, MARC 2 appeared, this being a general system for supervision and control. MARC consists of a platform upon which different applications are built. MARC 2 can handle up to 15 users simultaneously, and 10 simultaneous sessions to PABX´s. The project team consisted of six system engineers with an average of four years´ experience of software construction. Approximately 4600 semicolons of Ada-code were reused from the MARC 1bc system. 27900 semicolons of new code were developed. The system consists of only one Ada main program, the size of the executable image is 4 Mbyte.

4. MARC 3 prototype

During 1988, MARC 2 was enhanced with a prototype for automatic repair. In an expert-system environment, the Service Technician creates 'Service directives'. A ´Service directive´ can be activated when an alarm is reported. MARC then calls up the system and carries out automatic repair in accordance with the 'Service directive'.

5. MARC 3.1

Development of a Network Management interface in MARC. The size of the system was increased by another 6200 semicolons.

In the planning of each MARC project the waterfall model has been used. The following abbreviations for the different phase-names are used throughout this paper.

PaR   Planning and Requirements

PD   Product Design. Modularization of the system.

DD   Detail Design. Design of each individual module.

CUT   Code and Unit Test. Coding and validation of each module.

IT   Integration and System Test.

2.   DESIGN AND DEVELOPMENT EXPERIENCES

In the design of the MARC system, the aim was to use a object-orientated design methodology. Items that are logically related were collected together in objects. In the modularization, each object was implemented as an Ada package.

This strategy of combining object-orientation with Ada´s packaging concept has proved most successful. New functionalities have been added to the system at low cost. Significantly, it has only been necessary to modify the software in one place.

2.1   Product Design Phase

At the end of the Product Design phase, the Ada compiler was used to validate the program interfaces (i.e. the package specifications). All program interfaces in MARC are implemented at procedures and functions. This early compilation high-lighted some of the problems in the design.

2.2   Detail Design Phase

At the end of the Detail Design phase the design was validated once more with the compiler. At this stage all types, records and procedures in the program interfaces were declared. By compiling the system in the DD-phase, the coding phase could start with an executable system, with all package bodies implemented as empty stubs.

2.3   Coding and Unit Test Phase

In the coding phase a set of rules was followed to improve the readability of the software.

    A. Naming rules for source-code files, package names and object names.

    B. To ensure program readability, fullname references were required instead of using "use" clauses.

    C. Source program layout standards.

In the MARC system generic components are widely used. Experience of using generics in the MARC project is highly favourable. The conclusion drawn from the MARC 2 project was that generics should have been used to even a greater extent. Generic components are more expensive per code-line than non-generic, but the gains are obvious when the generic component is used several times in the project.

Already in the Design phase of an Ada software project, it is relevant to analyze where it would be appropriate to use generics, as well as taking an inventory of what can be reused from previous projects or retrieved from the component library.

Ada tasks have been used frequently in the MARC system. Approximately 100 tasks have been implemented in the MARC software.

Tasks are used for solving the following types of problem:

- IO-operations on serial ports.

- Parallel activities. One task checks that the terminal is not left inactive, and another that the modem connection has not been broken.

- Allocation of jobs. The clocks in the PABX's are adjusted upon transfer to summertime. A controller task queues a job for each PABX. A number of subordinate tasks carry out the connection, session and disconnection with the PABX. When a controller receives information that a modem port is free it allocates a job to the free port.

- External event standby. An alarm task stands by to read an alarm report from a computer port alerted by the alarm transmitters.

2.4   Integration and System Test Phase

The integration test phase proved to be a lot shorter in the MARC-project compared to the traditional project.

The analysis of the the MARC project confirms that Ada projects are front-end loaded. A traditional non-Ada project adheres, according to Reifer (3), to the 40:20:40 rule, where software effort is allocated 40% to requirements and design, 20% to coding and 40% on testing. According to Reifer(3), Ada developments tend to follow a 50:15:35 distribution.

In the MARC 2 project the distribution was 47:26:27. The fact that less effort had to be spent on testing can be due to Ada´s strong typing and Ada´s ability to check program interfaces.

In MARC the use of the pragmas Supress and Priority substanially improved performance when executing the program. Pragma Supress specifies that all checks are supressed unconditionally. This facility should, at the earliest, be introduced at the end of the IT-phase when all logical program errors have been sorted out. Pragma Priority is used to give some tasks higher priority than others. If several tasks are in a wait-state the task with the highest priority is run first.

In the Ada environment, in which the MARC system is developed, there is a good Library-manager tool. Other tools were badly missed. For example:

 - A tool to optimize task sizes. Tasks were declared as task types and it took much trial-and-error to optimize the size.

- Recompilation tool. A tool that checks the modification dates and only compiles the part of the system that has to be compiled.
- Configuration Management tool.

3. MAINTAINABILITY AND PORTABILITY

The maintenance costs have been extremly low for the various MARC releases. During a 24 month period, of operation of MARC 1 bc, bug-fixing has incurred work cost, amounting to less than 1% per year of the development cost.

For MARC 2, during the first 18 months of operation, bug-fixing has incurred work cost, amounting to approximately 2% per year of the the development cost. I.e. 200 hours per year, out of a 10000-hour development project

The portability issue has been important when developing MARC. The system has been designed to run on different H/W-platforms. The MARC 1a -prototype was ported from a M68000-computer to a VAX-computer in approximately two man-months. This is primarily explained by few dependencies to the operating system and the use of an IO-subsystem product.

The MARC 1bc-system was ported from the DEC-Ada compilation environment to Telesoft-Ada environment in one man-month.

4. A COST ANALYSIS

The MARC 1bc and MARC 2 projects used Boehms CoCoMo model (1) as the project estimation tool. CoCoMo is one of the most common models for costing software projects.

An estimate is made of the expected program volume. The semi-colon computation is used as a measure of program volume. Semi-colon count is generally accepted for measuring the size of Ada programs. According to Harbaugh,Saunders (2) semi-colon count is the best line of code metric for Ada.

For MARC 2, the total volume corresponds to 32,500 semi-colons from 98,400 compiled lines. After the code volume estimation is made, 15 CoCoMo cost parameters are set. There are parameters for weighing in the project group's capacity; the quality of the development environment; the prerequisites of the project and the type of system to be constructed.

All the input data is fed into the CoCoMo model, and out come suggestions regarding project time-scheduling and manning plans. CoCoMo also calculates time consumption for the various phases of the project.

From the results of table 1, we can draw the following conclusions:

• Productivity in the MARC 2 project is 31 percent higher than for the "average CoCoMo-project". This may be based on a number of factors, but the two most important are the use of Ada, and the well-known axiom that "each job fills the time available to it".

• Integration has required considerably less work in MARC 2 than in the average project.

• Ada projects do not appear to follow Brook's Law, which states that consumption of resources increases exponentially when the program size increases (because of increased administration and increased internal communication). Instead, the results from MARC 2 show that the percentage of administration cost is reduced in larger projects.

• Normally, the first project should give 10-15 percent lower productivity, because of the learning factor. A comparison of MARC 1bc and MARC 2 indicates that the learning effect for Ada is greater than this.

Experience of using the CoCoMo model shows that it operates according to the principle of "garbage in, garbage out". It is important that the model be calibrated with at least 2-3 projects before results can be regarded as reliable. What saved MARC 2 from entering the statistics of non-delivered systems was that two miscalculations cancelled each other out.

Miscalculation 1 - the program size was underestimated. What had been estimated at 9,300 new semi-colons became 27,900 new semi-colons.

Miscalculation 2 - the CoCoMo parameters were incorrectly set, in particular the competence within the project group was undervalued.

Table 1 compares three CoCoMo runs with the actual result of the MARC 2 project:

Table 1:	Project phases (hours/phase)				
	PR	PD	DD+CUT	IT	Total
A. MARC2 Calc.	550	1,300	3,400	1,500	6,750
B. MARC2 as should have been	1,850	4,490	11,270	5,500	23,110
C. MARC 2 after calibration (The average project)	854	2,284	5,208	2,254	10,598
MARC2 result	423	1,335	4,666	1,689	8,113

Table 1: Shows a comparison of three CoCoMo runs. Calculation is based on 9,300 new semi-colons. In B, the actual number of 27,900 semi-colons has been entered. In C, the cost parameters have been calibrated with the knowledge obtained during the course of the project. See table 2.

Table 2:		MARC 1bc calc.	MARC 2 calc.	MARC 2 calibr.
HSM	(Hours per month)	130	140	140
Mode	(embedded-semi-org.)	embedded	semi	organic
PCAP	(Programmers capacity)	nominal	high	very-high
ACAP	(Analysts capacity)	nom	nom	high
AEXP	(Application experience)	low	nom	high
RELY	(Reliability requirements)	nom	high	high
DATA	(Database capacity)	nom	high	high
CPLX	(Product complexity)	nom	high	high
MODP	(Modern dev. methods)	nom	high	high
TURN	(Results waiting time)	low	nom	low
VIRT	(Changes in dev. env.)	low	nom	nom

Table 2 Shows the setting of the CoCoMo parameters for MARC 1bc and MARC 2 projects. The figures farthest right are a subsequent calibration of MARC 2 following knowledge obtained during the course of the project.

Table 3:	Program Size (Semicolon)	Productivity (Semicolon/month)
MARC 1bc	10,970	140
MARC 2	27,900	480
MARC 3 prototype	9,120	490
MARC 3.1	6,200	250

Table 3: Comparison of productivity within the various MARC projects.

5. CONCLUSIONS

The findings obtained from the MARC project indicate that the choice of Ada as the programming language has given the following positive results:

• Lower development costs. For individual projects such as MARC 2, productivity was shown to be 31 percent higher than the "average CoCoMo-project", in accordance with a calibrated CoCoMo-model.

• Better quality. During almost four years of operation of the MARC system, error corrections have required a work input of approximately 1.5% a year of total development cost.

• A systems architecture which reduces the cost of introducing new functions. With MARC, it has been possible to combine Ada with an object-orientated design method. Logically-related items are collected together in the objects and implemented as Ada packages.

6. REFERENCES

(1) Barry W. Boehm, Software Engineering Economics, Prentice-Hall, 1981.

(2) Harbaugh, Saunders: GKS/Ada Post mortem a Cost Analysis. Sigada, Ada Letters, December 1987.

(3) Donald J. Reifer: Ada´s impact , a Quantitative Assessment. Sigada, Ada Letters, December 1987.

COST EFFECTIVENESS OF USING ADA IN AIR TRAFFIC CONTROL SYSTEMS

By **Pierre ANDRIBET**

Director of ATC software development
THOMSON-CSF/SDC
18, avenue du Marechal Juin
92363 Meudon La Foret Cedex
FRANCE

Phone number: 33.1.4094 3214
FAX number : 33.1.4094 3229

The Air Traffic Control (ATC) Department of THOMSON-CSF's Division SDC (Defence and Control Systems) has been using the ADA language for developing Software in ATC centres for about 6 years, and since then, four complete ATC centres have been produced using ADA and four more are undergoing development.

Based on this experience, this paper intends:

-       to point out all the elements of cost of software development in ADA for ATC centres,

-       to describe the advantages of ADA from the standpoint of cost effectiveness:

    .   by quantifying the reusability ratio for each developed ATC centre,

    .   and coming from our experience, by giving some examples of reusability explaining the improvement induced by ADA.

This document breaks down in two main parts:

-       the first one describes what are the activities of the THOMSON's Air Traffic Control Department, the purpose of the software in these activities, and why ADA has been chosen in 1984,

- the second part identifies the main elements of software development cost, and analyses for each element what is the cost impact of using ADA.

1   INTRODUCTION : SOFTWARE IN ATC SYSTEMS

1.1   Activities of the THOMSON's ATC Department

For more than 25 years, the Air traffic Control (ATC) Department of THOMSON-CSF's Division SDC (Defence and Control Systems) has been supplying complete systems for in-flight detection and guidance of aircraft.

The attached figure 1 shows a simplified diagram of such a system.

The main elements comprising such an infrastructure are as follows:

- Primary Radars : conventional radar, operating through reflection of microwaves by the target,

- Secondary Radars : interactive radar, interrogating the target which returns information,

- Navaids : ground-based beacons used by aircraft for navigation and landing guidance purposes,

- Control centres : these centres receive pre-processed information from the various radars and synthesize this information by means of a set of processing computers.
  Pictures of the aerial situation, and data relative to evolution of the flight plans, are displayed to the air traffic controllers.

- Training simulator : the purpose of a simulator is to train controllers in the various procedures required in all air traffic control situations which may arise.
  This is achieved through simulation of radar information by a computer and selection of this information by an instructor (playing the part of a pilot).

1.2   Purpose of the Software

Every equipment unit we produce calls upon integration of software at a varying degree.

Naturally, from the beginning (25 years) ATC centres and simulators made the broadest use of software, but radars are increasingly calling upon software for data extraction, tracking and for the execution of their remote monitoring and remote maintenance functions.

In addition, this last function of remote monitoring and maintenance concerns also the navaids which are installed in unmanned buildings.

As a matter of fact, at each stage of the processing line, the part of the software is drastically increasing and is replacing hardware functions in order to provide more and more sophisticated capabilities and to improve the reliability and the availability of the system.

But for various reasons (use of different computers, CPU power problems) different languages was used on the different stages of the processing line; i.e FORTRAN, PASCAL, Assembly languages ...

To cope with this heterogeneousness, THOMSON-CSF ATC Department decided in 1984 to choose a common language for all the software on the whole processing line.

1.3   Selection of the Programming Language

Given this context, the selection of the proper programming language was of utmost importance.

In 1984 ADA was selected, and this selection was based on the following requirements:

-    Utmost final quality in order to achieve real-time reliability capable of meeting the required safety criteria,

-    Ease of teamwork (production of a control centre software project often calls upon more than 20 persons),

-    Ease of maintenance and evolution capability, the effective lifespan of a processing line often exceeds 10 or even 20 years,

-    Improving reusability of programs from one project to the other in order to lower costs in the international marketplace,

-    Providing utmost portability, some software modules having to run in different environnements.

NOTE :
>   The real-time constraint in the field of air traffic control is a specially critical one. Indeed, it would be utterly useless to display belatedly the position of an aircraft usually flying at 450 knots.

The ADA language was initially introduced in the ATC centre installed at KASTRUP/COPENHAGEN, the contract for which was signed in April 1984; the software for the central computers of this project (four DATA GENERAL MV10000), representing more than 300,000 source-code lines, was entirely written in ADA language.

This system was put in operational service on 17 February 1988.

Since then, other Air traffic control centres and simulators have been produced in ADA by THOMSON-CSF; these are:

-   control centres in KENYA,

-   control centres in PAKISTAN,

-   simulator in SWITZERLAND,

-   simulator in IRELAND,

Still others are undergoing development:

-   control centre and simulator for BELGIUM (CANAC system),

-   control centre and simulator for the DUTCH Air Force (PHAROS system),

-   control centres and simulators for NEW-ZEALAND (AMP system),

-   control centres for IRELAND (CAIRDE system).

2   COST EFFECTIVENESS OF USING ADA IN ATC SYSTEMS

To analyse the cost impact of using ADA in Air traffic Control systems, mainly five points must be considered:

-   initial investments; i.e, improvement of development environment, and development of real-time basic software,

-   marginal cost of each project; i.e development cost of each project, taking into account the reusability from other projects,

- cost of "maintenance"; i.e cost of the improvement of the system reliability, from the factory acceptance test and until the system is put in operational service,

- cost impact on hardware configuration,

- miscellaneous; i.e identification of all the other points important from the standpoint of costs but impossible to quantify.

2.1   Initial Investments

Ada is often said to be "complete" and to provide all the necessary capabilities in term of software engineering as well as in term of real-time operating system.

But when THOMSON-CSF's ATC Department tried to develop CATCAS project in 1984, it became evident that ADA is not "complete" enough.

Indeed, when starting to use ADA, two drawbacks mainly appeared in ADA environment that requires initial investments:

- The software development workshop was rather poor; i.e although it is compulsory for large scale project to have software configuration management tools, nothing is required, for this purpose, in the ADA Language Reference Manual (ALRM), except of course that ADA and associated Library manager provide an automatic check of consistency between all the modules.
  But this is not sufficient, and then THOMSON was obliged to develop a minimum set of tools to improve the management of the software development.
  To do that the amount of used manpower was 30 m.m (man.months).

- In term of real-time, ADA provides only a very basic mechanism (rendez-vous), then for quality reasons (simplicity, maintenability and readability) it is mandatory to develop real-time packages, in order to encapsulate the basic real-time mechanisms and to provide programmers with only high level services for inter-task communication and synchronisation (in our case, providing of a FIFO manager, and of locking services for shared memory access).
  In addition, some IO packages for serial lines and ethernet network management (radar input, inter computers transmission, Radar display connexion,...) had been developed.
  To do that the amount of used manpower was 70 m.m (man.months).

NOTE :

The tools that are compulsory to develop depends on
the environment provided by the computer, in 1984 the
ADA environment provided by Data General was the first
one, and because of that, the environment was strictly
limited to the requirements written in the ALRM.

In the present context, much more tools are available
on the different existing ADA environments and the
initial investments would be different for starting in
ADA.

For instance, we are now developing some systems - or
part of systems- on new computers based on UNIX and on
a new generation of ADA compiler.

In this new environment, we have decided to implement
the same real-time mechanisms than in the previous
generation of systems; but our new implementation
choices are based on the standard ADA tasking which
can be considered, now, as efficient enough.

This choice will improve our computer independancy,
and the cost of the basic environment to be developped
is expected to be lower than in the previous
environment.

2.2   "Marginal" Cost of Each Project

At this time, only four ATC systems can be considered as wholly
developed.

The following table shows the manpower used for the initial
development of each of these four systems.

	DANMARK	BELGIUM	KENYA	PAKISTAN
Number of source-code lines	300,000	370,000	150,000	170,000
Used manpower	440	520	109	54
Theoretical required manpower	460	560	230	260
"reusability" ratio	4 %	7 %	53 %	79 %

NOTE 1 :

"Used manpower" gives the manpower actually used for the development, and "theoretical required manpower" gives the manpower that would have been necessary in case of complete development (computed thanks to PRICE S model)

NOTE 2 :

"Reusability ratio" doesn't give the percentage of reused source-code lines, but the actual cost impact of reusability; i.e it gives in percent the following ratio:

$$\frac{\text{"Theoretical required manpower"} - \text{"used manpower"}}{\text{"Theoretical required manpower"}}$$

The following comments can be made about these figures:

-    the Danish system was the first system written in ADA, and then the reusability ratio is roughly equal to 1, because only specifications and multiradar tracking algorithms have been reused from the previous generation of systems (new language and new computer),

-    The Belgian and Kenyan systems began very shortly after the Danish one, and then were developped in parallel, that explains the poor reusability ratio.

-    The "reusability ratio" for future projects will improve, but it will be difficult to have a better ratio than 80 %

because each country is specific, and requires modifications in order to "customize" the ATC centre "product".

The use of the ADA language cannot explain wholly the reusability ratio, and it is necessary to analyse the contribution of ADA through the example of the following major components:

-       Track processing,

-       Flight plan processing,

-       Processing of operator actions.

These three components represents 90% of all the software of an ATC centre, and their functionnalities are as follows:

TRACK PROCESSING: The purpose of this processing is to acquire aircraft positions as provided by the radars, to translate them into a common coordinate system and to synthesize aircraft positions in order to provide the controller with one symbol per aircraft with the lowest possible average error.

FLIGHT PLAN PROCESSING: Every time an aircraft flies through the area controlled by the an ATC center, the information gathered on a flight plan must be transmitted to the civil aviation authorities. These flight plans are used by the air traffic controllers to identify the aircraft.

The flight plan processing manages this data and their association with radar data.

PROCESSING OF OPERATOR ACTIONS: This function pertains to processing of the commands issued by the air traffic controllers via the keyboards and rolling balls, or in processing of the operator commands on VDU's (creation, update and erasing of flight plans,...)

In each case, the reusability and the impact of ADA can be analysed as follows:

TRACK PROCESSING: The RADAR track processing procedure can be reused in full, since the algorithmics remain the same whatever the control centre. This processing is a mathematical algorithm which is used in all our air traffic control centres. It has demonstrated its performance and does not require modification. Regarding this function, the reusability ratio was already good in systems written in

FORTRAN; but the ADA language provides powerful typing, which enables standardization of input-output procedures, and that allows easy customization to the kind of RADAR to be received.

FLIGHT PLAN PROCESSING: Currently, this processing is very dependent on the methods of controlling Air Trafic.

Therefore, each country requires its own specific flight plan processing system.

But, based on the International Civil Aviation Organization (ICAO) standard (standardization of FPL data) and on our experience of the different systems we have developed, we have designed this system according to a bottom-up approach based on the Flight plan object, i.e development of basic "function libraries" to manipulate the FPL data and to offer methods which cover most of the possible events of the flight plan life.

Then, with these libraries, the writing of a customized flight plan processing system is limited to the main procedure which use basic methods to act on the flight plan life and data.

This kind of bottom-up design was very difficult to implement with language such as FORTRAN, so that the Flight Plan Processing subsystem was rewritten for each new specification in our previous ATC systems generation.

PROCESSING OF OPERATOR ACTIONS: This function varies widely from one project to another, since input/output facilities are often much different.

Some centres are using touch input device with menus, some others use keyboards with sequential commands.

Nevertheless, some operator functions can be retained, notably those associated with display, though most other functions have to be rewritten. Again, the structuring of the ADA language (notion of package) enables carry over of these functions from one project to the next.

In this area we have also developped several packages dedicated on the one side to the basic input/output management, and on the other side to the operator actions treatment.

2.3   Cost of Maintenance

In the field of Air traffic Control, a very high level of safety (reliability, availability,...) is required.

To match this requirement, THOMSON-CSF is obliged to ensure on-site maintenance until the required level of availability is reached before the beginning of operational service.

The cost impact of this phase is important, and when choosing ADA, THOMSON-CSF ATC Department hoped to reduce this cost because of software quality improvement induced by the main features of ADA (strong data typing, improvement of modularity,...).

As a matter of fact, based on the systems already installed, we can say that this phase cost is about:

-      about 12 m.m for ATC systems written in ADA,

-      about 25 m.m for ATC systems written in FORTRAN.

2.4   Cost Impact of ADA on Hardware Configuration

Using ADA for ATC systems has increased the needs for hardware configuration in term of:

-      CPU power (20% to 100%).

-      Main memory (200% to 500%).

-      Mass storage size (up to 400%).

-      Disk access time and I/O rate (not quantified).

This growth of the needs can be explained:

-      first by the overhead induced by ADA; i.e the same basic algorithm written in ADA needs, on the same computer, 10% to 20% more time than if written in "C".
       In addition, compilation time and mass storage of all the generated objects requires more powerful host computers in ADA than in any other classical languages.

-      and (this may sound somewhat heretical) by the improvement of the readability and maintenability (better modularity, multi-layered software architecture) which induces a loss of efficiency.

For example the flight plan data which is the atomic data processed by ATC data processing systems needed 0.5 KB in FORTRAN and needs up to 15 KB in ADA due to a very hierarchical structure.

In fact, this opposition of readability/maintenability versus efficiency is not really due to ADA, but ADA makes easier the improvement of readibility and maintenability and the software project manager must be very cautious to maintain the best compromise between these quality factors.

Furthermore, on our systems in the present context, the cost impact of this growth of needs is less than 20% of the computer price (about 10% of software cost), and since the ratio of price/CPU_power is always decreasing, it is evident that this cost impact will become negligible.

2.5   Miscellaneous

Miscellaneous points must be taken into account in the present evaluation although it is impossible to exactly quantify them,these are:

-   improvement of flexibility : in the field of ATC, a delivered software, once used in operational service, must allow easy evolution in order to stick to the evolutions of Air Traffic Control methods, because from an operational user's standpoint, evolution of an operational system is always easier to manage than installation of a brand new system.

-   improvement of portability that will allow, in case of computer change, a rehosting of existing software instead of rewriting.

-   commercial impact of using ADA.

3   CONCLUSION

Although the youth of ADA environments had entailed technical problems that required specific developments, although the choice of ADA induced some extra costs in terms of people training and initial developments, our latest control centres and simulators have provided evidence of the advantage, in term of costs, of using ADA.

Since this advantage is mainly due to the interesting features of the ADA language in the field of reusability, we have decided to go further in our Bottom-up design approach:

-    improvement of the identification of all the basic objects
     usefull in ATC software; and therefore growth of the basic
     package libraries,

-    using more deeply design methodology such as OOD, which
     exactly matchs to our requirements in term of flexibility.

FIG.1 PRINCIPE DU CONTROLE DE LA CIRCULATION AERIENNE

PRINCIPLE OF AIR TRAFFIC CONTROL

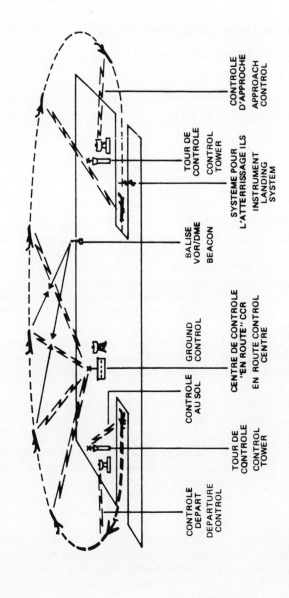

CONTROLE D'APPROCHE
APPROACH CONTROL

TOUR DE CONTROLE
CONTROL TOWER

SYSTEME POUR L'ATTERRISSAGE ILS
INSTRUMENT LANDING SYSTEM

BALISE VOR/DME
BEACON

CENTRE DE CONTROLE "EN ROUTE" CCR
EN ROUTE CONTROL CENTRE

GROUND CONTROL

CONTROLE AU SOL

TOUR DE CONTROLE
CONTROL TOWER

CONTROLE DEPART
DEPARTURE CONTROL

An Ada Case Study in Cellular Telephony Testing Tools

Harry Doscher

Motorola, Inc.

Radio–Telephone Systems Group

Arlington Heights, IL   USA

1 INTRODUCTION

Motorola Cellular is continually looking for ways to improve their software development process, and thereby, improve the quality of their delivered products. To that end, the Cellular management decided to undertake an Ada application to determine its effect on production of commercial software development. The initial Ada project was an application known as the M5000, which is a testing tool used internally to simulate all external interfaces to an Electronic Mobile Exchange (EMX) and to run regression test suites which simulate Land–to–Mobile, Mobile–to–Land, and Mobile–to–Mobile call events.

This initial Ada project was completed by a development team that had worked on cellular telephony testing tools, but had no prior Ada experience. A key factor in the success of the project was a commitment of time and resources by upper management. Each engineer who worked on the M5000 had a SUN workstation with access to both Telesoft and Alsys Ada compilers.

As with any initial venture, there were certain expectations by management, development problems that were encountered and overcome, and valuable lessons learned. Some of these problems encountered during the development and testing of the M5000 were:

- No member of the initial M5000 design team had any Ada experience
- No one associated with the project had experience with Object Oriented Design (OOD)
- The target hardware platform was a SUN workstation, meaning the M5000 application coexists with the SUN operating system
- When the project was started in 1988, the Ada compilers that targeted the SUN workstations could not properly compile all of the packages that comprise the M5000

In addition to lessons learned regarding improving the software development process, the results of the M5000 project were very positive. Regression test suites that previously took over two engineer years to conduct can now be run in less than 48 hours of test time. Motorola now has the beginnings of an Ada reuse library and has a core of engineers who can effectively use Ada oriented design techniques and produce high quality Ada code.

2 APPLICATION OVERVIEW

The Cellular Infrastructure Division (CID) of the Radio Telephone Systems Group (RTSG) of Motorola, Inc. produces among other things, Cellular Telephone Switches and the software that operates them. All of the software that runs on the switches sold and supported by CID is stress tested and regression tested before it is shipped to our customers. These stress and regression tests comprise the system level tests carried out on Motorola Cellular Switch Software.

There is no commercially available test equipment that will conduct system level tests on a cellular switch. While commercial test equipment can be used to test parts of a Cellular Switch System, there is nothing on the market that will adequately test the entire system, let alone conduct or assist in conducting a full functional regression test of the switch software. The problem lies in the fact that cellular load and regression test tools must simulate the entire outside world (land and mobile) to the switch under test. In response to this requirement for system testing tools, the original Cellular Load Simulator (CLS) was created. This tool generates a load on the switch(es) under test that consists of Mobile–to–Land, Land–to–Mobile, and Mobile–to–Mobile call scenarios. All scenarios are either answered or unanswered call attempts. Figure 1 shows a block diagram of an EMX system connected to a Public Switched Telephone Network (PSTN).

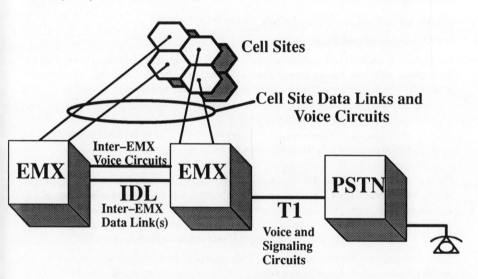

Figure 1. Cellular System Block Diagram

While the CLS satisfied the specific requirement of bulk call generation required to load test and stress test the cellular switches, CID was still faced with a monumental task when it came to regression testing each release of Electronic Mobile Exchange (EMX) software. A complete regression test effort took a little over two engineer years for a single software release. Two engineer years effort would not be especially bad if CID had only one software release per year. However, CID will have up to twelve releases in a single calendar year. The amount of time spent by the engineers and the amount of time the laboratory machines must be used for a full regression test quickly becomes prohibitive.

A full regression test consists of verifying the ability of the software to handle all normal telephone call scenarios and to correctly handle all of the possible call failure scenarios. The scenarios must be tested with and without handoffs. There are over 2000 different call scenarios that must be tested for each switch configuration. The number of call scenarios increases dramatically when we need to verify two or more EMXs connected to each other.

The solution to the problem of a lack of engineer and lab machine time was to create an automated regression test tool for cellular software, the M5000. The target processor for the M5000 is a Sun 3/x60 processor running the SUN operating system. Originally the software was to be designed using Structured Design techniques and implemented in C. The original development team had prior experience porting one cellular test tool application from a PDP 11/44 running RSX 11M+ to the same SUN platform and operating system.

3 THE APPROACH – PROBLEMS AND SOLUTIONS

3.1 Management and Engineering

The decision to use Ada for the M5000 was made by CID management who wanted to see if an Ada development would help to address the deficiencies that had been identified in our software production cycle. The following are some of the questions to which they wanted answers:

1. Would the use of Ada, with range and type checking accomplished by the compiler, aid in the integration of software units?
2. Would the use of Ada decrease the number of errors created by the development team?
3. Would the use of Ada provide a basis for a software reuse library?
4. Would the use of Ada enhance the overall quality of the delivered product?

The engineers who were scheduled to work on the project were concerned of the many problems associated with implementing the product in Ada, such as: learning both a new design methodology as well as implementation language. At the time of the change to Ada, in March of 1988, the schedule was in place showing a delivery date at the end of May 1989, a fourteen month schedule. The analysis phase had already been started using Structured Analysis, and functional areas had been identified.

The process generally followed today of hand crafting software for each application, reinventing and recoding worker routines time after time, waiting to write software test plans until after the code is finished, and having the designers and developers of the applications test their own work, in addition to determine whether or not their own implementations adhere to the letter of their own requirements is not conducive to the production of QUALITY software. In consulting current publications about Ada development, it was apparent that our existing development and testing methods were not conducive to the production of a well designed, Ada–based solution to our problem.

A significant engineering challenge was the creation of a test script language for the M5000. The logical choice turned out to be Ada. All test scripts run by the M5000 are compiled Ada procedures. All interfaces between the test procedures and the M5000 application are implemented using limited private types: the test creator is provided with a limited, yet robust, set of operations that are used to implement cellular call processing regression tests. The language is designed such that an engineer with knowledge of cellular call processing can easily construct new test procedures. The author of the test script is completely isolated from the inner workings of the M5000 and works only in the cellular call processing domain.

3.2 Building a Team

The first order of business was to form the team that would deliver the M5000 using Ada. The core group of engineers consisted of a development team of three senior software engineers, each of whom had three to five years experience at Motorola, one newly hired engineer with two years experience, and one engineer who had just graduated from college. The core group of three had been working as a team developing software testing tools for Motorola EMX systems.

One senior software engineer with five years experience at Motorola was added from the System Test and Evaluation Section. Also, one senior software engineer with six years experience at Motorola and one engineer with two years experience were borrowed from the switch software development groups. None of the developers had any background in Ada or OOD.

It was decided to establish a parallel, independent test organization for the project. The testing organization consisted of three experienced Motorola software engineers and was supplemented with two engineers who had just graduated from college.

Each of the engineers with software experience at Motorola were familiar with the development methods used by CID. Yourdon/DeMarco Structured Analysis and Structured Design techniques are used for CID software development adhering to a conventional waterfall model of the software life cycle. Normal implementation languages are assembly language, 'C', or Motorola Programming Language (MPL). For the M5000, it was learned that in order to realize the full benefits of Ada, the initial design needs to be done in an object oriented manner.

Another change in development methodology was introduced through the use of an independent testing group. They were able to concurrently develop the test plans and procedures in parallel with the application software development effort. In this manner, the system test plans were developed at the same time as the high level design, the subsystem test plans and procedures were developed along with the detailed designs, and the unit test designs and procedures were developed while the code was produced. In that manner, units could be tested as soon as they were written.

Four additional engineers were hired and assigned to the development team during the coding phase of the project. One more engineer joined the testing group during the creation of subsystem and unit tests. The engineers who were added had experience in Ada but none in telephony. A significant contribution to the generation of the M5000 was realized by the addition of the new engineers. The positive effects realized from adding engineers to a late Ada project were in direct opposition to Brook's Law [BRO75]. The average time taken to become familiar with the project, the development environment, and the organization was one week. The additional resources were effectively used and had a positive impact on the project schedule.

3.3 The Approach

Since none of the team members had any Ada experience, suitable training had to be obtained. A Senior Staff Engineer, took the assignment of evaluating Ada training courses. He discovered that many small and large companies advertise Ada training, but few companies combine Object Oriented Design (OOD) and Ada training. He looked for training that would encompass both Ada syntax and whatever properties of OOD that Ada supported. He was also assisted in course evaluation and procurement by an internal training organization and a contracts administrator.

The selected course was chosen because Object Oriented methods were stressed and the presentation itself was delivered in a layered fashion. Abstract ideas were presented initially while most of the details were deferred until all participants were versed in the concepts being presented. It is also important to note that the use of generics, limited private types, and tasks were also stressed in the training.

The course consisted of two weeks training in Ada–oriented design followed by two weeks on Ada syntax and semantics. Each course ran for two weeks, eight hours per day with a two–week break between the design and coding courses. The time between courses was used to work on the analysis of the M5000 and to practice the techniques learned in the design course.

All of the experienced engineers, the group leader on the project, and the section manager went through the four weeks of Ada design and coding classes. The recently graduated engineers only attended a two–week Ada coding class since they joined Motorola mid–way between the design and coding classes.

Team members prepared for Ada training by reading text books by Shumate [SHU84] and Booch [BOO87] [BOO87A]. Classroom instruction was augmented by having the team exposed to some of the Ada fundamentals before attending the training class. Additionally, a copy of an Ada compiler was purchased for the PCs available on our network. Most team members took advantage of the compiler and wrote small Ada programs before the start of class. As the M5000 project progressed, additional materials by Shumate [NIE88] [SHU88] [SHU89] were used.

As mentioned previously, the analysis phase had already been completed using Structured Analysis (SA) methodology. During SA, the problem was divided into five logical subsystems: land, mobile, billing, man–machine interface, and test script execution. An advantage was the fact that the team members had experience in the application domain, however, some problems were encountered in making the transformation from SA to OOD. Objects were identified and documented using a modified Booch notation, a tasking model was defined, and package specifications were created for high–level packages.

A deficiency in the initial documentation was identified, namely, the way in which objects interacted. Therefore, calling sequence charts were constructed to correct this deficiency. After an external review, 'withing' and 'withed' diagrams were added to the High Level Design. A major problem which had to be overcome was the lack of Ada design experience by the team members. This caused the design team to spend additional time on each phase of the project, since determining when to terminate a phase was uncertain. The experience gained on the M5000 allowed us to make clearer cut decisions on two subsequent projects.

During High Level Design, team members identified the GRACE* components [GRA86]which is a commercially available library of Ada packages that consists of source code for generic low–level 'worker' packages. The use of selected GRACE components eliminated the need to devote engineering time to the creation and testing of over 7,000 lines of generic Ada source code. Use (reuse) of these purchased components was accepted by the developers once it was demonstrated that the compiler being used could compile them without error.

3.4 Tool Technology

Two compilers were identified for use in the Ada training class: Alsys and Telesoft. Each compiler had strengths and weaknesses. Alsys was chosen for its robust diagnostics and Telesoft for its run time. Both development systems have improved dramatically since the initial evaluation in 1988.

4 THE RESULT

4.1 Statistics

The project managers and developers had the use of an on–line time accounting tool to record the M5000 development and testing efforts. A total of 25,479 hours, or 12.7 engineer years, were charged to the project. Development and test each accounted for 50% of the hours. This number does not include training time of 2,139 hours, or one engineer year.

The M5000 application consists of the following (All statistics are for Ada source code):

- 57 KLOC developed in–house
- 7 KLOC GRACE components (initial instantiation)
- 20.6 KLOC GRACE components (all instantiations)
- 108 KLOC test programs and procedures

It is important to look at the two totals given for Commercial–Off–The–Shelf (COTS) components. While accepted counting methods consider only the initial instantiation of a generic, there were enough significant differences in the instantiations of the generics used in the M5000 to count the total number of resulting lines of code from all instantiations. Implementing the different instances in C would have required doubling or trebling the effort that was required to use the Ada generics.

---

*GRACE is a Trademark of EVB Software Engineering, Inc.

4.2 Metrics

An analysis of the M5000 defect data was conducted by an independent internal organization [DAS89]. The analysis determined that the majority of the defects (70%) were introduced in the coding phase of the project as shown in Figure 2, and the majority of the coding defects (53%) were logic/control flow/ computation defects as shown in Figure 3. HLD refers to High Level Design and LLD refers to Low Level Design in the following figures.

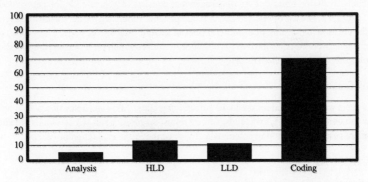

Figure 2. Percentage of Defects Introduced Per Phase

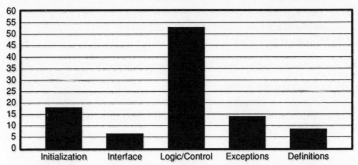

Figure 3. Percentage of Problems Introduced in Code (By Cause)

Those occurrences and types of defects identified were to be expected since rigorous reviews were conducted in the analysis and high level design phases. Phase containment effectiveness (PCE), shown in Figure 4, was approximately 85% for analysis and approximately 79% for high level design. The coding effort and portions of the detailed design were end date driven and reviews were much less rigorous. The effect was a phase containment effectiveness of just under 50% for detailed design and just over 30% for coding. Clearly, even with all the benefits provided by the Ada compilers, deviation from the established processes of rigorous reviews caused a decrease of defect containment effectiveness in the code generation phase of the M5000 project.

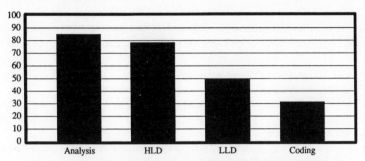

**Figure 4. Phase Containment Effectiveness Metric Values
For Each Phase of Software Development**

4.3 Reuse

Since reuse was a major goal of the M5000 project, it was addressed from the onset of the project. The M5000 designs were kept as generic as possible. In addition, the purchase of the GRACE library aided this effort. The fact that only the package specifications of the library components had to be examined and the fact that users of the library packages could understand the functions and procedures provided by the library were an important factor in making the decision to purchase rather than invent the code to implement the functions provided in the library.

Two additional tools have been produced to aid users of the M5000. The first tool is a Billing Record Verification Tool (BRVT) to verify billing files generated by the switch under test with records generated by the M5000. The second tool is a Log View Tool (LVT) which aids in viewing M5000 log files.

The BRVT application consists of the following:

- 13.8 KLOC of Ada code
- 45% newly generated code
- 18% reused unmodified M5000 packages
- 26% reused modified M5000 packages
- 11% reused GRACE components

The LVT application consists of the following:

- 5.6 KLOC of Ada code
- 48% newly generated code
- 7% reused modified M5000 packages
- 24% reused unmodified M5000 packages

- 21% reused GRACE components

The engineers who created BRVT and LVT had a background in Ada design and coding methods, but very little domain experience. No engineer on either project had been at Motorola for more than six months.

While the M5000 was not completed within the desired calendar time, both LVT and BRVT were delivered on time. The failure to meet the desired M5000 delivery date can be attributed to a number of factors:

- Lack of experience on the part of the implementation team group leader caused the high level and detailed design phases to consume more time than estimated
- Implementation and test teams were required to wait for a number of compiler updates
- Effort required to correlate the M5000 database with the database of the switch under test was underestimated
- Domain knowledge (cellular call processing experience) required to create the automated test procedures was underestimated

4.4 Comparison With an Equivalent C Language Project

At approximately the same time as the M5000 was being developed, another group in RTSG was developing an internal product in C that contained the same number of lines of source code. The number of source lines in the two projects were approximately equal, but the resulting quality levels and complexity of the delivered products were vastly different as shown in Figure 5. The method used to normalize the Ada and the C efforts was the Table of Programming Languages and Levels Version 4.0 [SPR88]. As can be seen from Figure 5, the M5000 has had 96% fewer post ship date defects reported than the C effort.

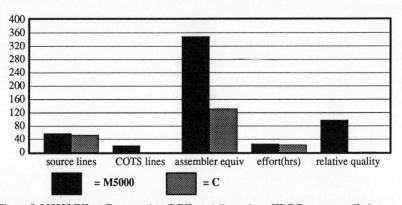

Figure 5. M5000 Effort Compared to C Effort (all numbers KLOC except quality)

The dramatic improvements in productivity and quality are attributable to Ada's enforcement of software engineering principles. A conscious effort is required to produce software with few defects. If the design takes advantage of Ada's strengths and if Ada is used as the implementation language, then software products with fewer defects can be realized.

4.5 Assessments

It was possible to integrate all the components of the M5000 within a three-day period. Ada's separation of package specifications from bodies (implementation details) allowed the designers to verify all of the interfaces between objects prior to implementing the package bodies. The fact that the compiler checked types and ranges of interface parameters eliminated many of the human generated code errors and tests. The use of generics eliminated another large human code generation and testing effort.

The Ada tasking model and the use of generics and limited private types were the largest obstacles encountered by the M5000 team. These concepts were, however, mastered as evidenced by the M5000 architecture. It is comprised of over twenty tasks. Generics make up over 26% of the M5000 application, and the M5000 testing language is implemented using limited private types.

The greatest benefit seen from the M5000 effort is the fact that proper usage of Ada **enforces** adherence to the principles of software engineering while other languages **allow** or discourage adherence to these principles. [CIP88]

The management objectives of decreased integration time, a decrease in system testing, software reuse and improvement of software quality were all realized. The developers have also recognized the benefits of using Ada and OOD in software development. Because of the successes realized in this project, they have expressed a desire to continue the use of Ada in future development.

5 CONCLUSIONS

A significant savings in development and testing time and effort was obtained from the reuse of Commercial–Off–The–Shelf software in the M5000. New engineers were added to the project when it was running slightly behind schedule without making it later. In fact, the engineers that were added made a significant contribution in a short time and the schedule was regained. This was due largely to being able to produce an understandable solution to a very complex problem. The quality and understandability of the design and implementation was demonstrated by the external review process and by the ability to add new employees to a project and have a positive effect on the delivery date.

An evaluation performed by the RTSG Software Quality Assurance organization has determined that productivity on the M5000, measured in lines of code generated per engineer per day normalized to lines of assembly language, was roughly twice that of projects done in C. Moreover, there have been even greater gains in delivered product quality.

Due to the differences in deliverables in an Ada project, it is important to get a complete commitment from management and to properly establish their expectations. We found that having first and second level managers instructed in Ada deliverables prior to their initial delivery avoided many anticipated questions concerning deliverable entities, e. g., package specifications as part of a high level design.

CID made a significant up front investment in training, materials, people, hardware and software. In return, the deliverables have been (1) a well documented, well structured design that can be easily maintained, (2) well structured components that can be reused on subsequent projects, and (3) a core group of engineers trained in Ada and OOD that can be used as internal consultants on subsequent Ada projects. Two follow on projects, the BRVT and LVT, were completed on time using both the lessons learned along with much of the actual code from the M5000.

As with any software project, problems were encountered during the course of designing, building and testing the M5000. Establishing a proper development environment is critical. Ada compilers that target workstations running UNIX* are not mature; there are defects in implementation, run–times, and tools.

Motorola RTSG has made a commitment to continue the use of Ada for software testing tools. Ada is also being evaluated on a project by project basis for use in product software. The experience gained on the M5000 project has been used to improve the software development process in Radio–Telephone Systems Group as many of the lessons that were learned on the M5000 were a result of Ada's enforcement of software engineering principles.

6 REFERENCES

[BOO87] Grady Booch, Software Engineering With Ada Second Edition, Benjamin/Cummings, 1987.

[BOO87A] Grady Booch, Software Components with Ada Structures, Tools, and Subsystems, Benjamin/Cummings, 1987.

[BRO75] Frederick P. Brooks, The Mythical Man–Month, Addison–Wesley, 1975, Page 25.

[CIP88] John Cipolla, Motorola internal memo, 1988.

[DAS89] Michael Daskalantonakis, Analysis of software defect data from the "M5000" project in CID, Motorola internal memo, 1989.

[GRA86] EVB Software Engineering, Inc., GRACE Components.

[NIE88] Kjell Nielsen and Ken Shumate Designing Large Real–Time Systems with Ada, McGraw–Hill, 1988.

[SHU84] Ken Shumate, Understanding Ada, Harper and Row, 1984.

[SHU88] Ken Shumate, Understanding Concurrency in Ada, McGraw–Hill, 1988.

[SHU89] Ken Shumate, Understanding Ada With Abstract Data Types, John Wiley, 1989

[SPR88] Capers Jones, Table of Programming Languages and Levels Version 4.0, Software Productivity Research, Inc., 1988.

---

* UNIX is a Trademark of Bell Laboratories

7 ACKNOWLEDGEMENTS

I would like to thank the members of the M5000 development and testing teams for their dedication and perseverance.

Bob Horvath	Michelle Howey	Tim Moran
Steve Turner	Brad Skrbec	Jim Peterson
Julie Stewart	Eileen Dyer	Steve Robinson
Mike Lyman	Dave Carpenter	Dan Eaglin
Andy Kojs	Jennifer Urbank	Scott Leschke
Brad Johnson	Carl Ekins	Diane Schulkowski
Heather Pence	Kley Cardona	Gerald Peppers
Paul Brandt		

Chuck Giese produced the initial functional requirements specification for the M5000.

Larry Svec did a great deal of the initial Ada course evaluations.

Michael Daskalantonakis has spent many hours collecting and interpreting the software metric data for the M5000.

Dennis Pratt and John Cipolla provided the impetus and resources to produce the M5000.

Michael Lightfoot spent many hours negotiating with vendors.

Jeff Cartwright provided timely procedural and managerial consulting.

Ron Borgstahl provided much needed and much appreciated editorial work on the final draft.

PART II: Ada Application Experience II - Defence Systems

Developing Maintainable and Reliable Ada Software: A Large Military Application's Experience

M. C. SPRINGMAN

TRW Space and Defense Sector
Redondo Beach, California

1. ABSTRACT

The Command Center Processing and Display System Replacement (CCPDS-R) project is a large Ada command and control application being developed by TRW for the U.S. Air Force that consists of approximately one million Ada source lines of code (SLOC). An innovative Ada process model is being employed for software development that features early evolution of foundation Ada architecture components, continuous design integration and demonstration, and incremental testing.

A combination of the Ada process model, layered software architecture features, enforced engineering standards, extensive development/test tools, and Ada-based design documentation has enabled the developed software to be integrated, debugged, and maintained more productively than on comparable non-Ada projects. Software quality metrics to date indicate a highly maintainable system with a manageable software change rate. Software reliability growth has been accelerated by exercising the complete software architecture skeleton and applications packages as they are developed using diversely varying scenarios to uncover problems that are not usually found until qualification or system test. This paper identifies the key features which are contributing to this highly maintainable and reliable system, and discusses some quality metrics which support the assertions.

2. PROJECT BACKGROUND

The CCPDS-R system will provide information during emergency conferences by the United States National Command Authorities and various nuclear capable Commanders in Chief. It is the missile warning element of the new Integrated Attack Warning/Attack Assessment System Architecture developed by North American Aerospace Defense Command/Air Force Space Command.

The CCPDS-R project is being procured by Headquarters Electronic Systems Division (ESD) at Hanscom Air Force Base and was awarded to TRW Defense Systems Group in June 1987. The project consists of three separate subsystems consisting of approximately 1,000,000 Ada source lines plus developed tools and commercial off-the-shelf (COTS) software. The first subsystem (350,000 Ada source lines) is 30 months into development. The other two subsystems will reuse major portions of the first subsystem.

CCPDS-R is characterized as a highly reliable distributed system with a sophisticated user display interface and stringent real-time performance requirements. All CCPDS-R software is being developed using DEC's VAX Ada compiler on DEC VAX/VMS machines, augmented with Rational's R1000 Ada environment. The operational software executes on a network of DEC mainframes and workstations. The first subsystem implements over 2,000 requirements using 11 VAX nodes, 73 VAX/VMS processes (Ada main programs), 275 Ada tasks, and 7,000 components/units. CCPDS-R is being developed, tested and documented per DOD-STD-2167A [2167A].

3. DEVELOPMENT/TEST APPROACH OVERVIEW

The CCPDS-R software development approach is the initial application of TRW's "Ada Process Model" [Royce 1990-1], which is based on early definition, demonstration, implementation and test of incremental capabilities. Incremental development is a well known software engineering technique which has been used for many years [Boehm 1981 and Boehm 1985]. Increments are defined so that the foundation architecture components that are relatively independent of the required application capabilities are developed, integrated and tested as early as possible, while the generally more volatile, application-specific components are allocated to later increments. The Ada Process Model requires that software capabilities be demonstrated at informal design walkthrough milestones (PDWs and CDWs) and at formal review milestones to provide tangible evidence of design progress. Reviews involving extensive capability demonstrations provide a better basis for the customer and the contractor to assess readiness to proceed with subsequent development activities than conventional design documentation by itself.

The primary advantage of Ada for incremental development as defined above is its support for partial implementations. Separation of specifications and bodies, packaging, sophisticated data typing and Ada's expressiveness and readability provide powerful features which can be exploited to provide an integrated, uniform development approach. The uniformity gained through the use of Ada throughout the software development cycle as a representation format is also useful for eliminating the class of errors of translation from design language to code and for eliminating the class of errors of translation from design language to code and for providing consistent development progress metrics for continuous assessment of project status [Andres 90, Royce 90].

The CCPDS-R software test approach [Springman 1989-1] benefits from the incremental structure because the software is partioned into manageable increments for software test, with software maintenance time planned to correct errors. Informal testing is performed by developers and integrators to ensure (1) that individual components function correctly in a standalone mode and (2) that the integrated components function correctly as capability strings. Although substantial informal testing occurs as a natural by-product of demonstration, this testing is not complete, nor is it intended to demonstrate requirements satisfaction. Formal testing is the responsibility of an independent test organization that verifies all software requirements are met. All testing is performed within a hierarchical configuration-managed tool set termed the Ada Testbed.

4. MAINTAINABILITY/RELIABILITY FEATURES

TRW has been very successful in producing a large volume of CCPDS-R software that is readily maintainable by the development team. The early increments undergo a substantial maintenance phase by the development team prior to delivery to the customer in the final product. The software exhibits impressive reliability even in its relatively immature state. A number of features contribute to this: (1) Ada language features and their contributions to the layered architecture; (2) the development methodology, which has been tailored to exploit Ada's contributions to software engineering discipline; and (3) the software tools being used to support development and maintenance on the project, each of which utilizes aspects of the Ada language for optimum effectiveness. The feature descriptions are grouped according to the above categories.

4.1 Ada Language Features

Software Architecture: The Network Architecture Services (NAS) [Royce 1989] software provides a consistent set of building blocks for constructing a software architecture skeleton (SAS) with standard control interfaces. This permits applications programs to interface with each other through pure data coupling implemented in System Global Interface (SGI) packages. NAS provides the objects and operations needed to construct real time networks which support flexible, open architectures. The CCPDS-R software design is described in terms of DEC VAX *nodes*, VAX/VMS *processes*, Ada *tasks*, and intertask communications *circuits* and *sockets*. The SAS is defined and baselined early, and consists of the top level executive structure for all processes and tasks and their interconnecting circuits and sockets. The process and task executives are all instantiated NAS generics, with the Ada source code produced by a tool which has all the architecture objects described in a database. The SAS concept enables rapid construction of a complete functioning network, which facilitates early discovery of design, interface and integration problems.

The NAS/SAS/SGI-based architecture contributes to maintainability and reliability because: (1) the standard SAS process and task executive structure; (2) design flexibility that enables creation of new process/task network architectures rapidly with no impact on the applications; (3) isolation of interfaces in centrally controlled Ada interface packages; and (4) isolation of complex real-time software issues in NAS.

Uniform Life Cycle Ada Representation: The use of compilable Ada as a design language is the key to providing uniformity of representation format through the development cycle. The terms Ada and ADL are virtually interchangeable with respect to our usage standards. ADL is compilable Ada with placeholders for pending design detail. The same Ada product standards apply to early design representations, which supports the concept of evolving designs into implementations without translating between two sets of standards and representation formats. This results in a design documentation set that describes the design throughout the life cycle in terms of the final Ada product representation. Maintainers only have to understand Ada and the NAS architecture to understand the documentation.

Continuous Design Integration: There is a continuous design integration which occurs as individual developers compile their evolving Ada components in the context of the SAS structural components and against the global interface packages. This eliminates a class of interface errors that are normally not found until the I&T team attempts to integrate the software. This is facilitated by a combination of: (1) using Ada as the design representation as well as the implementation language; (2) rigid interface control through global interface packages; and (3) the demonstration-oriented Ada process model. Integration of Ada program units is enforced mainly through compilation. Integration of components within builds is accomplished by constructing design walkthrough demonstrations composed of capabilities which span multiple components. Integration across builds is accomplished by constructing major milestone demonstrations of capabilities which span multiple builds. The continual integration results in software components that are rapidly integrated as a natural by-product of the design phase with high interface reliability.

Component Reuse: Already proven components are reused extensively throughout the architecture. This contributes to maintainability (consistent, repeated application) and reliability (already tested). Examples in our architecture include NAS, hundreds of instantiations and "withed library" units, the SAS components (tasks replicated in multiple processes and processes replicated on multiple nodes), and instantiations of a generic user interface for ten different operator positions in the system. Reuse has been greatly facilitated by use of Ada generics and judicious packaging of components.

Design Documentation Set: The design documentation exploits Ada's self documenting features. Our naming and commenting standards result in source code that is highly readable and understandable by reviewers and maintainers. Companion documents are produced that provide textual and graphical descriptions of the overall system architecture (System Description Document), the overall software architecture (Software Design Document), and individual component designs (Software Development Files) [Springman 1989-2].

4.2 Ada Development Methodology

Enforced Software Standards and Procedures: A detailed software standards and procedures manual was available for all developers and testers within two months of contract start. The manual includes procedures for all aspects of the development and test process, and standards for Ada design, coding, and commenting, including ADL guidelines. The availability of these standards very early in the project ensured that software would be developed consistently by each developer. Subsequent revisions incorporated lessons learned for process improvement. Most of the Ada/ADL standards are automatically audited by a Code Auditor tool. The combination of automated and manual quality evaluation audits results in consistent code and documentation, which makes the software maintainer's job much easier.

Incremental Test: Incremental testing is performed bottom up to achieve maximum test coverage and to ensure that components at a particular level operate properly before they are integrated at the next higher level. For requirements verification, a requirements allocation/traceability tool set ensures all requirements have been allocated to the design and that there are formal test cases to verify each requirement at some test level. Because requirements test coverage is assessed early and continuously as the incremental testing proceeds, requirement implementation holes are discovered early when they are relatively inexpensive to fix. Because each level of testing builds upon the previous testing, the key early builds are tested extensively as the software system is developed, resulting in highly reliable foundation components. The early availability of an executable Software Architecture Skeleton (made possible by our instantiation of generic process and task skeletons) is key to realistic early string testing. It would have been extremely difficult to convince our customer that string testing performed outside of the operational SAS environment was valid.

Development Progress Metrics: A by-product of our definition of ADL is a uniform representation of the design with a complete estimate of the work accomplished (source lines of Ada) and the work pending (source lines of ADL) embedded in compilable format in the evolving source files [Andres 1990]. A metrics tool was developed on CCPDS-R which scans Ada/ADL source files and size and complexity statistics at any level (component, program, build, subsystem). The metrics collection process is performed monthly, with results tabularized/plotted to provide development managers and the customer insight into status of the Ada product. These same metrics are useful for determining rework status for quality/maintainability assessment.

Early Software Reliability Evaluation: In parallel with other integration and test activities, software that is already integrated and functioning is used as the basis for assessing the reliability of the system's software. This activity concentrates on the foundation components (NAS and SAS/SGI), using application task stubs for initial assessments, and replacing the stubs with application components as they are completed. The objective is to execute the software in a stress environment using varying input scenarios to thoroughly exercise the logic over extended periods (e.g., overnight, in unattended mode). Such testing uncovers errors that are difficult to detect in normal, procedure-oriented testing, including errors dependent on subtle timing or sequencing relationships. By FQT, the software, especially the foundation components, will have been thoroughly exercised to provide a high degree of confidence in the reliability of the product. This process is greatly facilitated by the early availability of an executable SAS constructed by instantiating generics for all the processes and tasks in the system's software network.

Quality Evaluation Process: The software managers on the project are responsible for technically evaluating Ada code and documentation products for content quality. Developer peer reviews are conducted on the code to assure the proper use of Ada and to share implementation lessons already learned. Manager and peer reviews complement the Quality Assurance audits, which verify compliance with product standards. The structure and readability of Ada enables knowledgeable reviewers to rapidly become comfortable working with the code, which is an unambiguous representation of the design and the final product. The result is a set of software code and documentation products that are consistent and readily usable for maintenance. In addition, quality metrics (discussed in a later section) are compiled and analyzed to determine trends, corrective actions, and process improvement.

4.3 Development/Maintenance Tools

Source Code Generation Tools: Of the 350,000 Ada source lines for the first CCPDS-R subsystem, approximately 200,000 lines are generated by tools. The tools generate "cookbook" software such as the SAS task/process executive skeletons, display format databases, and message formatting/validation procedures and their associated Ada type specifications. The minor variations and coding/typing errors that inevitably arise when multiple individuals attempt to code similar functions are eliminated, which simplifies testing and enhances reliability. Because changes to the software are accomplished by simply editing text files and rerunning the appropriate tool, maintenance is simplified. For example, the CCPDS-R Message Tool uses the same flat files to produce source code for four different applications components, which centralizes configuration management and ensures consistency of a change across the four components.

Configuration Control Tools: The Ada testbed consists of hierarchically structured directories, build procedures, and supporting tools that provide the environment for the execution and configuration control of all developed and test support software. Its structure is designed to eliminate duplication of software among testbed users, minimize the software needed by each testbed user in his own area, and establish a uniform set of controls as the software moves from developer to baseline. The testbed exploits the Ada compiler's library management and obsolescence determination features to rapidly incorporate changes to the software baseline while minimizing the impact to user areas. The Ada testbed resides on the VAX cluster. It is essential for software maintenance because it enforces baseline control while providing visibility and access to modified components for checkout prior to formal baselining.

Software Problem Resolution Tools: The operational software has been designed to provide as much error isolation information as possible. Ada's exception handling features are key to the effectiveness of our approach. Anticipated errors are processed where they occur, while other errors are trapped at the lowest level practical by exception handlers. All errors are logged through the NAS Error Monitor process, which executes on each node of the system. All error messages are maintained in an Error Code Database, and are displayed and logged with detailed execution information as they occur. The detailed error information quickly directs the maintainer to the source of the problem. Other problem resolution tools include the NAS Network Performance Monitor logs, Realtime Data Recording logs, online Data Reduction capabilities, the VAX Ada Debugger, and the Rational R1000. These tools have been invaluable in isolating problems during development and integration, and will be equally useful for maintenance of the delivered software.

5. SOFTWARE QUALITY METRICS

TRW has devised a set of software quality metrics [Royce 1990-2] based on rework measurement that provide insight into current and projected maintainability of the software product. Software Change Orders (SCOs) are used to record changes to configured software components required to (1) fix problems or (2) incorporate enhancements. Useful metrics for software quality can be derived from the number of SCOs, the effort it took to implement them, and the number of changed SLOC resulting from their implementation. Metrics include:

Modularity (Q_{mod}): The average extent of SLOC breakage per SCO, which reflects the ability of the integrated product to localize the impact of change and thereby simplify maintenance.

Changeability (Q_C): The average complexity of breakage per SCO measured by the number of engineering hours required to resolve each SCO. This value provides insight into the ease with which the product can be changed.

Maintainability (Q_M): The ratio of SCO rework productivity and development productivity. This metric is based upon total SLOC, total reworked SLOC, total development effort, and total rework effort, and identifies the relative cost of maintaining the product with respect to its development cost. A value of Q_M much less than 1 indicates a very maintainable product.

CCPDS-R requires that statistics supporting the quality metrics be recorded on the SCOs. To date, over 1200 SCOs have been processed through the CCPDS-R formal change control process, of which 670 are relevant to the operational software product. The others relate to support tools, test software, commercial software, or initial turnovers. Each SCO includes an estimate of the effort to incorporate a fix/change, the engineering effort expended on the SCO, and identification of the number of changed SLOC.

The results of compiling and analyzing the quality metrics-related data from the SCOs are intuitively satisfying because they generally match what one would expect of an architecturally sound, well-managed software project staffed by an above average team. The SCO rate closely matches the configured SLOC rate, while the number of open SCOs has remained relatively constant, indicating that the SCO rework is being accomplished in a timely manner (Figure 1).

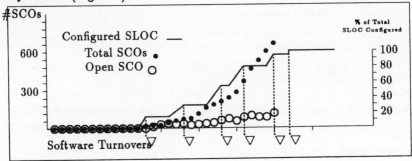

Figure 1: SCO Rate vs. Configured SLOC Rate

Figure 2 identifies the distribution of SCOs by the effort required for resolution, which suggests that the software is generally straightforward to modify.

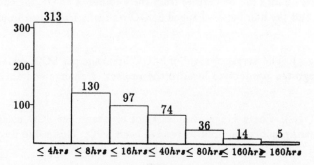

Figure 2: SCO Effort Distribution

The modularity metric (Q_{mod}) is 60 SLOC/SCO, which approximates the average CCPDS-R program unit size. Although each SCO generally affects more than one program unit, the overall design appears to display a high degree of change localization. The changeability metric (Q_C) is 16 manhours/SCO, suggesting that change is fairly simple. Figure 3 shows how Q_C has evolved for the software. Based on conventional experience, one would expect that changes become more expensive with time as more software is added to the configured baseline. However, CCPDS-R's cost per change has improved with time, indicating that the evolutionary development approach, early design investment in the foundation and riskier components, and a solid layered architecture have produced an integratable design with reasonable control of breakage.

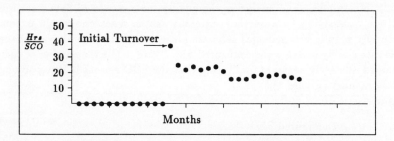

Figure 3: Rework Improvement: Changeability Evolution

Meaningful data for the maintainability metric (Q_M) requires analysis of software changes on the completed product. The project is still some months from this phase.

6. SUMMARY

TRW's innovative layered Ada architecture components and Ada development methodology have resulted in the successful development, integration and test of over 350,000

Ada source lines to date for CCPDS-R in a process rigorously monitored and reviewed by our U.S. Air Force customer. The resulting software has been straightforward to enhance and maintain, which is directly attributable to features associated with our use of Ada, our development methodology, and our tool set. Quality metrics show that the project is evolving with high probability of producing a very high quality product. The stability of these metrics implies that the remaining efforts are predictable, i.e., the software will continue to exhibit a manageable change rate that will converge to zero by FQT.

While these metrics are explainable and intuitively satisfying, there are few similar metrics with which to compare from past non-Ada projects or ongoing Ada projects. To enable meaningful comparison of Ada projects within TRW, an internal standard based on Ada COCOMO [Boehm/Royce 1988] is used for counting Ada SLOC. However, other companies and agencies will probably count Ada SLOC somewhat differently to make comparison of size and productivity metrics difficult. There are also few, if any, metrics related to maintenance of completed Ada products. Consistent data from other Ada projects must be collected and analyzed to determine macro trends that characterize Ada's contribution to maintainability. CCPDS-R's efforts are just a start.

TRW has found that new software engineers coming onto the CCPDS-R project have become productive in developing or maintaining the CCPDS-R software nominally within 1-2 months, using the top level documents and the Ada source code as their primary training mechanisms. The availability of experienced software engineers already familiar with the software clearly facilitates the learning process. TRW's experience is showing that a small group of highly trained Ada engineers with a background in the underlying software architecture concepts provides an effective nucleus for a maintenance team. With such a nucleus, a team trained in Ada and armed with the delivered CCPDS-R documentation and tools will find it straightforward to fix problems and incorporate enhancements.

7. BIOGRAPHY

Michael Springman is the Assistant Project Manager for Software Development on the CCPDS-R project. He is responsible for the development of approximately 1,000,000 Ada source lines to be delivered to the U. S. Air Force for this high-reliability, real-time system. He received a BS in Mathematics and Physics from Southwest State University (Minnesota) in 1973 and an MS in Applied Mathematics and Computer Science from the University of Colorado (Boulder) in 1975. Mr. Springman has been with TRW for 13 years, where he has been involved with various real-time C³ and avionics software projects. He has been responsible for all aspects of the software development life cycle, including system and software requirements definition, software design and development, and requirements verification.

8. REFERENCES

[Andres 1990] Andres, D.H., "Software Project Management Using Effective Process Metrics: The CCPDS-R Experience", *AFCEA Military/Government Computing Conference*, Washington, D.C., January 1990.

[Boehm 1981] Boehm, B. W., *Software Engineering Economics*, Prentice-Hall, 1981.

[Boehm 1985] Boehm, B. W., "The Spiral Model of Software Development and Enhancement", *Proceedings of the International Workshop on the Software Process and Software Environments*, Coto de Caza, CA, March 1985.

[Boehm/Royce 1988] Boehm, B. W., Royce, W. E., TRW IOC: "Ada COCOMO: Definition and Refinements", *Proceedings of the 4th COCOMO Users Group*, Pittsburgh, November, 1988.

[Royce 1989] Royce, W. E., "Reliable, Reusable Ada Components for Constructing Large, Distributed Multi-Task Networks: Network Architecture Services (NAS)", *TRI-Ada Proceedings*, Pittsburgh, October 1989.

[Royce 1990-1] Royce, W. E., "TRW's Ada Process Model For Incremental Development of Large Software Systems", *Proceedings of 12th International Conference on Software Engineering*, Nice, France, March 1990.

[Royce 1990-2] Royce, W. E., "Pragmatic Software Quality Metrics for Evolutionary Software Development Models", pending publication.

[Springman 1989-1] Springman, M. C., "Incremental Software Test Approach For DOD-STD-2167A Ada Projects", *TRI-Ada Proceedings*, Pittsburgh, October 1989.

[Springman 1989-2] Springman, M. C., "Software Design Documentation Approach for a DOD-STD-2167A Ada Project", *TRI-Ada Proceedings*, Pittsburgh, October 1989.

[2167A] "DOD-STD-2167A: Military Standard, Defense System Software Development", 29 February 1988.

Introducing Ada and Software Engineering in the Swedish Defence Community: Expectations, Experiences and Prospects

Ingmar Ögren

Romet AB Laxvagen 32 S-18131 Lidingo, Sweden

tel +46 87674314   fax + 46 87318624

The Swedish Defence Material Administration (FMV) has a long and acknowledged tradition of working in close cooperation with military personnel when producing systems where operators can cooperate with their weapon systems in an optimal way. Information handling was earlier done exclusively in the human part of the systems while during recent years it has been possible to support the human information handling with computer assistance and thus boost the total system performance concerning both speed and efficiency.

1. A FUNDAMENTAL PROBLEM

Computer technicians are often electronic engineers or mathematicians. This has led to a situation where we have excellent and reliable electronic computers and good, well-optimized algorithms for tasks such as tracking or ballistics. This is however not sufficient for production of large systems. We now know from experience that such developments seldom fail because of hardware or algorithm problems but that the reason for a failure can be simply problems to keep the project information in good order.

2. THE FIRST STEP: INTRODUCTION OF ADA

On the 18th of July 1985 FMV wrote: "FMV intends to make the Ada programming language standard within the Swedish defence". Still more important was probably that at the same time establishment of modern principles for Software Engineering (SE) was strongly recommended. FMV further made a commitment to support the introduction of Ada with Software Engineering through making sure that education was available and through producing recommendations for development systems.

3. WHAT HAPPENED THEN

One of FMV's intentions was that the introduction of Ada should be preceded by application of Ada-inspired Program Design Languages (PDL). Such a language, ADEL (Ada inspired DEsign Language) was developed together with a tool, ADELA (ADEL Analyzer). The language and the tool were made available to FMV's contractors.

In those projects where ADEL was used, it proved quite useful for creating understanding between users and system developers: sufficiently formal to be analyzable and to be a good foundation for programming while still so simple that it could be learnt by a military application expert in a couple of hours.

The introduction of Ada took time. Companies which had recently made substantial investments in development environments for other languages proved to be somewhat hesitant towards Ada.

Others who tried Ada soon found problems such as:

-    the early development systems showed great potential for improvement

-    some of the language constructs such as tasking and generics proved to be difficult to understand and to use, especially in mission-critical embedded systems.

These and other problems slowed the introduction process, but then PEAB (nowadays Bofors Electronics) decided to make a large commitment to Ada and to bring in a qualified development environment from Rational. This commitment with its publicity is one of the contributing factors behind the now spreading acceptance of Ada within the defence industry in Sweden.

"Software Engineering" includes models and methods for an orderly approach to specification, design, coding verification and testing of software.

This area proved to be difficult, mainly for two reasons:

-    the experts available in the area founded their expert status on too limited experience and did not agree with each other on important points

-    the tasks involved could not be solved with purely technical methods, but insights in psychology and sociology were required.

We did not even have an acceptable list of criteria for evaluation of development methods and tools.

In the SE area FMV supported development of the tool ASP (Ada Specification Producer) which supported the methodology described by Grady Booch in his book "Software Engineering with Ada". This first effort did for different reasons not lead to a production tool, but gave important experience concerning method issues and software tool production.

The Swedish Telecom, like FMV, realized early the importance of a single programming language and of Software Engineering and thus, through its subsidiary Telelogic, engaged itself in the compiler company Telesoft. (The two companies are now combined in Telesoft).

Telelogic also started development of tools to support the CCITT design language SDL. A continuous exchange of information was established between Swedish Telecom and FMV.

In the beginning of 1988 FMV, in cooperation with leading defence industries started SESAM (Defence industry's user group for Software Engineering with Ada). SESAM works with four subgroups which meet regularily:

-       software metrics

-       software development models/methods/tools

-       software reuse

-       target machines.

SESAM also publishes an internal paper, the Rendezvous.

4. TODAY'S PROBLEMS

For FMV's further work in the SE area with Ada as a vehicle, a number of problem areas can now be seen, where FMV must put in active work to be able to field modern systems in the future.

4.1. Acceptance of Ada
Some companies are still hesitant to accept Ada as the main programming language. For civilian embedded systems the language C is the main competitor. Ada's strengths are most obvious in the maintenance phase where the language's readability and strong standardization can be expected to give reliable systems through several modification cycles. These advantages may not always be obvious to a contractor and FMV will have to act strongly in two ways:

-       to support Ada for all development of embedded systems

-       to establish principles for handling of heterogenous systems (older systems with new parts written in Ada or Ada systems with parts developed in some foreign technique e.g. 4th generation data base languages).

4.2. Update of Ada
FMV must take an active part in the present process of updating the Ada language with special interest in:

-       update of the tasking mechanisms in order to get a reliable and clarified handling of mission critical hard real time systems

-       clarification of the meaning of some language constructs, including a means of broadcst communication when applying Ada to multi-computer and multi-processor systems

-       possibly extension of the language to make it better suited to application of object-oriented principles.

4.3. Optimization of principles for Software Engineering
Although we now see a great interest in object-oriented methods, large parts of the industry still live in the function-oriented world as it is represented by e.g. Structured Analysis (SA) and hesitate to accept object-oriented methods. This hesitation has several reasons:

-    Ada is not considered to be suited to an object-oriented way of thinking

-    our experience of object-oriented analysis is still rather limited

-    tools for object-oriented methods are few and unproven.

In order to support establishment of modern SE principles, based on object-oriented principles, FMV has sponsored some practical work in the area.

5. PROSPECTS FOR THE FUTURE

The age of Ada has only started and FMV expects Ada to be the main vehicle for software development for many years still. Thus FMV actively takes part in the 9x language update. Besides a number of SE activities are considered most important to enhance the industry's ability to deliver correct maintainable systems on time.

5.1. Establishment of an agreed list of criteria for Software Engineering methods and tools.
At present a substantial effort is put into developing a criteria list and some of the criteria found so far are:

-    confidence in vendor

-    maturity for method and tool

-    support for reuse

-    traceability (concerns requirements and test criteria)

-    support for production of maintainable systems

-    seamlessness

-    potential for designer acceptance

-    support for human factors

-    support for effective configuration management

-    support for hierarchical structure with independent modules

-    support for parallel processes

-    relative advantage compared to existing methods/tools

- avoidance of "write-only" documentation

- compatibility (with existing routines and education)

- complexity

- tryability

- visuality (concerns results compared with present)

- Ada-closeness (mainly applicability of Ada syntax and semantics in the analysis/design phases).

5.2. Establishment of a spiral "ball bearing" development model

Experience shows that there are mainly two kinds of systems:

- those that are continously changed and expanded

- those that are not used.

Experience further indicates that it may not be humanly possible to produce a complete and correct requirement specification for any system of non-trivial size (although people keep trying).

FMV has not found it very useful to design a development model for the systems that are never to be used. Thus we need a development model which allows iterative work with incremental definition of requirements and which can go through several development cycles in a natural way.

The answer we have found so far is called the ball bearing model to visualize a mechanism where several activities are going on simultaneously (the balls) acting on different objects which are interconnected in a hierarchical way:

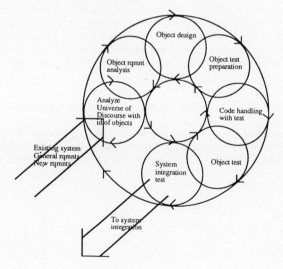

The basic model as shown above concerns the system development team. To make the picture complete it shall be supported by some extra activities:

- the user's activity to produce requirements and to evaluate prototypes and finished products

- a separate code production activity.

The model further presupposes that the three basic development elements specification, design and test are kept closely together so that as soon as an object is identified during analysis, its requirements are extracted, the object is given a preliminary design and tests are defined based on the requirements. Analysis and design will thus be layered throughout the development effort so that analysis will always be made on a basis of a partly established design structure. A problem may be the impact this model has on contract forms.

5.3. Gaining practical experience of object-oriented development of heterogenous systems with parts written in Ada

FMV has a large inventory of older software. Partly for this reason FMV has supported work in the object-based method ROSE (Requirement Oriented System Evolution) which handles existing systems simply as objects and thus can handle changes and additions in a modern object-based way without changing the existing system.

In order to gain broader experience of object-oriented and object-based methods, FMV also studies alternative methods such as ObjectOry from Objective Systems and OBS from Ericsson Radar Electronics.

5.4. Establishment of a modern prototyping environment for cooperation between military and technical personnel in system definintion

In order to build good systems the technicians need good requirements. The military cannot produce good requirements without knowing what is technically feasible. In order to make both good requirements and good systems possible, FMV now builds a modern reference lab for experimental and prototyping work for both military and technical personnel. When the lab is working it will be quite possible that requirements are expressed as one or more aspects of a working prototype.

5.5. Creating an organisation for production and maintenance of reusable components, written in Ada

Originally some people believed that Ada's standardization should result in production of reusable components " on the run" while producing application software. We know now that application software will seldom be reused for different reasons such as lack of generality or difficulty to understand.

Understanding is now spreading that system production is one thing and coding is something else. As a result discussions are now under way between FMV and leading defence contractors about establishing an Ada Reuse Center, to be used mainly by Swedish defence industry.

References
Carlsson (1985) FMV policy for Software Engineering and Ada. FMV doc id: LEDNING A 23:101/85

Booch (1983) Software Engineering with Ada. Benjamin/Cummins.

Jacobsson (1987) Object Oriented Development in an Industrial Environment. OOPSLA - 87. (Method ObjectOry).

ADEL PDL, ROSE method and ASP CASE tool. Sypro in Arbogå/Sweden tel +46 58912810 fax +46 58916901 telex 73904.

C2P Ada Shadow Program: Design, Prototype Development and Implementation of Command and Control Software

A. L. BRINTZENHOFF

SYSCON Corporation
3990 Sherman Street
San Diego, CA 92110-4393

K. NIELSEN

Hughes Aircraft Company
3970 Sherman Street
San Diego, CA 92110-4393

K. SHUMATE

Ada Systems Development Corporation (ASDC)
  a TeleSoft Company
5960 Cornerstone Court West, Suite 110
San Diego, CA 92121-9891

ABSTRACT

This paper presents experience, results, and lessons learned in the design, prototype development and implementation of real-time command control software in Ada. Specific issues discussed are the design methodology and resulting design, the initial prototype development and customer demonstration, and the subsequent implementation of the system, including transporting to a different host and target combination for the final development. Of particular interest is that the implementation was performed by a different group of software engineers - in a different company - from the original developers.

1. INTRODUCTION

The real payoff from Ada will come from the use of appropriate design methods that will allow Ada programs to be easily maintained and enhanced.

This paper presents concrete experience, results, and lessons learned in exactly such a situation for real-time command and control software designed and implemented using Ada. The project described is the Command and Control Processor (C2P) Ada Shadow project. The design and prototype development was performed by one company, Hughes Aircraft, while the implementation and evaluation is being performed by another, SYSCON Corporation.

Specific issues discussed are the design methodology, resulting designs and the design process; initial prototype development and customer demonstration; and development of the system, including tranporting it to a different host and target environment.

The project was performed in three phases: Phase 0, requirements definition, design, and prototype development; Phase 1, implementation; and Phase 2, evaluation. The following sections address each of these phases. Although Phase 2 had not yet been initiated at the time this paper was written, an overview of the primary objectives is provided.

2.   REQUIREMENTS DEFINITION, DESIGN AND PROTOTYPE DEVELOPMENT

A "shadow" project is one which provides a significant or meaningful subset, in an Ada implementation, of the corresponding parent project which is being implemented in another language. In general, the objective of a shadow project is to gain insight into the use of Ada in the context of a real-world application without being encumbered by all the attendant, extraneous issues of a large, full-scale engineering development project.

The C2P parent system is a computer-based communications processor front-end for a U.S. Navy shipboard command and control system. This system implements several different types of communication protocols referred to as tactical digital information links (TADILs). One particular protocol, called Link 11, is structured as a collection of bit-oriented message types. The purpose of the C2P Ada Shadow project is to implement a subset of the Link 11 messages as a stand-alone system and to then evaluate the accomplishments as a means of providing lessons learned on various facets of using Ada.

The project was structured to be developed over three phases, with the first phase accomplished on a VAX computer using the DEC Ada compilation system. The final implementation is targeted to the U.S. Navy's current standard "mainframe" computer, the AN/UYK-43, as the embedded processor. The size of the Ada and Ada PDL of the top-level and detailed designs is approximately 23,000 source lines of Ada. Hughes Aircraft formed the Software Development Plan, the Software Requirements Specification and performed the top-level and detailed designs, including the Software Design Document and informal preliminary design review (PDR) and critical design review (CDR) from late 1987 to late 1988.

2.1   Requirements

The Command and Control Processor (C2P) system is primarily a "store-and-forward" message processing system between a data link terminal and a Combat System (CS) that resides in another computer. A context diagram for C2P is shown in Figure 1. The bit-oriented data link messages addressed to C2P are received from the data link terminal in a packed format. The messages are unpacked, and the data validated and interpreted. Track data is normalized to a standard, internal format and stored in the track store database.

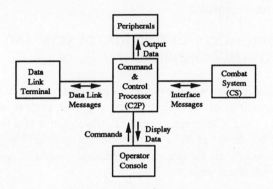

Figure 1. Context Diagram

Interface messages of a specific format are prepared from the data stored in the track store and intermediate-data tables, and sent to CS after a set of messages has been received from the data link terminal. Some of the incoming data link messages require an immediate reply without first being sent to the CS.

Interface messages are received from CS in a format that is very close to the normalized form and require very little conversion to the internal format.

Data link output messages are prepared for transmission during the next transmission cycle. Each transmission cycle takes place after all the incoming data link messages have been received, and after the data link terminal has been polled by a Network Communication Station. The outgoing data link messages are created from the data stored in the track store and the intermediate-data tables. These messages are packed and of the same bit-oriented format as the incoming messages.

C2P must be able to handle certain commands issued from the operator console, such as a set of track numbers to be used for a block of tracks. Display data must

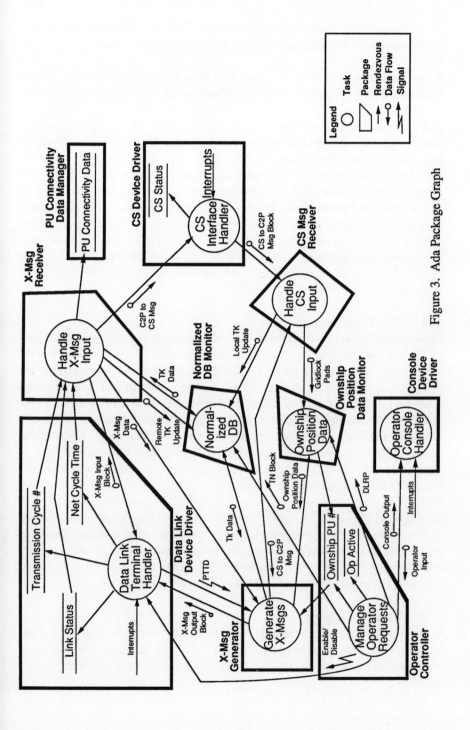

Figure 3. Ada Package Graph

be prepared for a number of output screens that provide status and control information and are viewed and manipulated by the operator.

If the data extraction option is active, C2P must prepare output data in distinct formats and send the data to certain output peripherals.

2.2 Design Methodology
The design methodology had been developed previously to apply specifically to real-time systems implemented in Ada. The major elements of the approach include: (1) the creation of a process abstraction to represent the concurrent elements of the system; (2) the transformation of the processes and their interfaces to Ada tasks and rendezvous; (3) the encapsulation of the tasks in Ada library packages; (4) the development of Ada support packages; and (5) the decomposition of large tasks into layered virtual machines. Every step of the design methodology is supported by a graphical representation of the design decisions made, and a set of heuristics to aid the transition from one design step to the next. The methodology is documented in [NIE88].

2.3 Top-Level Design
The top-level design was derived from a traditional data and control flow analysis of the stated requirements. Data flow diagrams (DFDs) that included control information, and a set of process selection rules were used to determine the process abstraction of the system. The concurrent elements and their interfaces were derived from the DFD shown in Figure 2 (a simplified version of the complete C2P functionality for this paper). The language-independent concurrent elements and their interfaces were transformed into Ada tasks. Some of the process interfaces were implemented as additional Ada tasks in the form of intermediary, or communication tasks. The tasks and their interfaces are shown as the circles and directed graphs in Figure 3.

With the aid of a set of packaging rules, the Ada tasks are encapsulated in Ada library packages ("application packages"). The application packages shown in Figure 3 (outlined as polygons) represent the major design objects of the system, and contain functionality that can be traced directly back to the requirements. (Figure 3 is a simplified version of the complete package graph.)

2.4 Detailed Design
Decomposition of large Ada tasks was performed using the Layered Virtual Machine/Object-Oriented Design (LVM/OOD) approach. Layered virtual machines were constructed as a set of high-level instructions from hierarchical functional

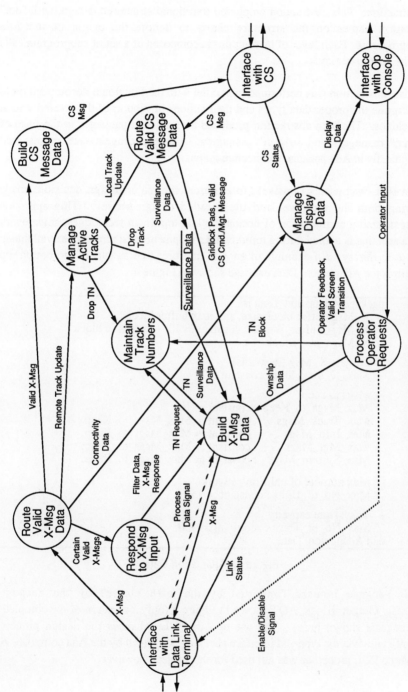

Figure 2. Top-Level Data and Control Flow Diagram

abstraction. This abstraction employed traditional structured design, with "dot" notation names on the structure charts to denote the origin of the Ada subprograms. Each layer of instructions is composed of a set of subprogram calls to the next lower layer.

A data abstraction was performed in parallel with the functional decomposition to determine the proper data types and their actions in support of the layered virtual machines. The data abstraction produced a set of Ada packages in the form of "type" managers and "object" managers. These packages were represented graphically in Ada package architecture graphs.

Ada PDL was used extensively to represent the major design decisions made during both the top-level and the detailed design phases. This approach necessitated a combination of bottom-up and top-down techniques, since every Ada unit that is *with*ed during top-down development must already be available in the Ada library. An example of an Ada unit prepared as part of the bottom-up phase is the Adaptation_Data package shown in Figure 4.

```
package Adaptation_Data is
-- X_Msg buffer block size, and max buffer blocks
    X_Msg_Buffer_Block  : constant := 10; -- words in block
    X_Msgs_per_Block    : constant := 5;

-- Largest X_Msg (in words)
    Max_X_Msg_Size : constant := 4;

-- Msgs to keep
    Max_Msgs_to_Keep  : constant := 10;
    Max_Track_Msgs    : constant := Max_Msgs_to_Keep;
    Max_Info_Msgs     : constant := Max_Msgs_to_Keep;
    Max_Mgt_Msgs      : constant := Max_Msgs_to_Keep;
    Max_System_Msgs   : constant := Max_Msgs_to_Keep;

-- Max number of units on network
    Max_No_of_Units : constant := 15;

-- Track store capacity
    Max_No_of_Tracks : constant := 100;
end Adaptation_Data;
```

Figure 4. Adaptation Data

This package is used (imported by the *with* clause) by the package X_Msg_Output_Block_ADT shown in Figure 5 (only a skeleton of the complete package is shown here). The use of Ada PDL enhances the design process significantly via the type and interface checking performed by the Ada compiler. A separate PDL processor was not used for this project, however.

```
with Adaptation_Data;  use Adaptation_Data;
with X_Msg_ADT;
package X_Msg_Output_ADT is
  Buffer_Empty : exception;
  Buffer_Full  : exception;

  type Number_of_Msgs is private;
  type Msg_Blocks    is private;

  procedure Init_Block_for_Retrieval
          (Msg_Block : in out Msg_Blocks);
  procedure Init_Block_for_Storage
          (Msg_Block : in out Msg_Blocks);
  procedure Retrieve_Msg
          (Msg_Block : in out Msg_Blocks;
           Msg      : out   X_Msg_ADT.X_Msgs);
  procedure Store_Msg
          (Msg_Block : in out Msg_Blocks;
           Msg      : in    X_Msg_ADT.X_Msgs);
private
  type Number_of_Msgs  is range 0 .. X_Msgs_per_Block;
  subtype Msg_Locations is Number_of_Msgs
                  range 1 .. X_Msgs_per_Block;
  type X_Msg_Buffer is array (Msg_Locations)
                  of X_Msg_ADT.X_Msgs;
  . . .
  type Msg_Blocks is
    record
      Num_of_Msgs   : Number_of_Msgs;
      Next_Msg_Block : Number_of_Msgs := 1;
      Last_Block    : Boolean := False;
      Msg_Buffer    : X_Msg_Buffer;
    end record;
end X_Msg_Output_ADT;
```

Figure 5. Importing and Using Adaptation_Data

2.5   Prototype Implementation

The top-level and detailed design was implemented with a subset of the functionality on a MicroVAX II using the DEC Ada Compiler. The prototype implementation was demonstrated with a realistic scenario of a tactical military communications system. A limited set of the total number of data link messages was chosen to exercise all of the major parts of the system. This included reception and analysis of incoming data link and CS messages, creation and maintenance of tracks for a certain number of moving objects, message translation to a "normalized" format in the track store, database access, message display to an operator console, and the creation and transmission of outgoing messages to the data link terminal and to CS.

64   *A.L. Brintzenhoff et al*

3.   IMPLEMENTATION

The implementation phase consists of the unit design, coding and unit testing, integration testing; and system testing subphases. The issues involved in these phases in transitioning from the prototype with totally new personnel are described below.

3.1   APSE-related Transition Issues
A key aspect of the project was making the transition from the VAX DEC Ada environment to the new host and target environment, the Ada Language System/Navy (ALS/N).

The ALS/N is a Minimal Ada Programming Support Environment (MAPSE) which is under development and is hosted on the DEC VAX family of processors. The compilers, which have a common front end, are targeted to the VAX itself, and the U.S. Navy's current generation of "standard" processors, the AN/UYK-43 ("mainframe"), the AN/UYK-44 ("mini") and AN/AYK-14 ("airborne") processors. The AN/UYK-43, the target for the C2P Ada Shadow program, can be configured as a dual I/O controller, dual processor CPU (2.5 MIPS per CPU) with up to 10MB of non-contiguous real memory. In its current state, the ALS/N components for software development for the AN/UYK-43 target consist of the compiler (Ada/L), the linker, the exporter, run time environment (RTE), a general purpose text editor and text formatter and an on-line interface between the VAX and the AN/UYK-43 for program loading and control during development. Although various areas were carefully reviewed with respect to host/target differences, several unanticipated problems and issues occurred.

3.2   Implementation Issues
One of the key areas addressed in moving to the AN/UYK-43 target environment was how to structure the implementation phases (code, unit test and integration test). The principal issue here was how to most effectively utilize what had been produced in Phase 0, yet not be overly ambitious in the context of the new target environment and the advanced-development status of the Ada/L system, for which we were the first user. Although the original approach called for targeting on the VAX in Phase 1 followed by transition to the actual target environment in Phase 2 (primarily due to AN/UYK-43 access limitations) this was altered to begin implementation on the AN/UYK-43 target environment as early as possible in Phase 1 in order to gain as much information as possible regarding (1) the C2P Ada design, (2) the AN/UYK-43 architecture, (3) the use of ALS/N, (4) the performance of the run-time environment, and (5) Ada programming language features.

As a result of the above factors, a phased development approach consisting of three separate "builds" was selected. Build 1 was designed to consist of the Phase 0 prototype, the inclusion of several of the simpler application packages and the activation of the entire tasking architecture. Build 2 was designed to consist of adding portions of the more complex application packages that include the Link 11 and CS interfaces and the Data Extraction interface which was to be used as part of the testing capability. Build 3 was designed to consist of completing the subset of Link 11 and CS interfaces and conclude with a fully integrated program ready for system testing.

The motivation for including the entire tasking framework in Build 1 was two-fold: (1) to evaluate the operation of the framework of the entire program in the target environment and gain meaningful feedback which could influence the remaining development process; and (2) to provide an operational framework to which the remainder of the software components could be added as they were developed. By contrast, if a completed design (midlevel) and working prototype had not been available, the approach would have been oriented toward more initial prototyping of the tasking architecture on the AN/UYK-43 and other AN/UYK-3 specific Ada features.

3.3   Design-related Transition Issues

Although the overall structure of the design is sensible from an Ada standpoint, some task interfaces, and possibly even the overall tasking architecture, may need to be revised to reduce the time spent in repeated rendezvous. Thus, the granularity of the data exchanged is an area being monitored.

One change necessitated by the transition to the AN/UYK-43 environment is the reduction in the size of tasks by moving internal subprograms to external support packages. An additional change was the conversion of all single object tasks to task types from which the corresponding task object is then declared; this approach permits the task storage size to be adjusted accordingly. In addition, the size of various compilation units was reduced by creating new units to conform with Ada/L size limitations.

Since the AN/UYK-43 memory architecture consists of a virtual memory space that is smaller than the physical memory space, an additional level of "design" is required in the linking process. This additional design is required to assure that the established portions of a complete program, known as "phases," fit within the addressability scheme of the hardware. In addition, since inter-phase calls incur additional RTE overhead, the software must also be organized optimally (ultimately) with regard to dynamic caller-callee considerations. One area that will receive careful evaluation is the impact that software layering, resulting from the LVM/OOD design methodology, has on real-time performance.

Ultimately, however, a very significant portion of the software will need to be operational and undergo evaluation to determine what additional aspects of the design need to be revised. Of particular concern is the interdependency of various elements, for example, the software architecture design and the RTE efficiency.

3.4   Lessons Learned

One important lesson is that any Ada compiler used on a software development project should undergo some precisely focused and germane user evaluation before its use for implementation, even if it is, *a priori*, the only compiler that can be used, as is the case here. Here "focused" means addressing those features which will be used and are most critical to project success, and "germane" means realistic software size and combination of features. A specific objective here is to, at the least, be informed of deficiencies or limitations and, at the best, provide suitable coding or design guidelines or restrictions that obviate problems later or permit easier transition to the proper features when they become available. Because the ALS/N was not available for use during Phase 0, the design and prototype were performed with very limited knowledge of the ALS/N characteristics.

One of the extremely difficult areas of the development process was the lack of any type of debugging facilities on the target environment. As a result, components were implemented and tested on the the host environment using the DEC Ada compiler. The code was then instrumented, compiled, linked, exported and executed on the target environment. In addition, portions of code that were peculiar to the target environment had to be enabled or modified. To the extent that problems which exist with the target compiler or architectural configurations are complex, plans should be devised to seek viable debugging and testing alternatives as part of the overall software development planning.

One of the positive aspects of the Ada development was the ease with which the development team comprehended the design and prototype implementation of the C2P Ada Shadow program and began the transition. This resulted because the complete software architecture diagram (similar to Figure 3) and the corresponding Ada PDL, including executable Ada source code for the prototype, provided the new personnel with a familiar Ada-based representation for the C2P Ada Shadow program.

Other areas that warrant attention when making a transition to a new environment are the program library characteristics, compilation times and program storage capacity requirements since these can significantly affect software productivity and MAPSE hardware configurations.

3.5 Current Status
Currently a portion of the initially established development objectives, which include implementation of a portion of Build 1 and initial testing on the AN/UYK-43, has been accomplished. This includes operation of portions of the operator interface and limited processing of a small number of messages.

4. EVALUATION

During the Evaluation phase several key elements and aspects of the project will be reviewed. First, the viability of the ALS/N (Ada/L) to effectively support, as a MAPSE, full-scale engineering development projects at acceptable levels of productivity will be evaluated. Second, the viability of the Ada/L RTE to provide the necessary functionality and performance required for the types of projects anticipated will also be evaluated.

An additional area will be devoted entirely to performance evaluation of the completed system in which realistic, simulated report/message scenarios and system loads will be used to assess performance. Here the goal is to enable one to allocate performance shortfalls to (1) the existing design and design methodology used, (2) the AN/UYK-43 architecture, (3) the quality of compiler-generated code and (4) the performance of the run-time environment and (5) Ada language characteristics so that specific corrective actions can be taken.

Finally, it is planned that a portion of this work will address alternative designs and the viability of extending the existing designs to the implementations of additional TADILs.

REFERENCES

NIE88   Nielsen, K. W. and Shumate, K. C., *Designing Large Real-Time Systems with Ada*, McGraw-Hill, New York, NY, 1988.

ACKNOWLEDGEMENTS

This project is funded by the U.S. Government STARS (Software Technology for Adaptable, Reliable Systems) Program Office, sponsored by the U.S. Navy Space and Naval Warfare Systems Command, and directed by the U.S. Navy Naval Ocean Systems Center.

PART III: Design Aspects

Software Reuse in Ada

A.T. Jazaa
O.P. Brereton

Computer Science Department, University of Keele, Keele, Staffs, U.K.

ABSTRACT

The Ada programming language has a number of good features that support software reusability. It has also a number of weaknesses. We propose a logic-based framework for software reusability, paying particular attention to additional features that overcome Ada's reusability limitations. The proposed model that supports software reusability and dependency traceability is discussed and described.

1. Introduction

This paper introduces a logic-based framework for software reusability in Ada. The proposed framework has facilities to support many of the activities of the life cycle of a product. Source code modules are parsed and certain information is extracted and inserted in a knowledge base. Other information obtained from users is also registered in the knowledge base.

A cataloguing and retrieving mechanism based on keywords is proposed. It has advantages over traditional keyword-based approaches by giving users more freedom in formulating their requirements. Extra conditions and constraints can be imposed on retrieval to make the retrieval process more precise. The framework provides other facilities such as abstraction, inheritance and traceability.

The remainder of this paper is divided into a number of parts. Firstly there is a brief introduction to software reusability. This is followed by a discussion of the issues relevant to Ada's advantages and weaknesses for software reuse. The third part proposes and describes a logic-based framework for software reuse. The fourth part describes cataloguing and retrieving software components. The additional features of the framework that overcome Ada's limitations are discussed and described. Finally, a conclusion and summary are drawn.

2. Background

Within software engineering, as in other engineering disciplines, *reusability* is an important factor from the viewpoints of cost, reliability and productivity [Wood(1988) , Boehm(1984), Boehm(1987), Goldberg(1986)]. The ACARD report [ACARD(1986)] suggests that the *reuse* of software is a key factor in improving the production of software. Software *reuse* also offers the opportunity for the emergence of specialists in designing specific software components. Knowledge and experience can be accumulated (as is the case for hardware designers) in the modification of components to produce new versions to meet new needs. In addition, reuse will encourage developers to build software components which closely follow programming guidelines for documentation, design and implementation styles.

Although software *reuse* is believed to be a 'good thing' there is little evidence that it is widely practised. Reasons for this include:

- the difficulty in expressing the functionality and applicability of components
- deficiencies in methodologies for storing and retrieving software components
- the inherently different natures of software components and hardware components.

Software reuse, we believe, can be more effective if the following facilities are provided:

- a mechanism to create and modify a knowledge base that contains information about every stored component. For example the knowledge base should contain component abstractions relating to phases of the life cycle such that if new requirements are matched with an existing requirement abstraction then such abstraction should be traced through to the program that satisfies the requirement,

- A proper mechanism for cataloguing and retrieval,

- facilities for browsing and reasoning about a retrieved component, and for analysing its structure in order to assess the suitability of a retrieved component. An estimate of the amount of effort required to make a reused component fit into the new requirements is a necessary criteria,

- mechanisms for software construction to form a complete system or sub-system (using so called module interconnection languages for example).

3. Ada Support for Reuse

It is expected that considerable *reuse* of software components will be practised in the future as a result of the capabilities that have been provided by the programming language Ada [Boehm(1987)]. Horowitz and Munson [Horowitz(1984)] claim that any future efforts to develop reusable code will be influenced by the semantic rules of Ada mechanisms even if Ada is not used as a coding language.

Ada also provides powerful constructs for *reuse* such as abstraction, information hiding, and generic library units. Ada has an attractive facility for calling (or reusing) software modules that are written in languages other than Ada. Although it is possible to create a good software design in other languages by using one's own software design experience, in Ada, however, the basic concepts of good design are supported through the language itself.

4. Limitations of Ada

The above features of Ada enhance and encourage the ability to assemble a program from independently produced software components. However, a number of deficiencies are recognised as limitations for software reuse in Ada. These weaknesses are:

1. Generic Package Instantiation: Ada has no facilities to show the actual parameters of the generic program unit interface,

2. Inheritance: Ada has no facilities for inheritance which is more expressive than the generic package itself,

3. Program Development: Ada supports top-down and bottom-up program development. Top-down development has the following limitations:

    i-   due to the separation of specification and bodies each specification has only one body and vice versa,

    ii- a body stub needs to be connected to its parent where the specification of the stub was defined. This means a stub can not be used freely.

    Bottom-up development is supported through the use of "context-clauses". These in themselves limit component reusability (see for example [Bott(1988),Goguen(1986), Levy(1987)]),

4. Semantic Information: package interfaces carry no semantic information.

We attempt to overcome the above deficiencies by paying particular attention to additional features of environments. This is supported by Goguen [Goguen(1986)] as he reports:

Ada has some convenient features for reusing and interconnecting software components ... . The discussion of Ada's various limitations shows that a programming environment must supply additional features to support a flexible programming methodology for software reuse.

Our framework, as mentioned above, provides a number of additional features such as the ability to enable a user to view the actual parameters of the instantiated units. It also provides inheritance through the use of facts and rules to capture properties of the parent unit. Some properties of the new unit may be redefined or new properties may be added. The framework also has facilities to trace automatically all dependencies of a unit. These capabilities overcome many of the limitations of Ada program development. The above features are discussed in later sections.

5. The reusability Model

Our model of reusability is based on a logic-based framework for the management of Ada program libraries, configuration management and version control. This framework has a knowledge base containing information about many entities including program libraries, code (both compiled and uncompiled), documentation, specifications, requirements and others. The knowledge base contains information on the compilation status of each program unit and the relationships between compilation units. The knowledge base is created or updated by automatically parsing source code and extracting the necessary information [Jazaa(1988)]. Other information, obtained from users, can also be added.

The contents of a knowledge base is expressed in a simple form as *Prolog* facts such as:

generic_specification(Unit_Name).

package_specification(Unit_Name).

subprogram_body(Unit_Name).

with_clause(Unit_Name, ListOfUnits).

and so on.

The knowledge base provides a mechanism for expressing the functionality of components as a fact in the form:

reusable(Component_Kind_Description, Component, DescriptionOfFunctionality, Status).

where 'Component_Kind_Description' represents the component type (for example, package specification, generic procedure, subunit package body, . . .), 'Component' represents the name of the component, 'DescriptionOfFunctionality' is an attribute describing the component functionality in a natural language form, and 'Status' is an attribute whose values can be [Hutchinson(1988)] :

reusable,
reusable with modification,
not-reusable, or
others.

Certain software components are designed to perform a specified function therefore modification is not expected. In this case, components can be made ready 'on the shelf' for reuse and designated *reusable*. On the other hand, certain software components are required in the lower levels of implementations (or for other reasons) and therefore are not intended for reuse (i.e specified as not reusable).

When a component is designated *'reusable with modification'*, it is useful to provide the component with a specification or description of the ways in which the component can be changed when it is reused in other applications. This description adjunct clarifies component behaviour as well as improving productivity [Matsumoto(1984)]. Soldderitsch, Wallnau, and Thalhamer [Soldderitsch(1989)] give the reasons behind having components 'reusable with modification' and also the reasons for providing a description associated with a software component:

"Another has been in making use of code which may have been written for a quite different purpose, with different assumptions and needs. Modifications must be made with care, without inadvertently violating some assumptions and therefore introducing errors."

In practice, the reusability status could be set by the component designer, automatically, or, perhaps more sensibly, by the quality controller.

The (re-) user of a component can specify the required status or can retrieve components regardless of their status. The status information, we believe, is useful for later analysis of the retrieved component.

The knowledge base contains other useful information such as:

- creation time of a version of a component with its description,

- derivation of a version and the reasons for this derivation,

- statistics such as the number of times a component is reused,

- description of the state of the component such as reliability, or

- component attributes.

Other information can also be deduced from the knowledge base by means of rules. For example, a query could be issued to find a version of a software component that is:

- reliable,
- implemented in Ada,
- created before july 2, 1989,
- a subunit of a task body, and
- considered as a separate compilation.

When a component is created certain information is registered in the knowledge base. In addition, if the component is a source file it will be parsed and the necessary information will be extracted (as mentioned above) and registered in the knowledge base. Once a component is created the prototype system would automatically asks the developer to supply a description of the functionality of the unit under consideration. This description is in the form of natural language statements.

To retrieve a software component it is necessary to issue a query by describing the required functionality. If no component satisfying the given requirements is found the proposed system will assist the user in formulating his/her requirements.

The description of a component's functionality for both cataloguing and retrieving is tokenised and, for retrievals, the best match or matches are returned.

Cataloguing and retrieval are based on keywords but have advantages over traditional keyword-based approaches by giving users greater freedom in formulating functionality descriptions. Retrievers can use any expression with as many words as necessary. The proposed model also assists users if no component is retrieved at the first attempt. In addition, other conditions can be imposed to increase the accuracy of retrieval. The proposed approach also does not put any restrictions on users (i.e. no form filling, or training), compared with Wood and Sommerville's approach [Wood(1988)].

This proposed model is based on simple overall concepts which are straightforward to understand and use. It provides management support for component *reuse* from the very beginning of a software project from requirement and design through implementation and maintenance. This framework for reuse provides a basis for prototyping functional description methods and could accommodate modifications of the method or alternative methods.

The underlying logic framework for the management of Ada program families provides a mechanism for tracing component dependencies and correspondence between items throughout the software development cycle. These facilities, plus the pattern matching capability of Prolog, provide a good basis for investigating this or other approaches to reusability.

Understanding the behaviour of a retrieved component is a major reuse problem. Traceability is a key factor in overcoming this problem [Biggerstaff(1984)].

6. Cataloguing and Retrieving Software Components

Cataloguing and retrieval of information about software components is an active research topic. Most of the research on software reuse has concentrated on the identification of components. It follows two main approaches. The first one deals with cataloguing and retrieving information based on keywords, while the second one is based on natural language understanding.

We have proposed an approach based on expressions (keywords) provided by the user in natural language statements describing a component's functionality. In addition, rules and facts are used to impose restrictions on retrieval.

6.1. Cataloguing

Cataloguing requires the storage of information concerning software components in a form suitable for future retrieval with sufficient information to establish a full analysis of component applicability and dependencies. A component is stored in the knowledge base as follows:

1.   a tool 'catalogue' is invoked with the component's name and 'kind' description,

2.   a developer then needs to provide a functionality description of the component,

3.   the functionality description is then tokenised and words other than nouns and verbs are deleted, and

4.   the status of the component is determined through interaction with the user. When the status of a component is designated *reusable-with-modification* a description of the component's range of applicability needs to be provided.

6.2. Retrieving

The retrieval of software components is discussed within a prototype framework. A component is retrieved as follows:

1.   a tool retrieve is invoked using the command:

   retrieve_component.

2.   a functionality description of the required component is provided by the user,

3.   the functionality description is then tokenised as in the cataloguing above.

A developer, as mentioned above, can provide a description of the functionality of a (reusable) software component, which needs to be catalogued, in the form of sentences. We call this set of words P. When a component is required a user needs to provide a description of the required functionality. This description, we call Q. P and Q are transformed into tokens where words other than nouns and verbs are deleted from both sets.

Suppose P represents the following description:

   "The reuse of software components should focus not only on executable code, but also on higher levels of abstraction, on design and specification."

And suppose Q represents the following description:

   "The whole life cycle of software components needs to be addressed as the greater proportion of development time is spent on requirements, specification, design and

maintenance."

The descriptions above would respectively be transformed into tokenised forms as follows:

P = [*reuse, software, components, focus, executable, code, higher, levels, abstraction, design, specifications]*

Q = [*whole, life, cycle, software, components, needs, addressed, greater, proportion, development, time, spent, requirements, specification, design, maintenance]*

A component is retrieved if both sets have a non-empty common subset S. i.e.

$$S \ = \ P \ \cap \ Q \ \text{and}$$

$$S \ \neq \ []$$

Therefore S would be:

S = [*software, components, design, specification]*

At first the prototype system tells a retriever how many components match the requirement in order that he or she can be more specific before actually looking at them. The retriever can then set a minimum number of elements in S. That is, he or she can retrieve components that have at least n elements matching the requirement.

When a component is retrieved three types of attributes are retrieved with it. These attributes are component name, component kind description, and status of the component. These attributes enables one to determine other information concerning the retrieved component.

Retrieval can be made more accurate by including different criteria for selecting the right component. For example, one can say:

> *retrieve components if a component 'A' has description D1* and *Status* **not** *reusable,* **or** *has description D2* and *Status reusable_with_modification,* **and** *it was created before June 15, 1988,* **and** *it is a specification of a generic package.*

Or:

> *retrieve components if a component 'A' has description D1* and *Status reusable* and *contains the Bessel function.*

The proposed system is also applicable to the cataloguing and retrieval of complex arithmetic expressions by considering each expression as a keyword in its own right. It would also incorporate other cataloguing and retrieving models such as that of Wood and Sommerville. Once a component is retrieved a complete analysis of it can be carried out.

7. Abstraction and Inheritance

The 'description' information associated with a reusable component is most usefully expressed in an abstract form. This abstracted information reflects the essential points relevant to the required purpose (i.e reuse). Shaw [Shaw(1989)] suggests a simplified description or specification of a component to emphasis some properties while suppressing others.

According to Boldyreff [Boldyreff(1989)] *abstraction* is the key to software reusability and it is still an outstanding issue to be addressed. For example, the abstraction of the component and its contents can be achieved using facts as shown below:

   abstraction(Component_Kind_Description, Component, Abstraction).

Abstraction represents an abstracted specification. According to Muralidharan [Muralidharan(1989)]:

> "Proper abstraction gives the developer the flexibility to realize the specifications in many possible ways, and exposes to a potential client exactly what should be known to use the component, without having to be concerned about the actual implementation details".

This abstracted specification is provided by a developer through interaction with the prototype system.

In addition to a component's abstraction, a simple description of each entity (i.e. program unit) of a retrieved component is provided. The following example shows a simple description of each element of the component 'Complex_Relations' which will be displayed as in the table below:

Entities	Descriptions
generic_instantiation(int_IO)	instantiate integer numbers
subprogram_specification(read_in)	read matrix of N by M
subprogram_specification(inverse)	calculate inverses of imaginary numbers
subprogram_specification(impedance)	calculate impedance from real numbers
subprogram_specification(calculatedimp)	calculated observed data from impedance
subprogram_specification(getobservation)	generate observation from impedance and observed data
subprogram_specification(outobs)	printout tables of observations
subprogram_specification(f)	return a value for any mathematical function

Viewing or accessing the description of each element of a component, or the abstraction of the component itself, can easily be achieved in a number of ways using facts and rules.

The use of rules and facts allows entities to inherit the properties of their parents. New properties may be added and old ones may be modified. For example, if a package specification 'J' has properties 'X', 'Y', and 'Z' and its body has extra properties 'N' and 'M' then subunits of 'J' will inherit the properties 'X', 'Y', 'Z', 'N', 'M' as well as their own properties.

8. Life Cycle Traceability

The current practice in software engineering is to decompose a complex software system into its simple constituents. This decomposition facilitates the understanding and controlling of software systems. *Traceability* methods are needed to trace all decomposed system elements and their dependencies so that a software developer can easily control and manage the system.

According to Feiler and Smeaton [Feiler(1988)]:

"Traceability of a product's components refers to the ability of relating documents describing product components to each other, to trace their relationship through the development, and to browse and query the relationships. Examples of such relationships are the relationships between requirements and specification for components and their code, and between user documentation and the system it documents".

Traceability can make a significant contribution to understanding the behaviour of a component by allowing a user to trace all of a component dependencies and other connections. Tichy [Tichy(1988)] claims that traceability is an area which has not been given much attention. He classified it as an area that needs further research.

Looking at dependencies of a software component is extremely valuable for software reuse. Consider for example the context_clauses:

with_clauses(direct_io8921181443, [io_exceptions, 'SYSTEM'],
generic_specification(direct_io)).

with_clauses(direct_io8921181443, [stdio, unix], package_body(direct_io)).

The above 'with-clauses' facts have the same version number (direct_io8921181443) because both components were submitted as one compilation. The with-clauses dependencies are automatically traced, compiled if necessary, and a full analysis can be achieved.

Subunits can also be traced easily to establish quickly and efficiently the correspondence between them and other objects in the knowledge base. For example, all subunits of a component can be listed by issuing a query such as:

?- list_stubs_of('Complex_Relations', Version), Version > 11-7-1989.

Answer would be:

Version = 'Complex_Relations89654321',

subunits of Complex_Relations	
subunit	description
divide	procedure body
scalmult	function_body
impedance	task body
calculatedimp	package body

Traceability is a significant step towards understanding product components, structure, and both individual and collective functions. *Traceability* also provides developers with insight into the construction of their product.

Retrieving components, we believe, is more practical within a software framework based on logic programming. This type of environment provides opportunities to trace both the dependencies of a software component and the correspondence between objects throughout all phases of development. Identifying these 'development threads' is an important contribution to understanding and maintaining Ada systems.

If *reuse* is to become more widespread it is likely that a greater proportion of life cycle costs will cover component modifications and system maintenance. These component modifications are needed for many reasons, for example, for different applications or different environments. In order to tailor components one needs to view a component life cycle quickly and efficiently. Being able to view the life cycle of a component (as transformation between phases) is of central importance [McDermid(1984)] and , in our prototype implementation, can be accomplished through the procedure *connect-to*. The following set of rules demonstrate the implementation of the procedure *connect_to*:

> connect_to(A, B), **where**
>   A is a_version_of a_package_body, **and**
>   B is a_version_of its_requirements, **and**
>   A and B were_created_in July1988.

The information held can also be used to satisfy queries such as:

> "Give me the versions (of this component) that were created in February or April 1989."
> "Why was this component created ?"
> "How many times has this version been reused ?"
> "In which languages and for which operating systems is this component available ?"
> "How many versions of this component are there, and where are they stored ?"

The prototype system also provides system and sub-system building mechanisms and can automatically compute all the needs (or dependencies) of a component submitted for compilation or recompilation.

9. Advances Made

Using the approach described in this paper an experimental system has been developed using a knowledge base containing many entities spanning the software development life cycle. This system allows a retriever to carry out quickly and efficiently a full analysis of retrieved components. In this way a retriever can better understood the structure of the components and their dependencies.

The proposed approach supports multiple versions of reusable components, building software systems and sub-systems, traceability, abstraction and inheritance of properties from a parent to a child. A cataloguing and retrieval mechanism is developed which has a number of advantages compared with keyword-based approaches such as:

* more freedom in formulating user requirements, and

* a capability to use constraints during the retrieval process to make it more accurate.

Although the retrieval mechanism has achieved its objectives in the light of results obtained from the experiments on the prototype, it takes a simplistic view of natural language description of components compared with other approaches of Wood and Sommerville [Wood(1988)], and Tichy, Adams, and Holten [Tichy(1989)].

10. Conclusions

The paper proposes a reusability model intended to encapsulate the properties of reusable components in a knowledge base which is automatically created and modified by parsing source code. This information is held as a set of Prolog facts about Ada units and their relationships together with a functionality fact which contains a functional description in limited natural language. Other information concerning the other phases of the life cycle is also added either automatically or through interaction with developers.

We have attempted to eliminate some of Ada's reusability limitations by paying particular attention to additional features of environments. The proposed logic framework, we feel, provides a means of tracing component dependencies throughout the software life cycle. It can also provides system and sub-system construction.

References

ACARD(1986).
"Software: A vital key to UK competitiveness", UK Cabinet Office Report, Advisory Council for Applied Research and Development (ACARD), HMSO, 1986.

Biggerstaff(1984).
T. J. Biggerstaff and A. J. Perlis (Guest Editors), Foreword, IEEE transactions on Software Engineering, Vol. SE-10, No. 5, September 1984, pp.474-476.

Boehm(1984).
B. W. Boehm, "Software Engineering Economics", IEEE transactions on Software Engineering, Vol. SE-10, no. 1, January 1984, pp5- 21.

Boehm(1987).
B. W. Boehm, "Improving Software Productivity", IEEE Computer, Vol. 20, No. 9, September 1987, pp.43-57.

Boldyreff(1989).
C. Boldyreff, "Reuse, Software Concepts, Descriptive Methods and the Practitioner Project", ACM SIGSOFT Software Engineering Notes, Vol. 14, No. 2, April 1989, pp25-31.

Bott(1988).
M. F. Bott and P. J. L. Wallis, "Ada and software reuse", Software Engineering Journal, September 1988, pp.177-183.

Goguen(1986).
J. A. Goguen, " Reusing and Interconnecting Software Components", COMPUTER, IEEE Publication, February 1986, pp16-28.

Goldberg(1986).
R. Goldberg, "Software Enginering: An Emerging Discipline", IBM SYSTEMS JOURNAL, Vol. 25, Nos. 3/4, 1986, pp334-353.

Feiler(1988).
P. H. Feiler and Smeaton, "Managing Development of Very Large Systems: Implications on Integrated Environments", Proceedings of the International Workshop on Software Version and Configuration Control, Teubner Verlag, Stuttgart, FRG, January 1988, pp62-82.

Horowitz(1984).
E. Horowitz and J. B. Munson, "An Expansion View of Reusability Software", IEEE

transactions on Software Engineering, Vol. SE-10, No. 5, September 1984, pp.477-487.

Hutchinson(1988).

J. W. Hutchinson and P. G. Hindley, "A preliminary study of large-scale software reuse", Software Engineering Journal, September 1988, pp208-212.

Jazaa(1988).

A. T. Jazaa and O. P. Brereton, "A Configuration Framework for Ada", Proceedings of the Seventh International Conference on Ada, 19-22 September, 1988, UK.

Levy(1987).

P. Levy and K. Ripken, "Experience in Constructing Ada Programs from Non-Trivial Reuse Modules", Proceedings of the Ada-Europe International Conference, Stockholm, 26-28 May 1987, pp.100-112.

Matsumoto(1984).

Y. Matsumoto, "Some Experience in Promoting Reusable Software: Presentation in Higher Abstract level", transactions on Software Engineering, Vol. SE-10, No.5 September 1984, pp.502-513.

McDermid(1984).

J. McDermid and K. Ripken, "Life Cycle Support in the Ada Environment", Cambridge University Press, 1984.

Muralidharan(1989).

S. Muralidharan, "On Inclusion of the Private Part in Ada Package Specification", Proceedings of the Seventh Annual National Conference on Ada Technology, March, 1989, pp188-192, USA.

Shaw(1989).

M. Shaw, "Abstraction Techniques in Modern Programming Languages," IEEE Software, Vol. 1, No. 4, October 1984, p. 10.

Solderitsh(1989).

J. J. Solderitsh, K. C Wallnau, and J. A. Thalhamar, "Constructing Domain-Specific Ada Reuse Libraries", Proceedings of the Seventh Annual National Conference on Ada Technology, March, 1989, pp419-433, USA.

Tichy(1988).

W. F. Tichy, "Tools for Software configuration Management", Proceedings of the International Workshop on Software Version and Configuration Control, Teubner Verlag, Stuttgart, FRG, January 1988, pp 1-20.

Tichy(1989).

W. F. Tichy, R. L. Adams, and L. Holter, "NLH/E: A Natural Language Help System", Proceedings of the 1989 IEEE 11th Conference on Software Engineering, published by ACM 1989, pp.364-374.

Wood(1988).

M. Wood and I. Sommerville, " An information retrieval system for software components", Software Engineering Journal, September 1988, pp 198-207.

Controlling Complexity in Ada Design Representation

JOHN A. ANDERSON & CARL E. DAHLKE

Computer Sciences Corporation
CSC Technology Center
3160 Fairview Park Drive
Falls Church, Virginia   22042
(703) 876-1482

An Ada software design must be understandable for many purposes beyond design and code, such as software management, configuration management, system resource allocation, and customer or internal review.   Unfortunately, Ada designs differ substantially from traditional structured designs and are very difficult for nonprogrammers to decipher. This paper describes a method of organizing the essential aspects of a complex Ada software design into a traditional tree hierarchy that is consistent with the concepts of abstraction and information hiding and that reviewers with minimal Ada experience can easily understand. The organizational method can be used to evaluate the extent of visibility and localization, to identify opportunities for reuse, and to assist in allocating resources to software modules. This method, when applied to the construction of customer-required deliverable documentation, will ease communication between software developers and their customers, between development teams and their management, and among development teams performing different tasks on the same software project.

1. BACKGROUND

The Ada programming language [DOD83] was designed to control complexity by supporting and enforcing the software engineering principles of abstraction and information hiding. Ironically, as the Ada software community continually improves its techniques of designing and implementing systems to exploit these principles, the resulting designs and code are often unintelligible to many of the people who must review or control software development. Management, customers, independent verification and validation teams, and others must be able to understand the organization of and interrelationships among software components in a system.

Traditional structured design (e.g., Yourdon/Constantine) has established many precedents in software design and architecture. It gave developers a consistent, straightforward way to describe software architectures in terms of hierarchical trees. As we progress into more modern development methods such as Object-Oriented Development (OOD), we continue to evaluate software in terms of the qualities learned from those earlier methods, such as strong cohesion and loose coupling. In Ada, these design qualities are often exploited by limiting dependencies among components to localized references at lower levels of implementation. Although the design quality of a given software component is improved by localizing references to and dependencies on other components, the resulting network of interconnecting modules makes diagramming, understanding, and evaluating the system extremely challenging.

A system defined in terms of this kind of network differs dramatically from the traditional hierarchical static software architecture [DOD85] to which customers (especially Government) are accustomed. The traditional hierarchical representation of a structured design helped designers and managers construct and evaluate the software system. Designers evaluated control flow, data flow, and visibility by examining an abstract picture of the interaction between software modules. Management created work breakdown structures by assigning branches of the hierarchical tree to particular teams of developers, allocated memory resource requirements to partitions of the system defined by branches, and controlled configurations based on identification of nodes within the tree. Although these tasks are still required when developing Ada software systems, the interacting network of packages seems to complicate the process. Further, the U. S. Department of Defense has mandated standards that require that a system be decomposed into a hierarchy of Computer Software Configuration Items (CSCIs), Computer Software Components (CSCs), and Computer Software Units (CSUs). Even when not required to follow such mandates, other organizations choose these standards or variations of them (e.g., U.S. Federal Aviation Administration).

Software developers need to represent an Ada software system hierarchically to aid design evaluation, project scheduling and tracking, requirements allocation, and configuration management. Further, a given Ada design must be representable in a single unambiguous form no matter who constructs it, thus ensuring that the construction process is repeatable. Such a hierarchical organization of the software architecture will also aid in organizing and constructing contract-required documentation.

2. REPRESENTING ADA DESIGNS AS HIERARCHICAL TREES

This section of the paper describes a method to diagram individual software components, illustrate their relationships to other components, and summarize them in a single hierarchical tree without compromising design information. The method supports the representation of any Ada software system and has been used on several Computer Sciences Corporation IR&D projects. The method responds to the requirement that a software system be organized into a hierarchical collection of CSCs and CSUs that is present on many Government projects [DOD88].

The method starts by creating diagrams of dependencies within the system using directed acyclic graphs (DAGs), one for each software component. After the system has been graphically represented in a collection of DAGs corresponding to the layers of abstraction within the system, a hierarchical tree is constructed that uniquely identifies the system's CSCs and CSUs.

The components of a simple Ada software subsystem or CSC and their compilation dependencies are represented in Figure 1. Since the decomposition of a large system is analogous to the decomposition of a CSC, it will be a sufficient example for this paper. Figure 2 summarizes the unique graphical icons used to represent the CSC's various compilation units and CSC classes (subsystems, packages, and subunits with decomposable structure). Although the Ada system in Figure 1 is quite small and could be understood by novice Ada programmers, the numerous interconnections and interdependencies complicate the representation. Abstraction and information hiding were used to localize the dependencies within the system, but increased the number of interdependencies among units. At first glance these mechanisms for controlling complexity increased the complexity of the overall representation of the system. However, if the representation of the entire system is consistent with the software engineering principles used to construct it, complexity can indeed be controlled.

2.1 Diagramming The System Architecture

Diagramming begins by establishing a top-level architecture of the software system. The top-level architecture is constructed of CSCs that may be Ada modules or Ada software subsystems (collections of objects with limited visibility to other parts of the system [BOOCH87]). Actually, the entire top-level software architecture can be considered a subsystem in itself if it represents a CSCI in a larger system development effort. Although this stage of the representation process is quite flexible, CSCs in a top-level architecture should represent the major components of a system and collectively may exhaust the primary requirements of that system.

CSCs do not correspond directly with Ada code, but represent a specification together with collections of compilation units that are necessary for execution closure (that is, all of the code that is necessary to define and implement the CSC). Thus, the subsystem can be examined in terms of its definition and corresponding functionality (specification), separately from its decomposition (execution closure).

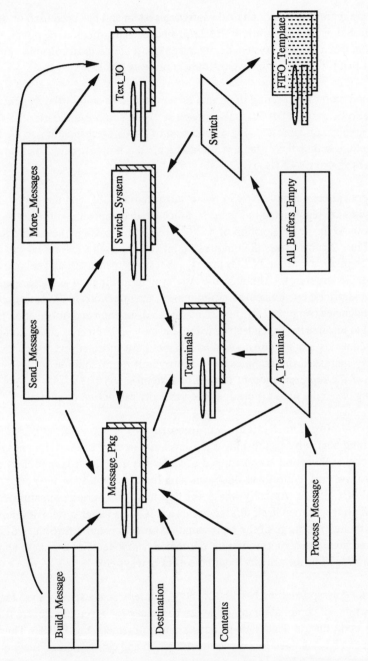

Figure 1. Message Sender Receiver System Components and Dependencies

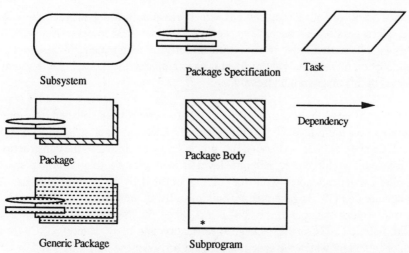

* An asterisk in the lower left corner of a subprogram or task icon
  indicates that the object has a further decomposition

Figure 2. Ada Architectural Icons

The top-level architecture of the example system is represented in Figure 3. Note that
the subprogram at the top of the diagram (Send_Messages 1.1) represents the main
executable process for this subsystem; this subprogram's specification can be
considered the interface to the subsystem. Send_Messages is not just a single
subprogram unit, but has some lower-level architectural information associated with it,
as indicated by the asterisk in the lower left corner. The packages that Send_Messages

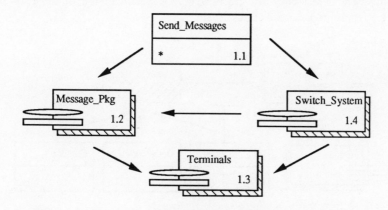

Figure 3. Message Sender Receiver System Top-Level Architecture

depends upon are also represented with corresponding dependency indicators. Send_Messages does not depend on package Terminals 1.3; however, it was included at this level because it implements significant software requirements in the application. The inclusion of Terminals at this level is an example of the flexibility allowed at the top-level of this diagramming technique.

Once the top-level architecture of the software system is established, the internal structure of each top-level CSC is diagrammed. Each top-level CSC is decomposed into CSCs and/or CSUs. Although this process may be similar to the construction of the top-level architecture, at some level it will include diagramming specific compilation dependencies within a CSC as defined by its context clauses. The architecture of a CSC is generated by building a list of the CSCs and CSUs needed to construct it. For example, if the CSC is a package, the lower-level CSC architecture would include CSUs for its package specification and body (if any), CSCs for any components upon which the specification and body depend, and CSCs and/or CSUs for its subunits. Subunits that hide further dependencies should be represented as CSCs to specify that they must be further decomposed. CSUs represent subunits that have no further decomposition. If new dependencies are identified in a CSU during the natural evolution of the design, subunits may evolve from CSUs to CSCs. The transition is represented graphically by simply adding an asterisk to the CSU's icon.

The internal architecture of Message_Pkg (1.2 in Figure 3) is represented in Figure 4. It consists of compilation units for its specification and body (CSUs 1.2.1 and 1.2.2 respectively), and subprogram subunits for Destination and Contents (1.2.5 and 1.2.6). The Build_Message subprogram (1.2.4) is also a subunit of this CSC; however, it is represented as a CSC (note its asterisk) because of its further internal complexity. The dependency of the Message_Pkg specification upon the Terminals CSC (1.2.3) is also represented at this level.[1]

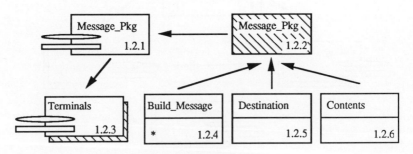

Figure 4. Message_Pkg

---

[1] This is the same Terminals CSC that appeared on the top-level Architecture (Figure 3). The numeric difference will be explained later in the paper.

Build_Message's localized dependency upon Text_IO is illustrated in Figure 5. Separating the internal architecture of Build_Message allows further design enhancement (such as the addition of a more sophisticated user interface) without disruption of the architectural diagram of its parent, Message_Pkg. Thus, the diagramming method supports the abstraction and information hiding principles in the Ada language.

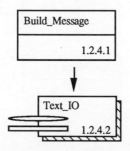

Figure 5. Build_Message

The above process is continued until all of the CSCs in a system are diagrammed. The architecture of any particular CSC should be diagrammed only once; however, it may be (and probably will be) referenced at various points in the architectures of other CSCs. Once a CSC has been diagrammed to a level that represents specific Ada compilation units, the diagramming process is completely repeatable. That is, given a particular Ada software design, one and only one correct graphical representation can be constructed with this technique. To clarify the relationships among all of the parts of the example subsystem, Figures 6 and 7 include the architectures of the rest of the CSCs within the example subsystem.

To maximize the effectiveness of the software system representation, a simple development standard should be followed: The program units should be separately compiled. The graphical representation of a software system should depict all of the program units within that system. Since this graphical method represents the relationships among Ada compilation units, enforcing the use of separate compilation of all program units will ensure that all of them are in the final representation. An alternative to this diagramming method might represent nested units without separate compilation. However, the corresponding nested graphical representations are cumbersome and outside of the scope of this paper. Besides, nesting without separate compilation inhibits further decomposition during system evolution.

The representations used in the example are simple, yet sufficient for organizing the software architecture. The layered representations illustrate the program units visible to a compilation unit as well as that unit's own internal structure. Additional

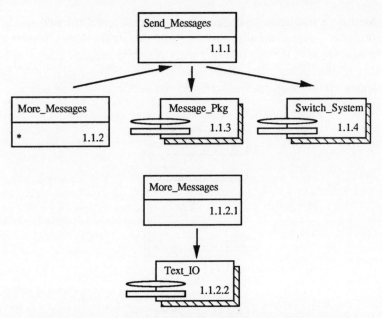

Figure 6. Send_Messages

information may be added to these representations. For example, if the simple package icons are replaced with package-specification icons that indicate the types and operations exported (like those used by Booch in his earlier books, e.g., [BOOCH83]), dashed arrows may indicate dependencies upon types and solid arrows indicate subprogram or task entry calls.[2]

At the end of the above diagramming process, the system is represented as a collection of DAGs, each DAG representing a particular layer of a CSC software architecture. This collection can be contrasted against a single DAG representing all of the dependencies within an Ada software system, which may be too complex to comprehend (e.g., Figure 1).

2.2 Translating To A Hierarchy
Translating the Ada software architecture into a tree hierarchy is greatly simplified by organizing the software into layers. Starting with the top-most layer of the system architecture, each element (CSC) in the particular layer of the software architecture is numbered. Each element in a layer below a particular CSC is numbered prefixed by

---

[2] The construction and maintenance of such diagrams can become unwieldy without automated support. For example, the detailed representation of a package specification would be replicated at every reference to that package, thus requiring unreasonable rework whenever the package interface changed.

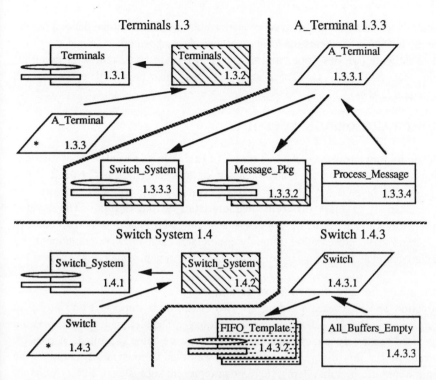

Figure 7. Terminals and Switch_System

its parent's CSC number, forming a unique numeric identifier. This process is continued until all CSCs and CSUs are numerically identified on all levels of the system. This numbering system can then be represented hierarchically as a tree. Thus the tree hierarchy for the software decomposition is not arbitrary, but reflects the information in the layered architectural representation. The numbering system has already been imposed upon the example architectural diagrams for reference. The decomposition of the example subsystem as a hierarchy of software components is shown in Figure 8.

A major consideration for the translation process is how to handle multiple references to software within a (sub)system. Because Ada software reuse is generally in terms of packages or subsystems, it is most likely that multiple references will be in terms of CSCs. As stated above, in order to completely represent all interdependencies in a software system, a single CSC may appear on several software architecture DAGs. To alleviate this problem, we recommend that a CSC's decomposition be represented only once on the hierarchy, and a reference be added to identify the unique CSC number corresponding to the location of its decomposition. This reference will aid the documentation process, because design documents often recommend that reused software components be defined in only one place and referenced everywhere else.

The double asterisk parenthetical references within the CSCs on the decomposition hierarchy in Figure 8 indicate the location of their decomposition. A single asterisk is used to indicate non-developmental software to remain consistent with notations within DOD-STD-2167A. (These references may also be added to the layered architectural DAGs.)

3. SOFTWARE DESIGN SUPPORT

The diagramming process results in a means of examining a complex set of relations among components so that the total complexity of the system need not be dealt with at one time. The layered and hierarchical representations of an Ada software structure can be used to evaluate different characteristics of the design. The layered representations illustrate the design of each module with regard to its own context. The hierarchical representation uniquely enumerates each software component and compilation unit and illustrates their relationships on a system-wide basis.

3.1 Abstraction and Information Hiding
Abstraction and information hiding are two of the most important and powerful aspects supported by the Ada programming language. The hierarchical representation can be used to identify and evaluate how much they are being exploited. A primary requirement for this diagramming method was that it consistently support the definition and use of subsystems. CSCs can represent subsystems, library units, or subunits with further decomposition. Thus, CSCs in the hierarchy supportt defining and identifying of abstract components while deferring their internal structure to a lower level. Further, the method does not focus only on the existence of a software component, but indicates the interdependencies among the components.

3.2 Visibility
A major consideration for an Ada software architecture is the extent that components have visibility to other parts of the system. Since the hierarchical representation identifies every software dependency within a system, a technologist can evaluate if visibility to a particular component is appropriate. On the other hand, if a service from a CSC was established for use in specified parts of the design, the technologist can also evaluate whether the CSC was used appropriately by searching the tree for its references.

Separate compilation in Ada with the use of subunits often causes software to "inherit" visibility to other packages via its parent. For example, all subunits of a package body inherit visibility to the library units referenced in that package body's context clause. The hierarchical tree can be used by the software developer to investigate whether a subunit has visibility to a component without necessarily referencing every file of PDL (or code) in its ancestry. In the same manner, redundant context clauses can be

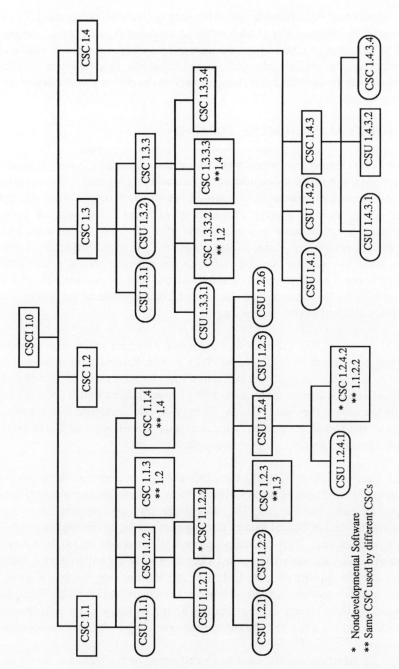

Figure 8. Message Sender Receiver System Decomposition

* Nondevelopmental Software
** Same CSC used by different CSCs

identified and removed. For example, if the package body of Terminals (1.3.2) were dependent upon Message_Pkg (1.2), it would be indicated as a CSC at that level of the hierarchy as well as at 1.3.3.2. Also, the extent of visibility to controlled modules can be monitored. For example, the visibility to Unchecked_Conversion on a package-wide basis may be identified and changed early in the design process before its use becomes widespread.

4. PROJECT MANAGEMENT SUPPORT

Software development involves much more than designing and implementing software. Management must coordinate and encourage cooperation among software teams performing diverse tasks throughout the software development life cycle. Proper management of a project depends on efficient communication between development teams, accurate estimation of the effort needed to complete the project, and effective monitoring of the project progress. The organization of a software design into a hierarchical tree that maintains the principles of the design process simplifies the construction of understandable documentation, thus aiding communication. This organization also creates a better picture of the project, aiding effort estimation and project monitoring.

The total number of CSUs in a software architecture hierarchy represents the number of compilation units to be implemented. With a normalization of the number of lines of code in a "typical" compilation unit, an estimate for the number of lines of code to be delivered can be determined by multiplying this normalized value by the number of compilation units in the current design. The one-to-one correspondence between the CSUs and the compilation units, which uniquely identifies all of the deliverable software files, also simplifies configuration management.

The tree hierarchy also provides the software manager with a mechanism for allocating parts of the development effort to software teams. When CSCs or sets of CSCs are allocated to teams, the hierarchy identifies which software components are shared among teams. Thus a critical path of development can be determined, and software reuse is encouraged. This allocation process also applies to required memory constraints. Since the hierarchy uniquely identifies all of the required code, memory budgets can be applied to specific CSCs, and the budgets can be balanced by examining which modules are shared among the system. Although the hierarchical tree provides little assistance in allocating timing constraints, its understandable organization can assist in building a call tree for examining critical threads of control.

Finally, the hierarchy can be used to closely monitor the software development progress. As components are identified, CSCs can be assigned to them and decomposed later. Since the decomposition below a CSC collectively represent the CSC's execution closure, no CSC is complete until absolutely all of the CSCs and

CSUs in its corresponding subtrees are complete. As portions of the system are implemented and tested, the status of each CSC can be determined by examining the status of its subtrees and constituent parts. CSCs that have yet to be decomposed can be easily identified as leaves of the hierarchical tree that are CSCs without further decomposition or cross-reference (e.g., FIFO_Template 1.4.3.2).

5. APPLICATION ON SOFTWARE DEVELOPMENT EFFORTS

These representations have been very effective for documenting and monitoring small-scale Ada software development projects (teams of three to eight developers). The hierarchical organization eased the development of a tailorization strategy for the Software Design Document (SDD) Data Item Description (DID) of DOD-STD-2167A [DOD88]. The resulting document organized the software components and Ada-PDL in a form natural to software designers and Ada coders. The techniques and representations have been reviewed by managers of established large-scale Ada and non-Ada projects and received a generally positive response. The discussions with the managers identified three major issues: (1) the method recommends that CSUs correspond to compilation units (which may cause a documentation burden), (2) the method recommends that any further information hiding corresponding to separate compilation require the creation of a unique CSC, and (3) the hierarchy has a great deal of (documented) redundancy due to the system's referencing CSCs from a host of locations.

CSUs corresponding to compilation units may increase the amount of documentation for some large projects, since the the definition of a CSU determines the granularity of documentation. Depending on the customer and the development process, CSUs require separate software development files, configuration management, specific reference in design documents, etc. Although developers may not prefer to produce and/or maintain documentation on this low a level, this level does correspond to past non-Ada development standards. For example, a CSU on a FORTRAN project often corresponds to a single "function," which can be analogous to a single subprogram exported from a package. Further, because the Ada compilation unit determines the grain of change within a system, auditing on such a level may be necessary. Finally, since a compilation unit's context clause determines its visibility, creating a software architecture at a higher level actually removes necessary design information from the architectural representation. A less detailed representation may be appropriate for some projects and can be extracted from that which this paper suggests.

The creation of a unique CSC due to lower-level dependencies on separately compiled subunits is intimately tied to the diagramming method's support for information hiding. Ada provides the capability to localize dependencies to the subunit level of the software architecture, and the creation of a corresponding CSC represents this kind of design decision. If necessary, this rule may be relaxed slightly for very simple lower-level structures. For example, the dependency of More_Messages (1.1.2.1) upon Text_IO (1.1.2.2) might have been represented on the same DAG as the decomposition of Send_Messages (1.1.1 through 1.1.4) (see Figure 6).

The final point regarding context clauses and visibility is also the justification for the multiple references to the same software throughout the system. Ada programs allow localized reference to library units from anywhere in the software architecture. The visibility gained is well-documented in the compilation unit's context clause. A graphical representation of the system architecture must emulate these dependencies to reflect the true design. These multiple references demonstrate the extent of software reuse within the project (often referred to as fan-in) and may indicate software components potentially reusable on future projects.

6. CONCLUSIONS

The proper use of software engineering principles such as abstraction and information hiding may seem to the novice or nonprogrammer like an increase in design complication. The organization of an Ada software design should be representable in a simple manner that is consistent with these powerful principles while supporting the activities necessary for managing the development process. The method described in this paper organizes an Ada software design into a simple hierarchy that emulates the design while supporting such activities as software management, configuration management, system resource allocation, and customer or internal review. Because this hierarchy resembles one constructed from traditional structured design efforts it will be more understandable to nonprogrammers and still support detailed activities of programmers and designers. Thus, the process facilitates communication between software developers and their customers, between development teams and their management, and among development teams performing different tasks on the same software project.

7. REFERENCES

[BOOCH83] Booch, Grady, Software Engineering With Ada (First Edition), The Benjamin/Cummings Publishing Company, Inc., Menlo Park, CA, 1983.
[BOOCH87] Booch, Grady, Software Components With Ada, The Benjamin/Cummings Publishing Company, Inc., Menlo Park, CA, 1987.
[DOD83] U.S. Department of Defense, Reference Manual for the Ada Programming Language, ANSI/MIL-STD-1815A, 22 January 1983.
[DOD85] U.S. Department of Defense, Defense System Software Development, DOD-STD-2167, 4 June 1985.
[DOD88] U.S. Department of Defense, Defense System Software Development, DOD-STD-2167A, 29 February 1988.

Does Ada Really Contribute to the Development of Embedded Computing Systems (ECS) ?

H.A. NEUMANN

MBB GmbH, Postfach 80 11 09, D-8000 München 80

Abstract:
This paper is a contribution to the dispute about the suitability of Ada for the development of Embedded Computing Systems (ECS), particularly if these systems are distinguished by severe timing constraints (hard real-time systems).

In this context the paper presents the principles of a particular procedure, termed *E-S-A/ProSpec*, that supports the formal model-oriented specification of ECS and allows for the transformation of the formal specification into suitable structures of Ada objects.

A major concern of the paper is the critical examination of the Ada objects resulting from the transformation in terms of complexity, safety and efficiency. Conclusions are drawn with respect to conceivable solutions that hold the capability to achieve more efficient Ada implementations.

Keywords:
Formal specification, operational objects, activation/deactivation of processes, activation predicate, multitasking, active/passive Ada task, monitor task, task scheduling.

1 INTRODUCTION

Immediate application of a software development language, such as Ada [Ada83], in the course of the development of Embedded Computing Systems (ECS) is restricted to the design and implementation of the embedded software in fairly small ECS. There are two essential reasons:

(1)   the notation of Ada does not reflect adequately the imagination of the system engineers about the structure, properties and/or behaviour of a more complex ECS

(2)   principles of scheduling of concurrent ECS components are very specific and restrictive in Ada, and communication between such components is restricted to the utilisation of a particular synchronous principle ("Ada rendezvous").

The first reason is very general. Nevertheless, it enforces the distinction of two major phases of ECS development, even if the development of the embedded software is of major concern [NEU89]:

(1) ECS specification

(2) embedded software design and implementation (in line with the ECS-oriented hardware/-firmware development).

The second reason is a specific one and refers to the application of the model-oriented approach to ECS specification. This approach is outlined in [NEU90] together with a powerful specification procedure and associated notation, termed *E-S-A/ProSpec*, that

(1) supports the conceptual decomposition of ECS into suitable operational and non-operational objects

(2) allows the easy construction from such objects and expressive formal specification of an abstract model, which reflects the ECS behaviour in terms of reactive and functional ECS requirements and physical constraints

(3) allows the computer-supported transformation of the formal model-oriented ECS specification into suitable structures of Ada design objects and associated implementations.

E-S-A/ProSpec has been proposed and elaborated by the author. Thereby *E-S-A* (*Enhanced Structured Analysis*) comprises a graphical and textual notation to support the conceptual ECS decomposition. It is based on Structured Analysis [DEM81], however is "enhanced" by suitable model-oriented principles that are related to predicate transition nets. *ProSpec* (*Process Spec*ification) is an elaborate notation that allows the model-oriented formal specification of operational objects that are identified during the conceptual ECS decomposition.

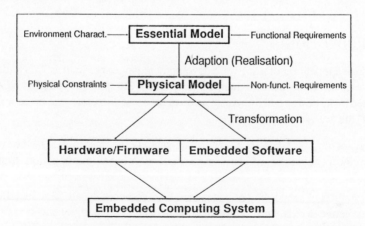

Fig. 1: ECS Specification Process supported by *E-S-A/ProSpec*

The basic principles of *E-S-A/ProSpec* and of the transformation process are presented. On this basis the characteristics of resulting structures of Ada objects are critically examined in terms of complexity, safety and efficiency. Conclusions are drawn and conceivable solutions discussed that hold the capability to overcome efficiency implications under the condition of ECS with severe timing constraints. As a conclusion of the presentation the view of the author to the question raised in the title of the paper is summarized.

2 ECS SPECIFICATION

2.1 Principles of the ECS Specification Process

The ECS specification process that is supported by *E-S-A/ProSpec* is indicated by figure 1. It results from the fact, that generally target-independent as well target- and solution-dependent requirements and environment characteristics can be distinguished. Consideration of the target-independent reactive and functional requirements, of environment characteristics and of the required ECS operation allows the establishment of the target-independent ECS behaviour representation, the so-called "Essential Model". This "engineer-oriented" ECS model must be adapted and extended to the "Physical Model" in such a manner, that the target- and solution-specific constraints and non-functional requirements (associated with quality, security etc.) are obeyed.

The phases of the *E-S-A* specification comprise the conceptual ECS decomposition (to achieve the model structure) and the model-oriented formal ECS specification. The phases reiterate until the verification of the Essential and Physical Models and their validation against the requirements and constraints are achieved.

2.2 Conceptual ECS Decomposition

In *E-S-A/ProSpec* operational and non-operational objects are distinguished.

2.2.1 Operational objects
Operational objects have the following characteristics:

(a)   they are building blocks that may be decomposed into less complex objects, which leads to a hierarchical structure - termed "ECS decomposition structure"

(b)   on each level of the hierarchical structure these objects are connected with other objects to form a net structure - termed "ECS flow structure".

Top level object of the structure is the ECS interfacing to special devices or terminators of the ECS environment and optionally to other ECS. Each ECS is decomposed into s levels of "subsystems", and each lowest-level subsystem into p levels of "processes", where s >= 0 and p >= 1 depend on the size and complexity of the ECS.

The operation of each subsystem and of each upper-level process is understood to be characterized by multiple concurrent threads of control, therefore the distinction of these objects is arbitrary. However, each lowest-level process is defined to be a concurrent object with only one single thread of control.

Lowest-level processes are decomposed into functions, where each function usually represents a distinct service. Functions are defined to operate alternately and in sequence. As a consequence always only one function of a process is specified to be active, and a conflict arises, if more than one function is ready to operate. In this case a "scheduling mechanism", i.e. the principle of selection of the next function to become active must be specified.

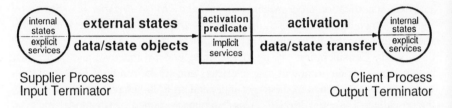

Supplier Process   Client Process
Input Terminator   Output Terminator

Fig. 2: Interfacing of ECS Objects

The interfacing of two particular operational ECS objects is defined to be achieved by means of a so-called "activator", which represents an external logical switch (termed "activation predicate") and associated implicit services - see figure 2 and [NEU90]. It is assumed that, on transition of an activation predicate, these implicit services effect the activation or deactivation of an associated function and effect optional queuing and transfer of data objects to this function. Therefore the required synchronization of concurrent processes and the communication between processes are specified indirectly by means of activation predicates associated with functions.

2.2.2 Data and Activation Flow Diagrams
The decomposition structure and the flow structure is visualized by so-called *Data and Activation Flow Diagrams (DAFD)*.

Within a DAFD the activators are depicted by named single bars, termed "activation element". For reasons of simplicity these elements are replaced by the name of a data object in case queuing and transfer of actual data objects are effected by the activator. If data objects are made available and are accessed by means of an explicit store or buffer, the activation elements are replaced by a named double bar.

A typical example of a DAFD is presented in figure 3. This DAFD represents a single-lift system that is a subsystem of a multiple-lift ECS. In figure 3 the circles represent processes. Isolated single bars represent signals that are transmitted from/to terminators, whereas the single bar named GOcond(j) represents a structured activation element. Named or bare arcs that directly connect operational objects represent queuing and transfer of data objects or of simple activation calls to the object addressed by the arrow. For example details please refer to [NEU88].

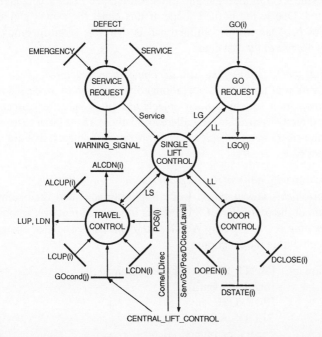

Fig. 3: Example of a Data and Activation Flow Diagram (DAFD)

As can be seen from the example DAFD, the processes react upon different signals, generate signals, accept state information or data objects, transfer updated states and data objects to other processes. This means that the specification of the orderly operation of the ECS in terms of *ProSpec* requires each distinct and competitive activity of a process to be represented by a separate function.

2.2.3 Non-operational objects
The non-operational objects represent "external states", "internal states" and "data objects". These objects usually mirror the hierarchical decomposition structure.

External states are logical representations of physical signals that are transmitted from/to the ECS environment or are suitably defined ECS-internal switches. They are logically combined to form the activation predicates and therefore determine, if a particular function is active or not active at a particular point of time. Internal states control the local flow of control inside an active function of a process.

2.2.4 Object Dictionary
The hierarchical structures of non-operational objects down to the lowest-level elements and the logical and physical attributes of these elements are specified by means of a special symbolic languages within the so-called *Object Dictionary (OD)*.

2.3 Model-oriented Formal Specification

In the following sections the highlights of the formal specification language *ProSpec* are presented. Due to the limited scope of this paper the syntax and associated semantics of *ProSpec* is only outlined and is therefore often incomplete or not necessarily precise to the last detail.

2.3.1 Formal specification of the ECS decomposition structure

The specification of upper-level operational objects down to processes reflect the ECS decomposition structure. Such objects are either specified directly, or are specified indirectly by means of so-called object-types. In the latter case parameters represent non-operational objects or other operational objects, that are addressed by the object type.

2.3.2 Formal specification of the ECS operation

Operational objects are supposed to be implicitly activated for operation. The specification of the particular ECS operation in terms of reactive, responsive and timing behaviour is expressed by WAIT-statements and associated operations that are embedded within the functions:

    function ::=   [WAIT_FOR activation_predicate;]
                    function_identifier:
                    [PURPOSE: any_text]
                    BEGIN
                    {operation I function}
                    END function_identifier [RETURN]

Functions are classified into "repetitive" and "non-repetitive". A repetitive function offers repeated service and is therefore headed by a WAIT-statement and closed with a RETURN-clause. Repetitive functions, which are specified one after the other, are interpreted as a block of competitive functions that run alternately with proper selection provided in accordance with defined selection principles (see section 2.3.5). A non-repetitive function is terminated after completion of its first operation. It allows for the initialisation of states and, if associated with a WAIT-statement, for the exit from a group of alternative functions.

If the transformation of input data (other than relevant states) to output data by means of a special algorithm is part of the operation of a function, the formal specification is restricted to an embedded function "frame". Operations of a frame are specified by "any_text" that is understood to be outside the scope of the semantics of *ProSpec*.

2.3.3 Activation predicates

The effect of the activation predicate on the associated function depends on the actual state of the function, which is defined to be active, ready, waiting or terminated. A function is switched to the ready state on transition of the associated activation predicate from FALSE to TRUE. This enables the function to be selected for activation as soon as the active function is switched to another state. A repetitive function that has completed its service, is switched to the waiting state, if the associated activation predicate is found to be FALSE at completion, and is switched to the ready state otherwise.

An activation predicate is either represented by a simple waiting condition or is composed of simple waiting conditions that are logically combined by logical operators OR I AND. Simple waiting conditions are defined in accordance with the following syntax rules:

```
simple_waiting_condition ::=
    boolean_variable [TO_RESET] I
    CALL_FROM alternative_callers[(formal_data_object)] I
    state_variable relational_operator state_expression
```

```
state_variable ::=                 state_expression ::=
    integer_variable I                 integer_expression I
    userdefined_state_variable I       userdefined_state_value I
    predefined_state_variable          predefined_state_value I
                                       state_variable
```

where:

(a) boolean_variable represents a simple state, i.e. either a two-state external signal or a two-state ECS-internal switch

(b) alternative_callers addresses either an anonymous caller or alternative callers that are identified. In both cases a recall is possible by means of a predefined internal data variable CALLER[identification], where: identification ::= [process_identifier.]function_identifier.

(c) formal_data_object is a formal parameter that represents a structured data object that is specified in the Object Dictionary

(d) userdefined_state_variable represents a state that may assume any of the values defined by the user and specified in the Object Dictionary

(e) predefined_state_variable represents one of the following predefined external states:

PERIOD I TIME I QUEUE[(identification)] I STATE[(identification)]

PERIOD holds the actual time period elapsed since the last encounter of the associated WAIT-statement, TIME holds the actual time available from a central clock, QUEUE holds the number of calls that have accumulated (see below) and STATE holds the state of the function that is addressed.

Simple waiting conditions are set to TRUE by means of activation operations. Reset of a simple waiting condition to FALSE is either by means of an explicit activation operation or is supposed to be implicitly provided, if the simple waiting condition has contributed to the transition of the activation predicate to the value TRUE and is one of the following types: boolean_variable TO_RESET I CALL_FROM.

Simple waiting conditions of the type CALL_FROM are defined to be associated with an implicit queue, where calling functions and associated actual data objects accumulate in accordance with the principle "first-come first-served".

2.3.4 Activation operations

The operation of each function of a process is specified in sequential order by means of three types of elementary operations, that are defined to be "indivisible":

(a) activation operations that control the activation or deactivation of functions in processes:

SET_operation ::=	SET boolean_variable; I
	SET state_variable = state_expression;
RESET_operation ::=	RESET boolean_variable;
CALL_operation ::=	CALL process_name.function_name
	[(actual_data_object)]
	[AFTER PERIOD = p I AT TIME = t];
WAIT_operation ::=	WAIT_FOR waiting_condition;

(b) assignment operations that switch internal states and thereby change control flow conditions or function selection conditions

(c) control flow operations or decision tables, that specify the required logical sequence of operations.

The SET-, RESET- and CALL-operations are defined as no-wait-operations that effect the transition of simple waiting conditions. Whereas the SET- and RESET-operations enable "indirect activation/deactivation" of functions, the CALL-operation offers "direct activation". The WAIT-operation causes a function to be temporarily suspended, if the stated waiting condition is found to be FALSE. Waiting conditions are composed from simple waiting conditions as activation predicates, however may include internal states. The application of WAIT-operations may result in rendezvous situations, if mutual calling of functions in different processes is required.

2.3.5 Function Selection Mechanisms

Selection of a function inside a block of alternative functions is defined to be in accordance with the rank of the functions that is expressed by the order of its specification within the block. Ranking of functions is a frequent case in real ECS, because very often functions that react upon urgent events and update associated internal states must be selected with higher priority than functions that depend on the actual internal states.

In order to provide for a more flexible function selection, alternative functions inside a block may be grouped into function groups, and a priority and a particular selection principle may be optionally associated with each function group. The priority may assume any integer value ranging from 0 (default value) to 255 (highest priority).

Selection principle is one of the following alternatives:

(a) FCFS, that expresses "first-come - first-served" as the principle of selection within the associated function group (default)

(b) ARBI[TRARY], that addresses arbitrary selection within the function group

(c) PRIO[RITY], that addresses selection based on the priority of the calling function.

In addition to the priority-ruled interruption of functions, two special operations are defined that allow the specification of condition-ruled interruption:

(a) INTERRUPT ON waiting_condition;

(b) BREAK [TO_REPEAT [process_identifier.]function_identifier] ON waiting_condition;

After (a) or (b) has been passed, the function is interrupted at any subsequent point, as soon as the stated waiting condition has become true. In case (b) the function is not queued for continuation, instead the optional process/function is called.

The available CALL-operations and selection principles along with priority- and condition-ruled interruption allows the straightforward specification of any of the following basic scheduling mechanisms or any suitable combination thereof:

(a) cyclic activation of functions by periodic function calls (cyclic scheduling)

(b) pure operation-controlled activation/deactivation of functions, i.e. no priorities and interruption conditions are specified (wake-up scheduling)

(c) interrupt-controlled activation/deactivation of functions (e.g. pre-emptive scheduling)

(d) condition-ruled interruption of functions (e.g. time-sliced scheduling).

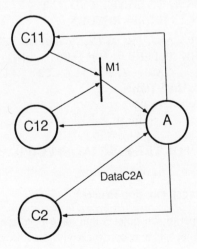

Fig. 4: DAFD of a Typical Example

2.4 Example Specification in *ProSpec*

The essential principles and basic formal elements of *ProSpec* are applied in the following typical example specification - see figure 4.

The specification comprises processes *C11*, *C12*, *C2* and *A*. Process *A* enclose two alternative function *F1* and *F2*, where *F1* is indirectly activated by processes *C11* and *C12*, and *F2* is directly called by process *C2*. Non-repetitive functions *INIT* in *C11* and *C12* provide for the initialization of external states *B1* and *B2*. The processes *C11*, *C12* and *C2* are synchronized by calls from the function *F2* in *A*.

```
C11:  BEGIN
          INIT:   BEGIN RESET B1; END INIT
          WAIT_FOR CALL_FROM A.F2;
          F:   BEGIN ... SET B1; ...  END F RETURN
      END C11

C12:  BEGIN
          INIT:   BEGIN RESET B2; END INIT
          WAIT_FOR CALL_FROM A.F2;
          F:   BEGIN ... SET B2; ...  END F RETURN
      END C12

C2:   BEGIN
          WAIT_FOR CALL_FROM A.F2;
          F:   BEGIN ... CALL A.F2(DataC2A); ...  END F RETURN
      END C2

A:    BEGIN
          WAIT_FOR B1 TO_RESET AND B2 TO_RESET;
          F1: BEGIN  ...  END F1 RETURN
          WAIT_FOR CALL_FROM C2.F(Data) OR PERIOD = p;
          F2:   BEGIN  IF PERIOD /= p THEN ... END (IF)
                       CALL C11.F; CALL C2.F; CALL C12.F;
                END F2 RETURN
      END A
```

3 TRANSFORMATION OF THE FORMAL SPECIFICATION INTO ADA OBJECTS

3.1 Principles of the Transformation Process

The transformation of operational objects that have been specified by means of *E-S-A/ProSpec* to Ada objects is in accordance with the following table:

E-S-A/ProSpec objects:	Ada objects:
process	active task (specification + body)
implicit activator providing interfacing and associated activation /deactivation of processes/functions, expressed by a WAIT-statement or WAIT-operation and associated activation operations (SET/RESET)	procedures and associated external or internal states encapsulated by a package, where activation and deactivation of active tasks that import and call the procedures is effected by means of a local "monitor task"
implicit activator providing a buffer mechanism for no-wait calls of a task with optional one-directional data transfer, expressed by simple WAIT- and associated CALL-statements	procedures as above with optional parameters to provide for the one-directional data transfer
non-repetitive function embedded in a process	procedure/function or accept statement and associated code section embedded in an active task
repetitive functions or group(s) of alternative functions embedded in a process	select statement, that is embedded within a loop of an active task and encloses select entries (waits) and associated code sections representing the alternative functions, where the calling of the selective waits is effected by "translator tasks" that are triggered by monitor tasks
frame function representing a special algorithm inside a function	procedure specification
assignment operation / control flow operation inside a function	assignment statement / control flow construct

3.2 Characteristics of the Resulting Ada Objects

The essential result of the transformation process are Ada tasks that correspond to the specified *E-S-A/ProSpec* processes. These "active tasks" are interfaced by means of "passive tasks" that represent the implicitly specified activators. The passive tasks act as "monitor tasks" or as "translator tasks".

Figure 5 presents the active and passive monitor and translator tasks that are the result of the transformation of the example specification. Active tasks are represented by bold circles. The arc heads indicate the calling of entries in tasks.

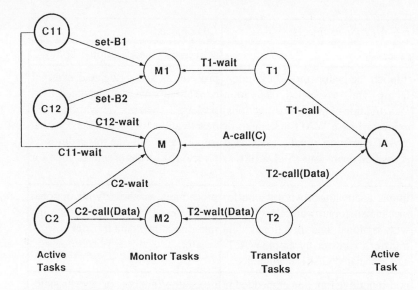

Fig. 5: Interfacing of Active Ada Tasks by Passive Tasks

3.2.1 Passive tasks

Monitor tasks provide for the interfacing and associated activation or deactivation of and one-directional communication between active tasks as specified by means of WAIT-statements/-operations and associated no-wait SET-, RESET- and CALL-operations. Direct calling of Ada task entries contradicts no-wait activation operations, because it causes the mutual coupling of active tasks by the mutual waiting for the "rendezvous", which is the basic mechanism to express task synchronization and communication in Ada.

Active tasks are calling tasks, whereas monitors are called tasks that accomplish selection of called entries [BUR85]. This principle distinction of active and passive tasks is disrupted, if an active task must reflect the specified selection of alternative functions. Since Ada tasks only offer selection among called entries, a translator task is required in such cases to reverse the calling direction between a monitor task and a selective active task. The translator task calls the wait entry of the monitor task on behalf of the active task and calls the active task on completion of the rendezvous associated with the wait call. The direct call of the monitor task by the active task and direct recall by the monitor to avoid the translator task would lead to the coupling of the alternative functions in the active task to the allocated monitor tasks.

3.2.2 Active tasks

The specification and body of an active task are fairly straightforward in case the selection of alternative functions is specified to be arbitrary. However, in other cases the entries to the alternative functions must be guarded and a suitable algorithm must be provided that opens and closes the guards in accordance with the specified selection principle. If priorities are specified with function groups, a task must be established for each function group.

3.2.3 Resulting Ada packages

The final result of the outlined transformation of an *E-S-A/ProSpec* specification into suitable Ada design objects and associated object implementations are packages as follows:

(a)   packages encapsulating active tasks that represent processes allocated to upper-level objects

(b)   packages designed as special abstract data types (as so-called "abstract machines") that export procedures used by the active tasks to call locally hidden monitor tasks

(c)   packages encapsulating passive translator tasks that act on behalf of active tasks that utilize selection among several entries to alternative "functions".

These packages provide for the "structured multitasking" by the systematic inter-facing of active tasks by passive tasks and thereby contribute positively to the software safety. However, the resulting nets of Ada objects are characterized by a high degree of complexity. This may lead to efficiency implications under the condition that an ECS must respond to severe timing constraints.

3.3 Possibilities to Achieve More Efficient Ada Implementations

3.3.1 Reduction of the complexity

A major contribution to the complexity results from the fact that selection among functions in active Ada tasks requires the calling of associated entries. This requirement prevents the simplifying rule, that active tasks are callers of passive monitor tasks, instead it requires the introduction of translator tasks.

An adequate solution to this problem would be achieved by the extension of the entry calling mechanism beyond conditional and timed entry calls to selective entry calls that correspond to selective waits. Since arbitrary selection does not match the usually required scheduling in real ECS, different principles of selection among entry calls should be offered in this context - see section 2.3.5.

The proposed extension of one of the Ada tasking language constructs would eliminate the translator tasks and the associated task switching, and therefore would also contribute to the increase of efficiency. Under the assumption that the tasks presented in figure 5 would run on one processor with equal priority, 14 context switches would be required until the tasks C11, C12 and C2 would reach the starting situation to again compete for the processor. By the elimination of the translator tasks 4 context switches would be saved.

3.3.2 Increase of the multi-tasking efficiency

The number of context switches reduces to the minimum of four that is necessary to activate the tasks C11, C12, C2 and A, if also the monitor tasks would be eliminated. However, this would require the application of task synchronization and communication concepts that are more primitive than the Ada rendezvous, such as [BUR85]

(a)   monitor procedures (and associated primitive wait and send operations) that would allow the specified wait and associated activation operations to be completely allocated to the calling tasks and thereby would avoid the context switching to the additional monitor task

(b)   semaphores (and associated primitive P- and V-operations) that would provide for the mutual exclusion of the access of the active tasks to code sections manipulating common states (critical sections) and thereby would reduce the context switching to active tasks as above.

Both concepts (a) and (b) increase the complexity considerably, because task switching is explicit by means of primitive operations, although (a) is superior to (b). Furthermore, both concepts require the global visibility of the states that influence the wait and go of the active tasks. This requirement contradicts the information hiding principles that are observed by monitor tasks and therefore does not comply satisfactorily with safety criteria.

Result is, that the Ada concept of monitor tasks is superior to concepts that extend indirectly or directly the active tasks to provide for task switching, such as monitors and semaphores, if complexity and safety are considered. Therefore it is not recommended, that the Ada tasking constructs are extended to provide for more efficient asynchronous task switching.

There are other solutions that hold the potential to achieve a more efficient Ada implementation:

(a)   optimized programming (explicit optimization)

(b)   optimizing compilation (implicit optimization)

(c)   suitable extension of the Ada run-time system

(d)   ada-oriented hardware or firmware to support task switching.

ProSpec allows the so-called "sequentialization" of an ECS, which means the transformation of n processes into alternative function groups that are embedded within only $m < n$ processes. Case (a) is addressed, if $m = 1$ and the resulting *ProSpec* specification is transformed into one Ada task. Increase of efficiency depends on the required scheduling of the alternative *ProSpec* functions and resulting complexity of the Ada task and on the quality of the Ada run-time system.

Another case (a) solution is achieved, if calls by active tasks to monitor tasks are reduced to cases that really require switching of a task to the waiting or to the ready state. Since checking of the states associated with the waiting conditions by the active tasks is needed here, a safe application of the method is restricted to wake-up scheduling. Other solutions utilize busy waiting and polling, which are more efficient, if average waiting times are below average task switching times.

Case (b) is addressed, if the compiler utilizes implicit wait- and send- operations to allow the monitor tasks to be transformed to monitor procedures, or if a suitable transformation is based on implicit semaphores and associated P- and V-operations [HAB80]. Case (c) is addressed, if special Ada packages offer operations that support a more efficient task communication or synchronization, e.g. operations that utilize message passing or mailboxes or semaphores.

3.3.3 Scheduling of Ada tasks

There is a strong impact of the scheduling of Ada tasks on the complexity, safety and efficiency of the resulting software. Ada implementations that require scheduling that is based on particular function or task selection principles are cumbersome and complex and therefore are inefficient. In this context it is particularly annoying, that reactions of the run-time system and associated task interruption rules are not precisely defined, or are unsatisfactory [CHI90]. This refers to cyclic scheduling, wake-up scheduling, pre-emptive scheduling and time-sliced scheduling - see section 2.3.5.

It seems necessary that at least the first three types of scheduling are supported in such a manner, that a standard configurable ada-oriented run-time system can be achieved.

4 CONCLUSION: WHAT DOES ADA CONTRIBUTE TO THE DEVELOPMENT OF ECS?

The basic principle for task communication in Ada is the rendezvous, which supports and simplifies mutual communication, however causes the mutual coupling of Ada tasks. Decoupling and suitable interfacing of tasks can be achieved by means of separate monitor tasks that are implemented locally within special abstract data types in accordance with information hiding principles. These tasks can be understood as "specifications" of the task switching mechanisms that are required by specific ECS and that can be provided by reusable generic packages.

Both, communication and interfacing of tasks in Ada, contribute considerably to the reduction of the ECS complexity. Major reason is the fact, that active tasks are no longer overloaded by task switching functions and therefore are reduced to their actually specified workload. The important result is, that verification efforts decrease and that software safety is improved.

However, reduced efficiency compensates for the gain. The net effect gets even worse in real ECS due to the fact, that translator tasks are required to accomplish the calling of selective waits via monitor tasks, that selection among alternative entries is restricted and that task switching and interruption are not precisely defined and satisfactorily supported in Ada.

This fact has caused heavy discussions and disputes about the complexity and resulting efficiency and safety of ECS implemented in Ada in comparison to what can be achieved in this respect by the application of other programming languages. Despite or because of these disputes, the author is convinced that Ada has contributed more than any other programming language to a better understanding of the implications of software development for large, complex and hard real-time ECS, and that Ada has provided some of the key concepts that have really advanced the development of ECS.

In order to achieve the undisputed suitability of Ada for the development of safe and efficient high-quality ECS, the respective drawbacks and restrictions of Ada must be removed. There is a change to approach this goal and turn Ada into a software development language that is superior to any other language: Ada-9X. This chance should be used!

References:

[Ada83]   The Ada Programming Language Reference Manual, ANSI/MIL-STD 1815A -1983, Springer Verlag, Lectures on Computer Science, No. 155

[BAR]   Barringer H., Hill A. (Editors): Specification Techniques for Concurrent Systems, intended for publication as the result of the Ada-Europe Working Group "Formal Specification and Verification"

[BUR85]   Burns A.: Concurrent programming in Ada, Ada Companion Series, Cambridge University Press, 1985

[CHI90]   Chitwood G., Jones B.: Ada in the Real-Time World, Contribution to the 5. Deutscher Ada-Anwenderkongreß in München, Jan. 1990

[DEM81]   DeMarco T.: Structured Analysis and System Specification, Yourdan Press, New York, 1981

[HAB80]   Habermann A.N., Nassi I.R.: Efficient implementation of Ada tasks, Technical Report CMU-CS-80-103, Carnegie-Mellon University, 1980

[NEU88]   Neumann H.A.: *E-S-A/ProSpec* (Enhanced Structured Analysis), contribution to [BAR], May 1988 (preprint is available from the author)

[NEU89]   Neumann H.A.: AIMS - Aerospace Intelligent Management and Development Environment for Embedded Systems, Proceedings of the Int. Conf. on SDE&F in Berlin, May 1989, Pitman Publishing

[NEU90]   Neumann H.A.: Specification of Embedded Computing Systems and Transformation to Ada, Contribution to the 5. Deutscher Ada-Anwenderkongreß in Munich, Jan. 1990

PART IV: Environments and Tools

The MALPAS Analysis System For Ada

R. H. Pierce

IPSYS Software plc, UK

J. T. Webb

Rex, Thompson & Partners Ltd, UK

1 INTRODUCTION

MALPAS (Webb, 1988, 1989) is a suite of software tools used for the static analysis and verification of program text. Versions of the MALPAS suite have been available for some time for Coral 66, Pascal and various assembler languages. Ada has now been added to the list of languages supported by MALPAS. This paper describes the analyses performed by the MALPAS system, the special demands which Ada places on the system, and the development methods needed in order to maximise the benefits of static analysis using the MALPAS tools.

2 THE USE OF STATIC ANALYSIS TECHNIQUES

A great deal of "high integrity" software is to be written in Ada. Projects which will use Ada for software of this kind include the US space station and its Canadian and European contributions, the Eurofighter project, and the new US and Canadian air traffic control systems. Such software must be verified and validated to a high degree of confidence. Traditional testing, when it is feasible at all (generating the data to exercise every path adequately is a formidable task), is prohibitively expensive for real programs of any complexity.

Over the last few years, however, the complementary technique of static analysis (examining the source text without actually executing it) has received proper tool support which makes it a practical method for real-life systems. By analysing programs at an early stage in the life cycle, these tools provide a comprehensive check of the software's integrity and, just as important, do so far more cost effectively than relying on conventional testing alone.

One such static analysis tool is MALPAS, which, in addition to supporting other languages, now has a uniquely comprehensive ability to analyse Ada programs. The MALPAS Ada translator will give developers, users and regulatory bodies an extremely powerful facility to establish confidence in the correctness of Ada programs.

The UK Ministry of Defence has published draft interim standards (00-55 and 00-56) which deal with the identification of safety-critical systems and then the development of safety-critical software itself. Currently, a significant degree of static analysis is mandated, and MALPAS is one of the tools available to support this.

This paper discusses the functions of the MALPAS system, the mapping of Ada to MALPAS, the construction of the translator itself, and the effective use of the system.

3 THE MALPAS SYSTEM

The MALPAS tool performs a number of different but related forms of analysis. These are discussed below in order of increasing sophistication.

3.1 Control Flow Analysis

This form of analysis attempts to find ill-structured code (which cannot be reduced to a combination of sequence, selection and iteration), unreachable code and dynamic halts (endless loops). The control structures in Ada are such that ill-structured code is unlikely to be written, unless **goto** statements are employed with unusual zeal, but control flow analysis can still be used as a quick check on the well-structuredness of Ada code.

3.2 Data flow analysis

Using techniques similar to those employed in global optimisers, data flow analysis computes the *definitions* of a variable (the statements which result in a new value being assigned to the variable) which reach each place in the code where the variable is used. The data flow analyser supplies information on how data is used. It does this by grouping the program's variables into sets, each set representing a particular class of use. Examples are:

a)   Data that is read before it is written. This means data that is either input data or has not been initialised.

b)   Data that is written without being read. This means output data or some problem such as a misspelled identifier.

c)   Data that is written twice without an intervening read. This could be an error or the result of some feature such as a polling loop.

The classes are given both for all paths through a program and some paths through a program. For example, data written twice may only occur with some combination of input data.

3.3 Information flow analysis

For each output parameter (and possibly global variable) used by a subprogram, the MALPAS information flow analyser lists the input variables and parameters on which its value depends. This may be used to confirm that output variables depend on all the input variables specified and that no output variable depends on an input variable which is not specified. For example, an output parameter TRUE_AIR_SPEED which depends on STATIC_PRESSURE, DYNAMIC_PRESSURE and AIR_TEMP is quite believable, but if it also depended on LATITUDE there would be cause for concern. The results of information flow analysis may be manually compared with the behaviour of the procedure as described by the documentation, but it is also possible to annotate the program text to allow the analyser to compare the declared and the actual relationship of inputs and outputs. This is done by means of a statement of the form

derives TRUE_AIR_SPEED from STATIC_PRESSURE,
    DYNAMIC_PRESSURE, AIR_TEMP;

3.4 Semantic analysis (symbolic execution)

The Semantic Analyser describes the mathematical relationships between input and output variables for every semantically feasible path through the loop free regions of a program by, for example, considering a region up to a loop head, then considering the loop itself, and so on. It therefore reveals exactly what the program will do under all circumstances, something which is impossible in any dynamic testing programme. This not only includes all the input values which the analyst expects to influence the output values but also those which are not expected. For example, if the Semantic Analyser indicated that an autopilot had anomalous behaviour if a height sensor was faulty and gave a negative value, one would ensure that the program was modified to cope with such an eventuality.

A built in algebraic simplifier reduces the complexity of the information given and three techniques are available to control the level of detail provided. These are the bottom-up analysis of a structured program, as described below, the use of "node-marking" to restrict analysis to a particular section of a program and the use of a "Partial Programmer" to restrict information provided to that relating to selected paths. The choice of a particular technique depends on the structure of the program being analysed and the implementation language used. Node marking tends to be of particular value when analysing assembly code programs, and the other techniques would tend to be used with Ada.

3.5 Compliance analysis

By using preconditions, postconditions and assertions inserted by the analyst into the program text to be analysed, the compliance analyser attempts to prove that a subprogram meets its specification by showing that, given the preconditions, the postconditions hold. Assertions are provided to state the functionality of the program at intermediate points as necessary. For examples, assertions are required to give loop invariants for the analysis of code containing loops; the choice of loop invariants is one of the more difficult aspects of compliance proofs. For Ada, the pre- and postconditions can include predicates to indicate the absence of exceptions arising from the code, although a full treatment of exceptions by compliance analysis can become extremely complex.

Initially the compliance analyser may not be able to show unambiguously that there is no "threat", i.e. that the program meets its specifications. This may simply be because the algebraic simplifier built into both the semantic and compliance analysers may not be able to completely simplify the expression. However, MALPAS IL permits the insertion of "replacement rules" similar to rewrite rules in OBJ. These enhance the capabilities of the algebraic simplifier, enabling the user to direct effectively the simplification of expressions and obtain a clear statement of conformance where possible. The use of these replacement rules requires a reasonable level of skill by the analyst in using the tool iteratively to achieve a correct set of rules.

4 HANDLING LARGE PROGRAMS

Special techniques are provided by MALPAS to aid the analyst in handling large programs. A Partial Programmer provides the means to perform semantic and compliance analysis on selected paths of complex programs, reducing the output from the MALPAS analysers to manageable proportions. Another technique, and one which is particularly appropriate to Ada, it to perform bottom-up analysis, analysing the lowest-level procedures first and feeding back the information from these levels to the analysis of the next level. In Ada, these levels will generally be reflected in the package structure of the program, and the analysis process will generally proceed by first analysing the subprograms in packages at the bottom of the seniority hierarchy, attempting to prove that the postconditions for each such subprogram are implied by the preconditions anded with the subprogram functionality. These postconditions can then be used in the proofs of other subprograms which call the bottom-level subprograms, and so on up the seniority hierarchy until the main program is reached.

5 TRANSLATING ADA INTO MALPAS

The MALPAS suite operates on an intermediate representation of a program text. The intermediate language is called MALPAS IL. It is a human-readable, textual language with some close similarities to existing programming languages and some fundamental distinctions. The practicality of translating a given programming language into IL depends on whether the model of the computation process provided by IL is sufficiently close to the model implied by the language. In the case of Ada, it has been possible to find a mapping from almost the entire Ada language into MALPAS IL. This is in sharp contrast to the approach used in the SPARK subset of Ada (Carré, 1988) which is designed for use with another set of static analysis tools. While it is likely that in certain projects only a "safe" subset of Ada will be analysed by means of MALPAS, this will by no means always be the case and it is not the business of the translator to impose a particular set of Ada features on MALPAS users.

One feature of MALPAS IL which may strike the ordinary user as unusual is that there is no concept of "conventional" nested procedures or blocks in IL, and therefore the effect of a subprogram on global data must be modelled by mapping the non-local variables accessed by the subprogram into additional parameters in the IL translation of the subprogram. This is a fundamental requirement of static analysis, resulting in the need to analyse subunits to determine the effect of each subunit on the variables in the parent unit before the parent unit can itself be analysed.

Another unfamiliar feature is the treatment of composite types; these are not directly supported by IL and functional models of array and record access must be generated. Thus, for example, a write to a component of a composite object is treated as a function which takes the new component value and the old object and returns a new object. For discriminated records, an explicit test that the discriminant has the correct value is included in the generated IL.

The major features which are not translated are representation clauses and certain tasking constructs, although it should be stressed that an Ada compilation unit containing these features will still be accepted by the translator. Representation clauses do not in general affect the outcome of static analysis, and can in most cases be ignored (although the correctness of any representation clauses used in a high-integrity program must of course be established by other means).

MALPAS can only model the sequential behaviour of a program. For this reason, only the sequential aspects of a task can be translated into IL, with entry calls and accept statements being treated in a manner analogous to procedure calls; the dynamic and concurrent behaviour of each task must be modelled or verified by other means. Expressions in delay and abort statements are translated (since they may raise exceptions), but the statements themselves have no equivalent in IL and the resulting values are discarded. Many high-integrity applications will not use tasking in any event.

Apart from these constraints, any legal Ada program will be handled by the Ada MALPAS system. In particular, the full Ada separate compilation mechanism is available, and it is envisaged that in later versions of the Ada-MALPAS system the program library will be used as a repository for analysis results. Generics are initially handled by analysing only the generic specification and body, each instantiation assuming that the generic has been verified. In some circumstances, it may be desirable to analyse each instantiation individually, using specific information about the generic actual parameters to provide a more refined analysis. This approach may be adopted in a later version of the system.

The handling of exceptions presents no real difficulty of principle, but many difficulties in practice, not least of which is the sheer volume of IL which would be generated if every run-time check and all the dynamic control flow of exception handling were to be explicitly modelled in the IL by means of tests, goto statements and additional subprogram parameters (the latter being necessary to model the exception propagation process). For this reason, the translator has an (optional) simplified mode of translation in which the intention is to show that an exception will not arise; this involves modelling the various constraint checks in a procedure and establishing that a "no exception" postcondition holds. Circumstances which could give rise to STORAGE_ERROR or PROGRAM_ERROR are not considered by the translator. If it is necessary to show that a program will not raise either of these exceptions, this must be done by other techniques (Pierce & Wichmann, 1989).

A simple example of an Ada procedure and its translation into MALPAS IL is given here. The procedure controls the fan and thermostat in a car engine. The thermostat aperture should be closed at a water temperature of 83°C and fully open at 96°C and should open linearly between these two temperatures. The fan should turn on at 95°C and off at 86°C.

```
procedure CAR_COOL is
    TEMP_CLOSE : constant := 83;
    TEMP_OPEN  : constant := 96;
    TEMP_ON    : constant := 95;
    TEMP_OFF   : constant := 86;
    CLOSED     : constant := 0;
    FULLY_OPEN : constant := 100;

    type FAN_STATE is (ON, OFF);

    TEMP : INTEGER;
    APERTURE : INTEGER;
    FAN     : FAN_STATE;

    procedure HOT_OR_COLD
        (OPEN_SHUT  : in INTEGER;
         ON_OFF     : in FAN_STATE;
         APERTURE   : out INTEGER;
         FAN        : out FAN_STATE) is
    begin
        APERTURE := OPEN_SHUT;
        FAN := ON_OFF;
    end HOT_OR_COLD;

begin
    if TEMP <= TEMP_CLOSE then
        HOT_OR_COLD(CLOSED,OFF,APERTURE,FAN);
    else
        if TEMP >= TEMP_OPEN then
            HOT_OR_COLD(FULLY_OPEN,ON,APERTURE,FAN);
        else
            APERTURE := FULLY_OPEN *
            ( TEMP - TEMP_CLOSE ) / (TEMP_OPEN - TEMP_CLOSE);
            if TEMP > TEMP_ON then
                FAN := ON;
            end if;
            if FAN /= OFF and then TEMP > TEMP_OFF then
                FAN := ON;
            end if;
        end if;
    end if;
end CAR_COOL;
```

The MALPAS IL which would be generated from this procedure is shown on the following page.

```
TITLE car_cool;

CONST temp_close : integer = + 83;
CONST temp_open : integer = + 96;
CONST temp_on : integer = + 95;
CONST temp_off : integer = + 86;
CONST closed : integer = + 0;
CONST fully_open : integer = + 100;
TYPE fan_state = (on,off);

PROCSPEC hot_or_cold(IN open_shut : integer
          IN on_off : fanstate
          OUT aperture : integer
          OUT fan : fanstate)

PROC hot_or_cold
    aperture := open_shut;
    fan := on_off
ENDPROC

MAIN
    IF temp <= temp_close THEN
        hot_or_cold (closed,off,aperture,fan)
        ELSE
        IF temp >= temp_open THEN
            hot_or_cold(fully_open,on,aperture,fan)
        ELSE
            aperture := fully_open * ((temp - temp_close)
                      / (temp_open - temp_close));
            IF temp > temp_on THEN
                fan := on
            ENDIF;
            IF fan =/ off THEN
                IF temp > temp_off THEN
                    fan := on
                ENDIF
            ENDIF
        ENDIF
    ENDIF
ENDMAIN
FINISH
```

5 THE CONSTRUCTION OF THE TRANSLATOR

The Ada-MALPAS translator is constructed in the classical manner of Ada compilers. A front end performs syntax and semantic analysis including name identification and overload resolution, and generates a tree-structured intermediate language, which is then read by the translator back end which produces the textual MALPAS IL output. It is important to produce IL which is recognisably derived from the original Ada source text, since the outputs of the MALPAS analysers are expressed in IL terms and not in terms of the original source language.

The front end is derived from the Ada compiler front end produced by the Ada Group Ltd during the M-Chapse project. Some simplification of the front end is made possible by imposing the restriction that only correct Ada source is to be submitted for translation; this allows the front end to omit certain semantic checks which would be necessary in a compiler. Incorrect Ada will however normally be detected and IL translation suppressed, since full overload resolution is needed for the translator back end and the overload resolution system and its associated mechanisms of necessity detect a large number of the possible semantic errors in an Ada program. Since MALPAS IL does not permit overloaded identifiers, all such identifiers in the Ada text must be distinguished by some means in the resulting IL text. This is achieved by adding a distinguishing suffix where necessary. The original form of the identifier is preserved apart from the suffix, so that the analyst can easily recognise the original names from the Ada program text. As an example, if there were three versions of the procedure WRITE, they would be given the identifiers WRITE, WRITE__02 and WRITE__03

In the initial version of the system, MALPAS annotations (such as preconditions and postconditions) will have to be written in IL rather than in Ada, although they may be inserted into the Ada program by means of a special pragma. Where these annotations refer to overloaded identifiers, they must use the names generated by the translator, and where they contain expressions, the expressions must be in IL notation rather than in Ada. Clearly this is somewhat inconvenient for the analyst, and a later version of the system will allow the analyst to write the annotations using Ada syntax (probably as "formal comments") and have the translator process them into IL format.

Both the front end and back end of the translator are written in Ada, with the resulting high productivity and low error rate that Ada users have come to expect. The translator is tested using both the ACVC tests in groups A and C (the executable tests) and by a specially written test suite. Ironically, many of the errors discovered in the front end have been the result of unset variables on certain paths; these would all have been discovered prior to testing had the MALPAS data flow analyser been available at the outset.

6 USING THE MALPAS SYSTEM EFFECTIVELY

The MALPAS control and data flow analysers can be applied effectively to any Ada program and will often reveal anomalies which would eventually lead to run-time errors. However, to make the best use of the more sophisticated analysers, experience has shown that it is desirable to design the program from the outset to take into account the fact that static analysis is to be the main method of establishing correctness. Thus the information flow into and out of each subprogram should be written down as part of the design documentation so that it can be compared with the output of the information flow analyser (this comparison will be made automatically by the information flow analyser if the appropriate annotations are included in the program text). If the compliance analyser is to be used, preconditions and postconditions for subprograms should also be stated at the design stage, and loops constructed if possible to allow straightforward proof using loop invariant assertions (this can be difficult in practice). The program structure should also be designed in such a way that bottom-up analysis can be achieved. Features of Ada which are difficult for analysis should be avoided where possible; use of exceptions for normal control flow is a case in point. This requires a more formal approach to design than is perhaps customary, but the benefits to be gained in increased confidence in the correctness of the program are enormous.

It should be stressed finally that the points on program design and construction noted above are desirable but not essential. MALPAS will work in the absence of any specifications at all; it will be more usable if the specification information is available but valuable work, even of the "reverse engineering" kind, can be done in any case.

7 REFERENCES

Carré, B. (1984) *Validation techniques*, **in** Software engineering for microprocessor systems, ed. P. Depledge. London: Peter Peregrinus Ltd.

Carré, B. (1988) *A subset of Ada for formal verification (SPARK)*, Proc. 7th Ada UK Conference, York, 1988 (Ada User, Vol. 9 Supplement, January 1989).

Pierce, R. H. & Wichmann. B. A. (1989) *Analysis techniques for Ada programs.*, Proc. 8th Ada UK Conference, York, 1989.

Webb, J.T. (1988). *Static analysis - an introduction and example*, Proc. International Workshop of Software Engineering and its Applications, Toulouse.

Webb, J.T. (1989). *Static Analysis using MALPAS. An introduction with examples*. Rex, Thompson & Partners Ltd, Farnham.

Projections From a Decade of CASE

Dick Schefström,
TeleSoft AB,
Aurorum 1, 951 75 Luleå,
Sweden.

The last decade has shown a sharp increase of the interest and expectations in the area of software development environments. From a niche position of computer science, the subject has evolved into an independent area of research, and has generated a growing market of products which is sometimes referred to under the name CASE.

This paper gives a personal, and slightly Ada-oriented, perspective on the background and expectations that generated all this activity. It discusses what then actually happened, and outlines a future where the two cultures of software tools, recently named the Back-End and Front-End CASE, are harmonized into a single concept covering a broad and novel perspective of software development

1.0 BACKGROUND AND EXPECTATIONS

During the initial process of formulating the requirements of the Ada programming language, it was recognized that any abstract language as such would not be a sufficient guarantee for getting the desired productivity increase. Rather, the actual benefits were concluded to be highly dependent on the level of support for the many different tasks involved in software development, ranging from editing, debugging, over configuration control to document production and project management. This emphasis on creating a good *environment*, was manifest in the so called Stoneman document, (Buxton 1979, Buxton & Druffel 1980).

The document had an important impact, since it introduced the vision of an "APSE", (the Ada Programming Support Environment), and focused attention on the idea of integrated support environments to a larger public. Ten years later, people are still struggling towards this vision.

Although Stoneman included a large number of requirements, the most central and influential ideas are summarized by the following citations, (Buxton & Druffel 1984):

> *"The toolset must not only support the appropriate functions, but must be integrated into a consistent environment"*

> *"The APSE must provide a well coordinated set of useful tools, with uniform inter-tool interfaces and with communication through a common database which acts as the information source and repository for all tools"*

The first of those sentences emphasizes *integration* - the recognition that for significant progress to be made, tools must cooperate towards a common goal to a higher degree than was currently the case. The second sentence introduces the idea of the *environment database*, the all-encompassing structured data storage, which would act as the most important integrating factor in the environment. All this was placed in the three level KAPSE/MAPSE/APSE model, with the database at the very kernel KAPSE level.

Those ideas were of course not completely new and original. Instead, the sources of inspiration can probably be sought in a trend that had started long before, some notable examples of which are the *Interlisp* environment, (Teitelman & Masinter 1981), which very early clearly demonstrated the benefits and viability of an environment oriented towards interactivity and tight integration of different services, and the *Smalltalk* environment, (Goldberg 1983), which similarly demonstrated integration and interactiveness, but also information browsing and what is today called a modern user interface. Even though *UNIX* , (Kernighan & Mashey 1981), was not an environment in the sense of Interlisp and Smalltalk, but rather a general operating system, it was an unusually well integrated example, which demonstrated the benefits and elegance of uniform mechanisms and the power gained from the ability of tools to cooperate.

During the same period, many people started to explore the idea of a language oriented editor, (see, for example, Teitelbaum & Reps 1981, Donzeau-Gouge et al 1984), utilizing knowledge of the programming language to support structured editing, viewing, and early syntactic error detection. Since those editors, as part of their work, took over tasks that previously were done by the compiler, (such as scanning, parsing, and generation of internal form), it was a very concrete example of the benefits of integration: the compilation process should take over directly where the editor stopped, and since the point of contact was very much focused around the intermediate program representation, it was natural to propose that many tools should use this common internal representation. In the case of Ada, there was even a standard proposed with the DIANA intermediate language, (McKinley & Schaefer 1986). In the early eighties, every university should have their own language oriented editor project, maybe with an all time high marked by the first conference on Practical Software Development Environments, (ACM 1984).

Much other early work on environments indeed took place, such as the Gandalf project at Carnegie-Mellon University, (Haberman 1980), where much effort was directed towards programming-in-the-large questions like configuration management and version control. An early documentation of various results in the area of development environments is (Hunke 1980).

The result was anyway that the area of software development environments had now established itself as an important area of research, this far shown mainly by an increased number of magazine articles and conferences. The Ada Stoneman document played an important role in this process.

Great expectations were building up, and knowledge of this area was considered of strategic importance as an enabling technology for competitive production of software. Because of its potential global leverage effect, the environment technology became a popular receiver of funding from different research and development programmes, spanning from the initial US DoD Ada fundings Ada Language System, (ALS), and AIE, (Intermetrics 1982), over national programmes like the UK Alvey,

(Brereton, ed. 1988), and European cooperations like PCTE/PACT, (Gallo et al 1986, Thomas 1989a, Thomas 1989b), ESF, (Fernstrom et al 1988, Fernstrom & Ohlsson 1989), and Atmosphere, (Boarder, Obbink, & Schmidt 1989).

2.0 THE OUTCOME

Although the Stoneman-envisioned database was occasionally confused with the traditional business processing databases, most people soon concluded that another kind of database was required, (UK DoI 1981, Intermetrics 1982, Narfelt & Schefstrom 1984, Bernstein 1987, Dittrich 1986). Over the next years, a very large number of projects were launched with the goal of developing such an environment database. Two projects reached a somewhat higher level of attention than others due to their official support from important organizations. The CAIS specification, (Munck et al 1988), supported by US DoD, and the PCTE, supported by the ESPRIT programme of the European Communities, (PCTE 1986).

Most of the database projects identified similar requirements and needs, such as that the datamodel supported should be some variant of the Entity-Relationship-Attribute model, and that it should have the following functionality or properties:

- Long transactions.

- Composite objects.

- Dynamic schema extension.

- Multiple views.

- Version and Configuration Management

- Triggering.

From an Ada point of view, it became clear that the *program library* must be an integrated subset of the environment database, and in fact even could be its starting point, (Narfelt & Schefstrom 1985). Recently there has also been a trend to include ideas from object orientation, such as inheritance and polymorphism into this context, (Williams 1988, Rudmik 1988).

From a now more distant perspective, one can note that although much work was invested in exploring the basic database, few attempts were made to utilize the database for achieving the other central Stoneman concept, of *integration*. This should have consisted of populating the database with a set of tools that used the common database to exchange information in a uniform way, making the complete environment more than the sum of its individual tools. Instead of thereby validating the concept, new database proposals were invented, and discussions were concentrating on issues like for which level of granularity should the database be used, and variations in the basic support for data modeling.

The PCTE proposal here took a very broad approach, and explained the database as a generalization of the filesystem. In this way, the disturbing discontinuity that is experienced at the border between the filesystem and the database would disappear: they would be indistinguishable. No tool would then escape the database, just as tools all the time very naturally have used the filesystem. Tools would make their data accessible by representing them in terms of the PCTE model, and a catalogue of available tool schemas would evolve. The integration with the file system does however imply a very tight, in kernel, integration with the operating system. This causes practical problems unless you are an established vendor and a major supplier of operating systems. Environments that utilize PCTE are under implementation, (Eclipse, PACT, EAST, Atmosphere), some of which are very ambitious. But it must be concluded that few, if any, are yet in serious practical use.

Other projects, such as ISTAR, (Dowson 1987), deemphasized the programming aspect of environments, claiming that we should instead provide support for the orderly management of projects, with all it implies in terms of visible organizations, responsibilities, project plans, and contracts. The latter word, *contract*, was made a basic concept, around which any project should be organized. ISTAR therefore supported the organization of a hierarchy of contracts, which defined what was the input and constraints, and what defined the expected deliverables. The holder of a contract was free to establish subcontractors. Traditional programming support was treated by loosely integrating existing products into the ISTAR framework.

Taking a more critical view, one could claim that this class of organizationally oriented attempts ignored the benefits of tight integration and support for coding, but also sometimes failed to fill the ideas on project organization with a detailed enough semantics, so that conclusions and support could be automatic. In some sense, many such attempts therefore reduced themselves to methodology handbooks. The exploration of how to support projects in the sense of working organizational units is still going on, usually under the name *Software Process research*, (Software Process Workshop 1988).

The European multi-company cooperation *Eureka Software Factory*, ESF, (Fernstrom et al 1988), Fernstrom & Ohlsson 1989), also has a strong emphasis on "software process", but on the other hand explicitly rejects the idea of the central database, partly on the basis that a large number of companies are unlikely to agree on a single standard database and schema. Instead, a so called *Software Bus* is recommended, which states that tools that are contributed by the different companies in the project should be made available by means of a remote procedure callable interface. Although no detailed standard is developed in this area, the hope is that a degree of uniformity will develop as the different tools start to utilize each other. As an architectural guideline for how to construct the software, it is advised that all tools be composed out of two parts - one implementing the user interface, and another implementing the actual application.

A possible criticism to this approach is the lack of central ideas and guidance on how to get real benefits from integration. It is furthermore questionable how beneficial it really is to strive for a very strong, (most of the time process-separated), distinction between two parts, (UI and application), in a software tool. The problems of using UI <-> Application separation as a general principle are discussed in (Hartson 1989,   Fischer 1989). The problem is very similar to what has been discussed and worked on in the area of User Interface Management Systems, (Myers 1989), where similar conclusions on the limitations of user interface separation have been reached.. The limitations of using processes, (at least as supported in current operating systems), as the basis for decomposition of tools is discussed in (Balzer 1987). The project is still in its infancy, and no products are available.

Another effort in the area of environment frameworks that also partly rejected the "grand database" approach was NSE, (Sun 1988, Adams, Honda & Miller 1989). Instead of taking the usual focusing on data modeling and common data representation, NSE emphasized the dynamics of change in a project, and implemented support for coordinating groups of people sharing a common configuration, making sure that the continuous reintegration of changes could be done in a systematic way. The resulting integration of configuration control into the everyday work of the development team, was probably the most innovative contribution of NSE. The data modeling and interrelating aspects, that engaged environment database designers for years, was essentially replaced by a relatively straightforward heterogeneous Hypertext, (CACM 1988), facility called "links". With its roots in the world of C and Unix file systems, the relationship between NSE and languages like Ada, that imply a highly structured *program library*, however became a bit unclear. In its straightforward pragmatism, and in this context relative simplicity, NSE appealed to many people.

The effort that most closely adhered to the original vision of an APSE was however the Rational Environment, (InformationWEEK 1985, Rational 1986, Morgan 1988, Ripken 1988). Starting as a small venture capital company, they took the spirit from Stoneman, Interlisp, Smalltalk, and the language oriented editor approaches, and implemented a tightly integrated development environment for Ada. Integration, and tailoring for the purpose, was taken very far, with a special purpose hardware supporting an operating system that is completely dedicated towards production of Ada software. The compiler was built to be incremental, and most tools work against the internal representation of the programs.

While almost all other language oriented editors provided mainly *syntax* oriented support, whose importance in a broader perspective can be questioned, the Rational environment could provide further services like interactive cross referencing and semantic completion. This, together with a number of well integrated services for configuration control and documentation support, made Rational be an environment that people really liked to work with. The same property that made it initially possible to explore the benefits of tight integration, was at the same time however a problem. The special purpose hardware and proprietary operating system, together with the implied major investment, can make many potential users hesitate. The Rational environment is however one of the few novel environments that has been made a stable product in industrial use.

The description above can of course not be claimed to be complete: it may even upset some people since numerous important results, especially from the US, were not mentioned. Anything like a complete survey would require a major volume.

This was however not the purpose, since the tendency is anyway clear in one interesting respect: very large resources have been invested in environments technology during the eighties, but still relatively few results are in actual productive use. The largest efforts have been different forms of cooperations, often at least partially government funded and controlled. No complete in-use environment has yet evolved out of those efforts. A number of smaller dedicated developments have also taken place. At least some of those are today products in actual use. A discussion of the different technical and organizational issues involved in building integrated environments is available in (Schefstrom 1989).

3.0 THE TWO CASE CULTURES

The discussion above concentrated on the culture and approaches related to the Stoneman document. In parallel, however, another trend grew stronger which more emphasized the design phase, providing support for drawing of dataflows, architecture diagrams, program decompositions, etc. Much of this work can be traced back to practices and methodologies as documented in books such as *Structured Design,* (Yourdon & Constantine 1979), and Jacksons work on JSP and JSD, (Jackson 1975, Jackson 1983). In the telecommunications area, the SDL language, (Rockstrom 1985), evolved into an accepted standard for graphic description of software systems. In the Ada context, the so called *Booch-,* (Booch 1983, Booch 1987), and *Buhr* diagrams, (Buhr 1983), became well known and the basis for many tools.

Even though the methods included much reasoning about design principles, using concepts like *Coupling, Cohesion, Object-Orientation,* etc, the most attractive aspect for many people was the graphics. How encouraging to be able to *see* such an intangible thing as software.

From initially being design methods, illustrated by more or less informal hand drawn figures, there evolved a need for easy maintenance of those drawings, and for making sure that they were made in a standardized way, using a proper format. Software tools supporting drawings were developed, and a market evolved offering products such as *Excelerator, Teamwork, Software Through Pictures,* etc, (Index 1987, CADRE 1988, IDE 1988), supporting a large number of notations, such as *Dataflow Diagrams,* different forms of *Structure Charts,* and more or less standardized methods like *HOOD, CORE, MASCOT-3, YOURDON, etc.*

In the area of compilers and language oriented editors, the maturing understanding of the subjects led to the development of a technology for generating parts of both compilers and editors, (Reps 1984). Similar attempts are now also made for the graphic design notations, exemplified by the product *VSF,* (Hale & Carmichael), allowing for easier production of editors for different variants of design notations. Since many design notations are still evolving, and since substantial development can still be expected in that area, the generation technology can probably here play a more central role than was the case for compilers and language oriented editors in the early eighties.

Anyway, it is the market of those diagramming and graphics editing tools that many people initially associate with the relatively recently introduced word *CASE,* or Computer Aided Software Engineering.

Given the background presented above, it does however seem more appropriate to view CASE as the gradually evolving merger of two cultures, one which we call the *Environments Culture,* and another one which we call the *Diagramming Tools* culture. Their relationship could be characterized by the following picture:

The Two CASE Cultures

Environments	Diagramming Tools
Interlisp, Smalltalk, Rational. ⟷	Yourdon, Gane/Sarson, Jackson.
Architecturally and Integration oriented. ⟷	Single tools.
Technical culture. ⟷	Administrative culture.
Back-End CASE. ⟷	Front-End CASE.
Fast turnaround time. ⟷	"Move work to spec/design phase".
Prototyping. ⟷	Waterfall model.
Fast, Creative, Exploratory. ⟷	Slower, larger, formal.

In the Environments case typical representatives, or carriers of culture, are Interlisp, Smalltalk, and Rational. At the Diagramming Tools side, we have the graphical notations and methods that are the basis for the tools. While the Environments culture always has emphasized the "whole", using words like *architecture, framework*, and *integration*, the Diagramming tools have usually been more localized in their scope, producing isolated tools rather than complete environments.

The Environments culture has been mostly honored in the academic and technical context, while the Diagramming tools have had more of an industrial and administrative flavor. Referring to the phases of the traditional life cycle, the Environments have been most interested in the later phases, while the Diagramming tools always have focused in on the earlier requirements and design phases. Based on this positioning, they correspond to Back-End CASE and Front-End CASE respectively.

Fast turnaround time in the edit-compile-debug cycle has always been a main goal within the Environments culture, while the Diagramming tools more or less ignore this, based on the assumption that a good work in the design phase makes the coding trivial. The Environments have been more interested in providing good prerequisites for allowing fast prototyping, while the Diagramming tools culture fully accepts the traditional phased Waterfall model, (Boehm 1981).

Finally, the Environments culture honors a fast, creative, and exploratory style of development to a larger extent than the Diagramming tools, which is more oriented towards larger, slower, and more formally controlled projects.

3.1 The Effects of Separation

As a consequence of the differences between those cultures, we today see a disturbing discontinuity in the support for software development. Two islands of internally reasonably well integrated tools exist, but they do not connect to each other to any extent comparable to the level of integration that is achieved within, for example, many Back-End CASE environments. The situation can be illustrated by the following figure:

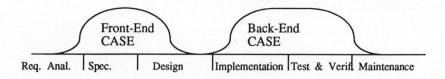

Current CASE Market

It is inherent in the basic purpose of earlier phases like "design", that the behavior of the program can not be given down to the detail where a computer could execute it. If we had such a "design-notation", it would then automatically make itself a programming language, creating a need for an even more abstract view of the software. Therefore, our definition of "design" is directly coupled to (a deliberate) incompleteness and abstraction at a level that is not fully executable.

Most design-tools today provide *code-generation*, which means that parts of a program are generated, based on the design. However, except for simpler applications, a mass of details must still be provided, a work that usually is done outside the control of the design tool generating the initial skeleton. This means that nothing guarantees that the program will continue to reflect the design. The usual argument is that when further developments must be done for a system, one should always go back to the design tool and update the design representation and generate new code. There are however usually no systematic ways of incoporating the refinement of this code that was produced during the previous cycle. The manual work implied could therefore easily outweigh the benefits.

3.2   The Need for a Homogeneous CASE.

How important is it to close the gap? Isn't just the enrichment of the code frames a trivial task, which we assign to our army of junior programmers? The answer, it is here claimed, is *no*, since the question has much deeper implications.

The current separation of FE and BE CASE is partly a reflection of the traditional waterfall model of development, where we apply a very phased development assuming that all work belonging to one phase can be completed before going into the next:

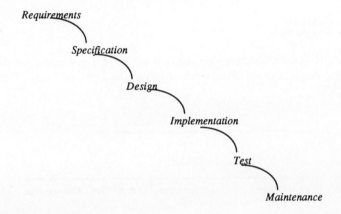

The name *Waterfall* model even suggests that it would be very painful, in fact almost unnatural, to go in the other direction. The rigid forms of this model are however questioned, (Agresti 1986), and many people instead favor a process including more of *prototyping*, (Agresti, ed. 1986), and *incremental development,* (Boehm 1981). This, together with the problems involved in even defining the differences between phases, (Swartout & Balzer 1982), should imply a strong need for being able to move freely and without pain between traditional development phases. Just as short turnaround time in the edit-compile-debug cycle has been a desirable thing, we must now extend the ambitions to achieve fast turnaround in the design-programming cycle.

Other arguments pointing in the same direction are the following:

- Much development, maybe most of it, is not creating something from scratch. Rather, development is most often a question of extending existing systems, or doing work in close connection to existing software. This implies a continuous circling in (at least) the design-programming cycle.

- Since most Front-End CASE tools are very much oriented towards new development, they to a large extent ignore reuse. Back-End CASE environments, such as for example the Smalltalk environment, (Goldberg 1984), have high reuse level.

- The maintenance phase, that is sometimes estimated to consume 80 percent of the cost in the complete lifecycle, does probably not consist mainly of correcting coding errors. Rather, substantial and legitimate needs for redesign occur because of unforeseen needs, new requirements, changing circumstances, etc.

Taken together, there are good reasons to conclude that for substantial progress to be made, Front-End and Back-End CASE must be integrated, closing the design-programming cycle. Neither technology alone is sufficient.

4.0 THE FUTURE

In the future CASE system, there are no discontinuities in the support for different tasks, but a single connected set of services covering the tasks of todays Front-End and Back-End CASE:

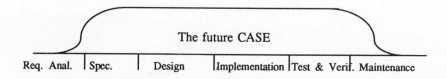

| Req. Anal. | Spec. | Design | Implementation | Test & Verif. | Maintenance |

This system should support the human equally well in the process of creating new systems as in the task of understanding and changing existing ones. It should allow for quick interactive browsing between different views of the same system, from a detailed programming oriented view to a design level over to the requirements that implied the corresponding modules. The system should support an approach to software that views design and programming as different views of the same system, rather than representing different phases on a time axis.

Instead of the traditional phased model, the future CASE system therefore should be required to support a model of development illustrated by the following figure:

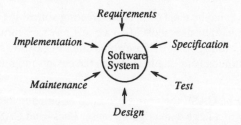

All the moments of the life cycle affect the resulting software, but not according to a fixed time sequence: results from implementation have side effects on requirements, and the experience of testing influences the way we would like to specify the system. Anyone who wants to apply the stricter time sequenced development paradigm can still do so, but he is not forced.

4.1 Architectural Implications

To achieve this kind of system, a careful coordination between different notations and internal representations must take place. Just as it was once concluded that the sharing of a common internal representation between an editor and a compiler was a sound architecture, the closing of the design-programming cycle calls for an extension of this idea to include the design and graphics information. The architecture can be illustrated by the following figure:

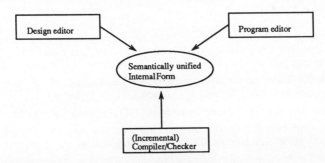

The requirement to be able to view and change software from either point of view, graphics/design and textual/programming, directly implies that at least conceptually, (although not necessarily physically), a single unified representation of the software system must be used. This internal form is acted upon both by the design editor and the language oriented program editor. The result is always checked and compiled by the same incremental compiler, no matter which tool produced or changed the program. Since all views are derived on demand from the single internal form, the problem of view inconsistencies disappears.

However, such a tight coordination between design and programming requires a very careful definition of the different notations involved. The graphics/design notation, and its semantics, must be designed together with complete compatibility as a major requirement. Although some design notations have been oriented towards certain languages, such as HOOD for Ada, (ESA 1989), there are few, if any, design methods that have been constructed with this requirement in mind. Therefore, we should expect that new design notations and/or languages must be developed, where the same semantics and concepts are propagated throughout both design and programming parts. Since programming languages have reached quite far in precision and detail of definition, and are stable, well standardized, and controlled, while design notations are usually less well defined and more in a state of development, it is reasonable to start the process by developing a tailored design notation to be compatible with an existing programming language. The Ada programming language is good candidate in this case, because of its rich set of concepts for programming-in-the-large, like packages, private types, tasking, generics, and well defined rules for separate compilation.

5.0 ACKNOWLEDGMENTS

The sketch above is a brief overview of thoughts and rationale from the future CASE planning at TeleSoft AB. I would like to thank Jack Schwartz and Jim Bladen of TeleSoft, San Diego, CA, for their unafraid visionary ideas.

6.0 REFERENCES

(ACM 1984), *Proceedings of the ACM SIGSOFT/SIGPLAN Software Engineering Symposium on Practical Software Development Environments*, P.   Henderson, ed., Pittsburgh, Pennsylvania, April 1984.

(Adams, Honda & Miller 1989), *Object Management in a CASE Environment*, in Proceedings of the 1989 International Software Engineering Conference.

(Agresti, ed, 1986), *New Paradigms for Software Development*, IEEE Computer Society 1986.

(Agresti 1986), *The Conventional Software Lifecycle: Its Evolution and Assumptions*, in New Paradigms For Software Development, IEEE Computer Society 1986.

(Balzer 1987), *Living in the Next Generation Operating System*, IEEE Software, November 1987.

(Barstow, Shrobe, Sandewall, ed. 1984), *Interactive Programming Environments*, McGraw-Hill, 1984.

(Bernstein 1987), *Database Systems for Software Engineering*. Proceedings of the 9:th International Conference on Software Engineering.

(Boarder, Obbink & Schmidt 1989), *ATMOSPHERE - Advanced Techniques and Methods of System Production in a Heterogeneous, Extensible, and Rigorous Environment*. Proceedings of the International Conference on System Development Environments and Factories, Berlin 9-11 May, 1989.

(Boehm 1981), *Software Engineering Economics*, Prentice-Hall 1981.

(Booch 1983), *Software Engineering With Ada*, first edition, Benjamin-Cummings, 1983.

(Booch 1987), *Software Engineering With Ada*, second edition, Benjamin-Cummings, 1987.

(Brereton, ed. 1988), *Software Engineering Environments*, editor Pearl Brereton, Ellis Horwood 1988.

(Buhr 1983), *System design With Ada*, Prentice-Hall Software Series, 1983.

(Buxton 1979), *DoD Requirements for ADA Programming Support Environments*, STONEMAN, DoD High Order Language Working Group, February 1980.

(Buxton and Druffel 1984), *Rationale for STONEMAN*, reprinted in (Barstow, Shrobe, & Sandewall 1984).

(CACM 1988), *Special Issue on Hypertext*, Communications of the ACM, July 1988.

(Dittrich 1986), *DAMOKLES - A Database System for Software Engineering Environments*. Proceedings of the International Workshop on Advanced Programming Environments, Trondheim, Norway, June 1986.

(Donzeau-Gouge, Huet, Kahn, Lang), *Programming Environments Based on Structured Editors: The MENTOR Experience*, in (Barstow, Shrobe, Sandewall 1984).

(Dowson 1987), *Integrated Project Support with ISTAR*, IEEE Software, November 1987.

(ESA 1989), *HOOD Manual*, European Space Agency, ESTEC, Postbus 299, 2200 AG Nordwijk ZH, The Netherlands.

(Fernstrom et al 1988), *Eureka Software Factory Design Guidelines and Architecture*, ESF Consortia, Hohenzollerndamm 152, 1000 Berlin 33, West Germany.

(Fernstrom & Ohlsson 1989), *The ESF Vision of a Software Factory*, Proceedings of the International Conference on System Development Environments and Factories, Berlin 9-11 May, 1989.

(Fischer 1989), *Human Computer Interaction Software: lessons Learned, Challenges Ahead. IEEE Software, January 1989.*

(Goldberg 1983), *The Influence of an Object-Oriented Language on the Programming Environment*, Proceedings of the ACM Computer Science Conference, Feb 1983. Reprinted in (Barstow et al 1984).

(Hale & Carmichael), *Which comes first, the method or the tools?*, white paper, Systematica Ltd, 7 St Stephens Road, Bournemouth, UK.

(Haberman 1980), *The Gandalf Research Project*, Dep of Comp. Sc. Research Review 1978-1979, Carnegie-Mellon University, Pittsburgh, Pennsylvania.

(Hartson 1989), *User-Interface Management Control and Communication*, IEEE Software, January 1989.

(Hunke, ed. 1980), *Software Engineering Environments*, North-Holland Publishing, 1981.

(IDE 1988), *Software Though Pictures*, product description, Interactive Development Environments, 595 Market St, San Francisco, California.

(Index 1987), *Excelerator*, product description, Index Tech Corporation, One Main St, Cambridge, Massachusetts.

(InformationWEEK 1985), *The Rational Idea of Commercial Ada*, InformationWEEK,, 25 November 1985.

(Intermetrics 1982), *Computer Program Development Specification for Ada Integrated Environment KAPSE/Database*, Intermetrics, Inc., Cambridge, MA.

(Jackson 1975), *Principles of Program Design*, Academic Press, 1975.

(Jackson 1983), *System Development*, Prentice-Hall International.

(Kernighan & Mashey), *The Unix Programming Environment*, IEEE Computer, April 1981. Reprinted in (Barstow et al 1984).

(McKinley & Schaefer 1986), *DIANA Reference Manual*, Draft rev 4, IR-MD-078, Intermetrics Inc.,Bethesda, MD.

(Morgan 1988), *Configuration Management and Version Control in the Rational programming Environment*, proceedings of the Ada-Europe Conference. Munich 7-9 June 1988.

(Munck et al 1988), *An Overview of DOD-STD-1838a (proposed), The Common APSE Interface Set, Revision A.* Munck, Oberndorf, Ploedereder, & Thall. Proceedings of the ACM Software Engineering Symposium on Practical Software Development Environments. Boston, Mass, Nov 28-30, 1988.

(Myers 1989), *User-Interface Tools: Introduction and Survey.* IEEE Software, January 1989.

(Narfelt & Schefstrom 1984), *Towards a KAPSE Database.* Proceedings of the First IEEE Conference on Ada Applications and Environments, St Paul, Minnesota, Oct 1984.

(Narfelt & Schefstrom 1985), *Extending the Scope of the Program Library*, Proceedings of the SIGAda 1985 International Conference on Ada, Paris, France, May 1985.

(Ripken 1988), Automated Support for Design and Documentation of Large Ada Systems. Milcomp'88 Conference, Sep 27-29, London, UK.

(Rockstrom 1985), *An Introduction to the CCITT SDL*, Swedish Telecom Administration, 1985.

(Software Process Workshop 1988), *Proceedings of the 4:th Intl Software Process Workshop, Devon, UK, 11-13 May 1988.*

(Sun 1988), *Introduction to NSE*, Sun Microsystems, 2550 Garcia Avenue, Mountain View, California.

(Swartout & Balzer 1982), *On the Inevitable Intertwining of Specification and Implementation*, Communications of the ACM, July 1982.

(Teitelbaum & Reps 1981), *The Cornell Program Synthesizer: A Syntax Directed Programming Environment*, Communications of the ACM, Sept 1981.

(Teitelman & Masinter 1981), *The Interlisp Programming Environment*, IEEE Computer.

(Rational 1986), *Application of the Rational Environment to Lifecycle Software Development*. White paper, Rational, 1501 Salado drive, Mountain View, CA 94043.

(Rudmik 1988), *Two Approaches to CASE Database Standards: OODB vs CAIS*. Proceedings of CASE'88, 2:nd International Workshop on CASE.

(Schefstrom 1989), *Building a Highly Integrated Development Environment Using Preexisting Parts*, in Proceedings of IFIP'89 XI World Computer Congress, San Francisco, CA, 28 Aug-1 Sep 1989.

(Thomas 1989a), *Tool Integration in the PACT Environment*, proceedings of the 11:th Conference on Software Engineering, May 1989, Pittsburgh, Pennsylvania.

(Thomas 1989b), *PCTE Interfaces: Supporting Tools in Software-Engineering Environments*, Ian Thomas, IEEE Software. November 1989.

(UK DoI 1981), *United Kingdom Ada Study Final Technical Report, Vol 2*, UK Department of Industry 1981.

(Williams 1988), *Object Oriented Data Management Systems: An Enabling Technology for the Next CASE Generation.*, Proceedings of CASE'88, 2:nd International Workshop on CASE.

(Yourdon & Constantine 1979), *Structured Design*, Prentice-Hall 1979.

An Expert System for Selecting and Tailoring Abstract Data Type Implementations

D.B. JOHNSTON

**Key Centre for Software Technology,
Department of Computer Science,
University of Queensland,
St Lucia, Qld, 4067,
Australia.**

1. Introduction.

One of the techniques which is improving programmer productivity is the use of standard modules for commonly used abstract data types. For example, abstractions such as sets and tables can be coded as standard modules and reused repeatedly. This is particularly true in languages such as Ada where a generic facility gives the ability to parameterise on types. In fact, for some abstractions such as those above, there is a wide variety of implementations available and the selection of an appropriate implementation may be one of the major decisions to be made in development of a program. For sets and tables, the implementation might use simple array structures, linked lists, binary search trees, balanced (AVL) trees, or hash tables in main memory, and sequential files, indexed sequential files, B-trees, or hash tables on secondary storage. Modern data structures texts such as Stubbs and Webre(1987) present this approach to data structure design. Booch(1987) provides a quite extensive library of abstract data types and their implementations in Ada together with some quite interesting rationales and classifications.

The selection of appropriate implementation data structures for an abstract data structure in the absence of a suitable library routine has often involved a compromise between machine efficiency and programmer efficiency. The need for programmer efficiency encourages a simpler implementation, but, at least for large structures, a more complex structure will often be used to obtain better machine efficiency. However, the availability of reliable library modules for these abstractions has somewhat simplified the decision by reducing the need to consider programmer productivity in making a choice. We believe that it is now feasible to have an expert system aid the program developer in the selection of implementation data structures and in the tailoring of the system to special needs in a particular application. A prototype of the selection component of this system has been developed.

2. Example of a General Library Module Interface.

An abstract data type which arises very commonly in programming, although many practising programmers may not recognise it, is the simple mathematical set type. As indicated above, there is quite a large number of implementations in general use for this data abstraction and it therefore is appropriate to use a set as an example of the technique.

Our definition of the set should include all operations available in any of the implementations. In Ada, the interface would be described by a generic package specification. Deciding which routines to include in the library for each structure involves a compromise between providing as many useful routines as possible and avoiding making so many available as to cause confusion.

```
generic
   type compnt_ty is private;
package set_package is
   type set_ty is limited private;
   procedure make_empty_set( set: out set_ty );
   function is_empty( set: in set_ty ) return Boolean;
   procedure copy( source: in set_ty; destination: out set_ty);
   function "="( set_1, set_2: in set_ty ) return Boolean;
   function is_in( compnt: in compnt_ty; set: in set_ty ) return Boolean;
   function cardinality( set: set_ty )return Boolean;
   procedure add( set: in out set_ty; compnt: in compnt_ty );
   procedure remove( set: in out set_ty; compnt: in compnt_ty );
   procedure union( set_1, set_2: in set_ty; result_set: out set_ty );
   procedure intersection( set_1, set_2: in set_ty; result_set: out set_ty );
   function "<="( set_1, set_2: in set_ty ) return Boolean;
   generic
     with procedure action( compnt: in out compnt_ty );
   procedure for_all( set: in set_ty );
   generic
     with function condition( compnt: in compnt_ty )return Boolean;
   procedure find( set: in set_ty; satisfy: out set_ty );
   procedure seize( set: in set_ty );
   procedure release( set: in set_ty );
   procedure open( set: in out set_ty; file_name: string );
   procedure close( set: in out set_ty );
end set_package;
```

Some of the less usual operations probably warrant comment. The generic procedures for_all and find are supplied as control abstractions to perform an action on all elements in the set (for_all), and to find the set of elements which satisfies the condition (in the case of find). The procedures seize and release are required in certain concurrent implementations. open and close are required for secondary storage implementations. In particular open is necessary to designate where the set is to be stored on secondary storage. In the case of secondary storage applications, the abstraction will often be used not just in a single program, but in a suite of programs operating on a particular structure.

It is quite likely that further operations would be provided. In particular, a full set of relational operators might well be made available to handle proper subset and superset operations as well as the <= given above. Some of the above operations such as union and intersection would also be made available in *in situ* forms as well as the form returning a separate result.

3.   Factors Affecting the Choice of an Abstract Data Type Implementation Method.

After deciding on the basic abstract data structure for which an implementation is desired, there are two general classes of information that the expert system requires in making an appropriate implementation method selection. There are some restrictions which will completely rule out particular implementations, but the more common situation is that additional detail will be required to select the preferred implementation on the basis of its efficiency in the context in which it is to be used. The first of these classifications could be regarded as defining different abstractions, but it is convenient to regard them as variations of the same abstraction, as that is certainly how the user sees them. For instance, in the absence of any restriction on the size of a structure (other than machine restrictions), we will normally rule out array implementations. It would be simpler in some ways to regard the set with a bounded size as a separate abstraction from the unbounded set, but we believe it is essential that our selection mechanism can handle them uniformly.

The first information provided, after selecting the data abstraction by name (eg set), would be to specify the operations required. This will affect both the feasibility and the efficiency selection mechanisms.

One major decision is, of course, whether persistent data structures are required, necessitating the use of secondary storage. It seems appropriate to have the user make the decision directly on which class of memory to use. Our current prototype has not considered compromises in this area, such as holding a structure on secondary storage, copying it as a whole to main memory as required, and saving it to file periodically. This will add additional considerations such as error recovery abilities of the implementations. We intend to do further work in this area.

Another example of characteristics which eliminate particular implementations is the concurrency characteristics required. Will the abstract data type only be used in strictly sequential situations, or which of a number of concurrency regimes will be applicable?
    a.   user control via a seize, release discipline,
    b.   mutual exclusion of all operations, or
    c.   allowing multiple concurrent readers but not concurrent writers.
In a case such as this we have to decide whether to provide separate implementations in the library for each case, or whether it is feasible to generate slightly different implementations from a common library routine. The latter alternative seems attractive from a point of view of keeping down the total number of library packages and is discussed further in section 5.

The system may need to be provided with details of the type of the components of the structure (eg the type of elements in the set). In a final implementation some of this would possibly be achieved by giving or referring to a type or module declaration. For example, the component size could be determined from the declaration. If the component is a subrange or enumerated type in the set example, a bitset implementation is likely to be competitive. This would be obvious from the declaration. However, the current implementation asks for specific details rather than a declaration. Some information would be harder to determine from the declaration. Is an ordering relation < available? Some such operation would be necessary if binary search tree, or B-tree based implementations are to be considered. Similarly, the availability of an appropriate hashing function would be significant. These operations could be provided as additional generic parameters. It is possible to make the module independent of these externally provided operations by treating the element parameters simply as bit patterns. Although this would, in the general case, require a potentially unsafe type conversion, there are significant advantages through the simplification of the interface to the module. This is particularly attractive in the case of hashing, where an appropriate function would normally have to be specially written for supply to the module, and furthermore, the randomising nature of the hash function means that there is no real reason for respecting types in this very special case. Where the component is a pointer type, particular care is required, for it is probable that the in-built assignment and equality operations have inappropriate semantics as they operate on references, rather than the referenced objects. In Ada, these should be treated as limited private types. In these cases, appropriate routines will need to be provided as generic parameters to replace equality and possibly assignment in the implementing modules. This could be handled by defining the package with further generic parameters. However, the difficulty is that assignment cannot be given as a generic actual parameter in Ada. For this reason, it seems more appropriate to use a generator to modify the library packages in cases where assignment is to be replaced by an appropriate routine.

The information so far discussed is used to select implementations meeting the essential requirements. Further information is required to select the most appropriate implementation. In an environment where a standard library of such implementations is not available, the coding difficulty will often be a major consideration in making this selection. Where a library of reliable modules is available, this influence, if not completely removed, is at least very substantially reduced. Our system does not consider it as an issue. Thus the issue can be reduced to one of machine efficiency and as usual there are both time and space considerations to be considered. The basic formulae for evaluation of space and time requirements are to be incorporated in tables in the selection system. The ability to incorporate new implementations in these tables as they become available is an important requirement for the system. At present, we believe that the most appropriate method for producing these evaluation functions is a mixture of analysis of the method and measurements on the implementations. For example, analysis of a simple implementation of the is_in routine for the set example would show that the execution time depends on the number N of elements as $C_1*N + C_2$ where C_1 and C_2 are constants. Use of performance evaluation tools on a simple driver program would enable determination of the values for C_1 and C_2.

Much of the information supplied by the user to allow selection on the basis of efficiency will necessarily be approximate. Maximum size (unless bounded only by memory availability), and average size in terms of numbers of components in the structure will need to be supplied for most structures and certainly for sets. This will be crucial in estimating space requirements and usually also important to speed calculations. An estimate of the relative frequency of use of the available operators on the structure is also important to time evaluation. In our prototype we also included an additional "importance of operation" so that if the speed of certain operations (say for on-line update) is regarded as more important than that of other operations, they can be given an appropriate weighting.

The prototype system had two separate evaluations, one on the basis of space, and the other on the basis of speed. We attempted to combine these into a single quality measure, but as the relation seemed rather arbitrary, we reverted to two separate measures, one for space requirements and the other for time for each of the feasible implementations.

4. Expert System Design

Our expert system was principally written in Prolog. Its database is built in the form of Prolog statements. This can be considered as two parts, the *fixed component* supplied when an abstract data type implementation is included in the library, and a *dynamic component* containing information supplied by the user who is selecting an abstract data type implementation. The control part of the Prolog program is responsible for obtaining the application characteristics from the user, incorporating it in the database, identifying feasible implementations, and then evaluating those feasible implementations.

The fixed component of the database has assertions of the form
> possible_struct(set).

for each abstract data structure for which an implementation is provided. For each operation provided on this structure there is an assertion such as
> possible_op(set, is_empty, struct(1)).

which indicates that the operation is_empty is available for a set. The third parameter gives the parameter style for is_empty. For each implementation, it is necessary to provide an assertion of the form
> possible_impl(set, bin_search_tree).

The dynamic component of the database records information about the specific abstract data type required by the user. Such information is recorded by means of assert clauses and includes information required for all structures — such as memory class, whether the structure is bounded, and the average number of elements in the structure. Similarly recorded will be specific information such as the relative frequency of use of the various operations.

The control part of the Prolog program will include a rule to decide if a particular implementation is compatible with the user's requirements. For example, we might specify that the binary search tree is only feasible where the implementation is to be in main memory and has an ordering operation.
> feasible(set, bin_search_tree) :- element(orderable),
> struct_ind(memory, main).

element is used to assert a property of the structure components. struct_ind asserts a structure independent property which the user requires. We then need to provide rules for evaluating the time and space requirements of particular applications. For example,
> space_of(set, bin_srch_tree, Space) :- element_size(1, Size),
> struct_ind(avg_size, Avg),
> Space is Avg * (Size + 2).

The first clause on the right accesses the dynamic component of the database to find the size of the elements in the set. The first parameter indicates which of possibly a number of components is being referenced. In this case there will only be one. The second clause on the right accesses a structure independent property, its average size in number of elements, also in the dynamic component of the data base. The final line establishes the required Space. A similar but somewhat more complex rule will need to be provided for evaluating the speed performance of each operation in a particular implementation. We found it necessary to provide access to some routines written in C for use in some of these rules. For example, the log function required for the time for a search routine in a binary tree was not directly available in our version of Prolog.

The Prolog program has three main phases: finding details of the required abstract data type and incorporating them in the database of Prolog assertions, determining which implementations are feasible, and evaluating the feasible implementations. Considerable care has been taken in the first phase to ensure that the questions asked of the user are in a logical order. In general, the questions work from the general to the specific, finding out first the required interface, then the structure independent information, then the more specific characteristics such as frequency of use of the operations.

5.   Tailoring the Implementation to the User's Requirements
In a simple system, each possible specification of an abstract data type interface and each possible implementation could be stored as a separate library module (a generic package in the Ada context.) However the number of modules stored could become quite large, and it seems appropriate to consider the possibility of storing the modules in a suitable way to that minor variants can be produced without completely replicating the code. Variations which could be handled in this way include
   a.   excluding particular operations from the visible interface,
   b.   *in situ* forms of the operations,
   c.   the simpler forms of concurrency,
   d.   handling **limited private** element types with explicit routines for as-
        signment and/or equality.
It is believed that it does not generally matter if some redundant operations are included in the package body as it seems that the better Ada systems have loaders that will not load modules unless they are required. However, it is desirable to be able to limit the visible routines to those actually required by the user, principally in the interests of simplicity in the user's program. The implementations of procedures with the abstract data type as an **in out** parameter are very similar to the corresponding functions returning the resultant abstract data type and could be described as a transformation of the basic structure.

Simple forms of concurrency could be handled similarly. For example, mutual exclusion could be enforced on the routines by insertion of a *seize* operation on entry to each procedure, with a corresponding *release* at each exit.

Such transformations could be handled at the textual level. However, it is our belief that it would be preferable to store the routines in a more structured form to simplify these manipulations. In particular, an intermediate code representation such as a Diana tree (abstract syntax tree for Ada —see Goos and Wulf(1981)) would be easier to manipulate for these transformations and can be easily and efficiently converted back to Ada code.

6.   Effects on Program Development

What do we see as the advantages and disadvantages of use of this system? Firstly, it is obvious that the hope of benefits from this system is predicated on an acceptance that abstract data type modules are a significant benefit in program development. This proposition seems to be well accepted in the Ada program development literature, although it remains to be fully accepted in a wider community. The major benefits are:

    a.   in avoiding rewriting program modules for this type of work over and over again for each application,

    b.   in improved reliability in the standard modules,

    c.   in improved efficiency as more effort can be devoted to this in a standard module than in an individual application and later users can benefit from improvements in performance made as a result of earlier experience.

The costs are

    a.   in the additional difficulty in writing generalised modules,

    b.   in suitably organising the libraries so that the appropriate module can be found when it is required,

    c.   in loss of the efficiency which might be obtained by optimising the module for a particular application.

In this paper, we do not wish to argue this case, but rather to point out how our system for selecting modules impacts on the development of software. However, this will necessarily relate to the advantages and disadvantages of the underlying methodology as outlined above.

Secondly, it is necessary not only to have standard library modules for abstract data types, but also to have a variety of implementations for the one abstraction. This has, to my knowledge, not been argued in the literature, although it is taken as obvious by the followers of this style of development. The situation is, of course, that no one implementation will give the best performance or even acceptable performance in all situations. When the factors presented in section 3 are taken into account, one implementation may be clearly superior in one situation, and another implementation preferred in a different context. For a small set, an array implementation may be ideal, while for a large and varying set a binary search tree may meet the requirements very well. This does cause a minor difficulty in Ada. The language does not provide directly for more than one implementation of the same package to be included in the same program. We would like the users of the set abstraction to be able to use a single interface. However, we don't have the ability to say that a particular implementation will be used in one part of the program, and another in a second part with the same semantics with different efficiency related characteristics. However, this problem is not too serious as we only need to make the package names different, and the only place where a change will need to be made to substitute a different implementation is where the generic package is instantiated. This is, we believe, the most reasonable place for such a decision, at least if we are to follow Ada's approach to separate compilation, and accept the need for private parts in specification modules.

What advantages do we see from the use of an expert system such as this for making the choice of a data structures implementation? To answer this we must look at how this decision has been made traditionally. The program designer has normally made this decision by mentally weighing up the various factors we have discussed, and where appropriate, the programming difficulty, and has decided on a particular implementation in a pretty subjective way. We believe that the ability to make such decisions appropriately is one of the most important technical skills of the program designer. The advantage of our system for the highly skilled designer, is that this system quantifies the factors that would have been used anyway. In clear cut cases, this designer would undoubtably have made the correct decision anyway. However, in more marginal cases, the quantitative efficiency measures will assist in making the appropriate selection. For the less skilled program developer, the system will be even more helpful, because the more unreasonable implementations will be clearly shown, and also because the system will draw attention to the factors which need to be considered in selecting an implementation. The user of this system may initially worry about having to provide details such as the relative frequency of use of the operators acting on the abstract data type as it is often difficult to provide such information accurately. However, we believe that this quantitative approach has advantages over the subjective way in which this has been handled previously. Furthermore, we would encourage the user of this system to run it with a variety of values for parameters which they believe to be critical, thus giving them a much better idea of the way in which various parameters affect performance in a particular situation. It would also be fairly simple to monitor the usage of the module in operation, and thus obtain more accurate information on such things as average size and relative frequency of use of operations and use our system to select a revised implementation which could then be simply substituted in the user's program to improve its efficiency.

What are the costs involved in this style of development? We firstly have the cost of developing, or obtaining the appropriate libraries and organising them appropriately, for example, converting them to a common interface. This is a cost which is related to the underlying method, rather than the use of our expert system. An additional development cost in our system is that for the construction of the tables in the form of Prolog assertions. This involves analysis of the various operations in each module at least using appropriate monitoring tools, probably assisted by code reading to assess the general form of the expressions for the time and space requirements of each module. With our current system, it also requires a basic familiarity with the Prolog language.

Both the construction of the libraries and the entry of the information into the Prolog tables are significant tasks and to achieve a nett benefit, it is necessary that the system be used quite often. Thus this cost is effectively amortised by the savings made in the many uses of the module. The side benefit in improved reliability should not be ignored.

7.   Conclusions

I believe that this system for assisting in selection of abstract data type implementations could be of significant benefit in encouraging the development of software using appropriate library modules. This will assist in reducing overall development effort, and improving efficiency and reliability in the resulting products.

Acknowledgements

I wish to acknowledge the substantial contributions to this work made by David Duke, who did some of the early work on this project, and Kathryn Andersen, who wrote the Prolog implementation.

References

Booch, G., *Software Components with Ada*, Benjamin/Cummings, 1987.

Stubbs, D.F. and Webre, N.W., *Data Structures with Abstract Data Types and Modula-2*, Brookes/Cole, 1987.

Goos, G., and Wulf, W.A., *Diana Reference Manual*, Institut Fuer Informatik II, Universitat Karlsruhe. 1981.

PART V: Reliability and Testing

EXPERIENCE AND SUGGESTIONS ON USING ADA TO IMPLEMENT INTERNAL PROGRAM REPRESENTATIONS

ARTHUR G. DUNCAN

General Electric Company, Corporate Research and Development

1. INTRODUCTION.

The Ada programming language was designed with the goals of reliability, modifiability, and efficiency in mind. The Ada package facility, with its clean separation between the interfaces and implementations of modules, together with Ada's ability to do type checking across modules, should make Ada programs more reliable and easier to modify than comparable programs written in such languages as C and Pascal. Moreover, this increased reliability and modifiability should not (in principle) entail any loss of efficiency, since we can use the pragma INLINE to avoid potentially costly function calls to frequently used interface functions.

Our experience with Ada at the General Electric Research and Development Center, has, on the whole, been positive; however, in this paper we present an example, based on our experience, where the Ada language, as it currently stands, was not a convenient match to our implementation requirements.

The remainder of the paper is organized as follows:

- We discuss our experience in implementing the internal program representation for a system to support reengineering of existing software to meet new requirements.
- We try to identify the reasons why Ada did not adequately support our application.
- We show how our application would be implemented using an enhancement to Ada proposed by colleagues of ours at GE.
- We briefly mention the Ada/9X effort.
- Finally, we offer our conclusions and recommendations.

2. REPRESENTING PROGRAMS IN A REENGINEERING ENVIRONMENT.

At General Electric we are currently developing a number of tools to support software reengineering. The user starts with an existing system, usually written in a language other than Ada, then uses the tools in the environment to produce a system written in well-structured, well-packaged Ada.

The key ingredient in such a system is a common internal program representation, called *IRep*, that enables all the tools in the environment to work together in a tightly integrated framework.

2.1 Requirements on the IRep.

IRep must satisfy a number of requirements, some of which may conflict.

- IRep must have a simple and consistent logical interface.

- This interface should not depend on peculiarities of the physical data representation.

- One should be able to take advantage of efficient implementations for different kinds of IRep data.

- Each tool should be able to use specialized IRep information not needed by other tools.

- IRep should be easily extendible to support new tools.

- Each tool should have its own local name space, in order to avoid name clashes when the tool is used in conjunction with other tools.

To give the flavor of our actual IRep, we will present a simple IRep, for a small language.

2.2 The Logical View of IRep.

IRep logically appears as a large graph-like structure consisting of a number of *nodes*, each having a number of *attributes*, or logical fields. The nodes themselves are grouped into *classes* whose nodes all have the same kinds of attributes; moreover, the classes are related by inheritance relations, whereby one class of node can ''inherit'' all the logical fields possessed by one or more other classes.

To describe IRep, we use a notation based on IDL, a specification language developed at Carnegie-Mellon University and used to represent the design of DIANA, the standard intermediate language for Ada [Nestor 89, Evans 83].

IDL defines data structures by means of two kinds of productions: *node* productions, which define attributes (or logical fields), and *class* productions, which define inheritance relations. The symbol ''=>'' denotes a node production, while ''::='' denotes a class production.

A sample node production would be the following:

    SUBPROGRAM =>
      parameters : Seq of FORMAL,
      declarations : Seq of DECL,
      statements : Seq of STMT;

This production states that every node of class *SUBPROGRAM* contains three logical fields, a *parameters* field, a *declarations* field, and a *statements* field. These fields are strongly typed. For example, the parameters field must be a sequence of nodes of class FORMAL.

We can also have node productions with an empty right hand side. An example is given by

    built_in_procedure =>;

This means that the class *built_in_procedure* has no specific attributes of its own, but must inherit all its attributes from other classes.

An example of a class production is

    SUBPROGRAM ::= procedure | function;

which states that the classes *procedure* and *function* are both subclasses of *SUBPROGRAM* and will inherit all of its logical fields. In particular, each node of class *procedure* or class *function* will inherit the three fields described in the previous production. The inheritance defined in IDL is *multiple* inheritance, i.e., a class may inherit directly from more than one other class.

Some sample IDL productions for a simple IRep might be

    NAMED_OBJECT => name : symbol;
    NAMED_OBJECT ::= DECL | FORMAL;

    DECL ::= SUBPROGRAM | variable | FORMAL;

    SUBPROGRAM =>
        parameters : seq of FORMAL,
        declarations : seq of DECL,
        statements : seq of STMT;

    SUBPROGRAM ::= PROCEDURE | FUNCTION;

    FUNCTION => return_type : Type;

    PROCEDURE ::= built_in_procedure | user_defined_procedure;

    FUNCTION ::= built_in_function | user_defined_function;

    built_in_procedure =>;
    built_in_function =>;
    user_defined_procedure =>;
    user_defined_function =>;

2.3 Desirable Properties of an Actual IRep Implementation.

The above productions present a great deal of information in a compact form. They show the classes of all information fields as well as the subclass relationships among the various nodes. A good implementation of the specification should

1. support both the field type information and the subclass relationships in a declarative manner.

2. support space-efficient encoding of the information in the fields,

3. support the type system defined by the productions and check statically that nodes of appropriate classes are assigned to particular fields.

2.4 The Ada Implementation of IRep.

At first glance, Ada would seem a good language for implementing the internal program representation, since Ada provides strong typing, variant record structures, subtypes, and a separation between interfaces and implementations of modules.

Our current implementation, based on suggestions by D. A. Lamb in his paper on implementation strategies for DIANA [Lamb 87], uses the following variant record structure.

```
type IRep_Node_Kind is (... k_built_in_procedure, k_built_in_function, ...);

type IRep_Node_Record(Kind : IRep_Node_Kind);

type IRep_Node is access IRep_Node_Record;

type IRep_Node_Record(Kind : IRep_Node_Kind) is
  record
    case Kind is
       ...
       when k_built_in_procedure =>
          built_in_procedure_name : Symbol;
          built_in_procedure_parameters : Seq_Of_IRep_Node; -- seq of FORMAL
          built_in_procedure_declarations : Seq_Of_IRep_Node; -- seq of DECL
          built_in_procedure_statements : Seq_Of_IRep_Node; -- seq of STMT
       when k_built_in_function =>
          built_in_function_name : Symbol;
          built_in_function_parameters : Seq_Of_IRep_Node; -- seq of FORMAL
          built_in_function_declarations : Seq_Of_IRep_Node; -- seq of DECL
          built_in_function_statements : Seq_Of_IRep_Node; -- seq of STMT
          built_in_function_return_type : Predefined_Type;
       ...
       when others => null;
    end case
  end record;
```

Access to this record structure is provided by an interface package containing a a well-defined set of access functions. Two examples are:

```
...
function  Get_Name(N : IRep_Node) return  Symbol;
procedure Set_Name(N : IRep_Node; To_Be : Symbol);

function  Get_Parameters(N : IRep_Node) return  Seq_Of_IRep_Node;
procedure Set_Parameters(N : IRep_Node; To_Be : Seq_Of_IRep_Node);
...
```

3. PROBLEMS WITH THE ADA RECORD IMPLEMENTATION OF IREP.

The Ada record implementation of IRep is unduly complex and provides inadequate type-checking, which requires us to insert run-time type checks into our code.

3.1 Unnecessary Complexity.

The record type definition is unduly complex for two reasons:

1. Case variants in Ada must be nested to form a tree, and

2. The field names, even among different case variants, must be unique.

As a result, in order to support multiple inheritance, we need to duplicate similar information across several case variants; moreover, we have to create artificially long field names, in order to keep the names unique across variants.

At this point, we should observe that, had the "::=" productions described a strict tree hierarchy of classes, we could have created a nested variant record structure that would have avoided the possibility of field name clashes among case variants. This would simplify the record structure itself (at the expense of some flexibility in the expressiveness of the IDL-like specification); however, it would still not handle, by itself, the more serious problem of inadequate type checking.

3.2 Inadequate Type Checking.

Since the IRep information is inherently strongly typed, we would like this strong typing to be reflected in the Ada implementation.

Consider the production

STMT ::= assignment_stmt I proc_call I return_stmt I exit_stmt I goto_stmt I if_stmt I loop_stmt;

We would like to be able to declare a variable or parameter of type *STMT* and have it accept nodes of type *assignment_stmt*, *proc_call*, *return_stmt*, *exit_stmt*, *goto_stmt*, *if_stmt*, and *loop_stmt* as acceptable values. On the other hand, it should exclude nodes of type *function*, since such a node is not a *STMT*.

Unfortunately, the Ada subtyping facility is not powerful enough to handle these inheritance relationships at compile time, even if we limit ourselves to single inheritance. We can define subtypes at the leaves of the hierarchy, such as

```
subtype Assignment_Stmt_Node is IRep_Node(k_assignment_stmt);
```

but we cannot define a more general subtype that would include some subset of the case variants, such as

```
subtype Stmt_Node is IRep_Node(assignment_stmt I block I proc_call I return_stmt
    I exit_stmt I goto_stmt I if_stmt I if_then_else_stmt I loop_stmt);
```

Another disadvantage of Ada subtyping is that it is not required to be checked by the compiler.

While Ada has legitimate reasons for not allowing this more general kind of subtyping, it tends to make the implementation of data types with inheritance more difficult and less safe. In order to accommodate all the types of *STMT* nodes, we must declare fields of type *STMT* to be of the most general type, *IRep_Node*. In order to ensure that only nodes of type *STMT* are used in these fields, we must resort to run-time checks on the discriminant of the individual data items. For example, suppose that all statements have a *label* field, which can be either a symbol or _*UNDEFINED*_. The interface function *Get_Label*, would then need to be implemented using a run time test for the class of the node. This code might look like

```
function Get_Label(N : IRep_Node) return Symbol is
begin
    case N.Kind is
        when k_assignment_stmt => return N.assignment_stmt_label;
        when k_proc_call => return N.proc_call_label;
        when k_return_stmt => return N.return_stmt_label;
        when k_exit_stmt => return N.exit_stmt_label;
        when k_goto_stmt => return N.goto_stmt_label;
        when k_if_stmt => return N.if_stmt_label;
        when k_loop_stmt => return N.loop_stmt_label;
        when others => raise CONSTRAINT_ERROR;
    end case;
end Get_Label;
```

In hand coding these access functions, it is easy to leave out an important case. Even if we generate these access functions automatically, many user-defined functions that operate on statements will still have to insert run-time checks to determine the exact kind of statement that has been passed in a particular situation. If we were to add a new kind of statement, we would then have to change the code to all these functions.

3.2.1 Run-Time Inefficiency. The Ada type facility attempts to achieve two goals at once: (1) to ensure that type mismatches are caught by the Ada compiler and (2) to produce efficient machine code by compiling direct calls to procedures. To achieve the first goal Ada requires *static typing* of variables and parameters, while to achieve the second Ada requires *static binding* of procedure calls to the actual code to be executed with the call.

While static binding of procedure calls is generally more efficient than dynamic binding, static binding can actually introduce inefficiencies is some situations. For example, suppose we have a function that takes an argument of class *DECL*. We do not know in advance what kind of *DECL* will be passed. Since we expect to treat variables differently from procedures, say, we will insert tests in the code to handle all the possible cases of *DECL*. These tests will generally appear in the form of a large **case** statement. This leads to code that is repetitive, verbose, hard to follow, and possibly inefficient. We must depend on the compiler to optimize the **case** statement for us.

If, on the other hand, dynamic code binding were an integral part of the language, we would expect dynamic binding to be handled in an efficient way; moreover, we could could dispense will all the extraneous tests.

One other source of inefficiency lies in the management of the heap. Complicated, graph-like data structures must, of necessity, be constructed of pointers to the heap. In the absence of a built-in compacting garbage collector, which validated Ada compilers are under no obligation to provide, the program memory tends to become fragmented, requiring more disk accesses than necessary.

4. A POSSIBLE SOLUTION: OBJECT-ORIENTED FEATURES IN ADA.

The concept of inheritance was fundamental in describing IRep; moreover, one can think of many other systems, such as window systems, graphical CAD systems, etc., where inheritance plays a major role in describing the system.

We have seen that inheritance is difficult to express in the current version of Ada; however, if Ada were extended to include explicit support for inheritance, we could achieve much more natural implementations for these kinds of systems. Support for inheritance should also include support for dynamic code binding.

4.1 An ObjectAda Implementation of IRep.

ObjectAda is an object-oriented extension to Ada, developed at the GE Research and Development Center [EB 89].

ObjectAda allows packages to be types and also allows one package type to inherit features from one or more other package types. Our IRep implementation could be expressed with the following ObjectAda code:

```
package IRep is

    package type IRep_Node is
        ...
    end IRep_Node;

    package type IRep_Named_Object is
        inherit IRep_Node;
        function Get_Name return Symbol;
        procedure Set_Name(To_Be : Symbol);
    end IRep_Named_Object;

    package type IRep_Decl is
        inherit IRep_Named_Object;
        function Get_Name return Symbol;
        procedure Set_Name(To_Be : Symbol);
    end IRep_Decl;

        ...
    package type IRep_Subprogram is
        inherit IRep_Decl;
        function Get_Parameters return Seq_Of_Formal;
        procedure Set_Parameters(To_Be : Seq_Of_Formal);
        function Get_Declarations return Seq_Of_Decl;
        procedure Set_Declarations(To_Be : Seq_Of_Decl);
        function Get_Statements return Seq_Of_Stmt;
        procedure Set_Statements(To_Be : Seq_Of_Stmt);
    end IRep_Subprogram;

    package type IRep_Function is
        inherit IRep_Subprogram;
        function Get_Return_Type return Predefined_Type;
        procedure Set_Return_Type(To_Be : Predefined_Type);
    end IRep_Function;

    package type IRep_User_Defined_Function is
        inherit IRep_Function;
    end IRep_User_Defined_Function;
        ...
end IRep;
```

The code for handling particular kinds of data will be defined locally in the package bodies of the various package types, while the inheritance and dynamic binding mechanisms will ensure that the correct code is executed in each case.

Note that in this definition, we gain the advantages of strong typing, down to the subclass level; more concise code; better information hiding, since we do not have to create a large variant record type; and the ability to extend our system incrementally by defining subclasses.

One final note. ObjectAda could be used simply as a preprocessor to Ada, allowing one to write programs in an object-oriented style, while still producing conforming Ada code; however, a better solution would be to have a native code compiler for ObjectAda.

This would have the following advantages over a preprocessor:

1. It would eliminate an additional pass in compiling programs.

2. It would make it impossible for programmers to make modifications to the preprocessed code, thereby guaranteeing that the ObjectAda source is the *actual* source of the program.

3. It would allow for more efficient implementation dynamic binding than with a preprocessor, since dynamic binding in a native code compiler can be tailored to the specific target machine.

4. Finally, it would allow an interactive debugger to work with the ObjectAda source code, rather than the preprocessed code.

5. OBJECT-ORIENTED FEATURES AND ADA/9X.

Eddy and Brown [EB 89], among others, have advocated that the addition of object-oriented features be considered as part of the Ada/9X effort. Our experience with using Ada to develop a software reengineering environment suggests that object-oriented enhancements to Ada would be desirable for systems that handle complex multifaceted data objects. The larger question, however is

What are our intended applications for Ada?

In other words, what do we really want out of the Ada language?

The original requirements for Ada were that it should provide support for the creation of safe, reliable, modifiable, and efficient embedded systems. If our aim is to handle tight real-time constraints, we might choose to give up automatic garbage collection, dynamic procedure binding, and inheritance, in order to achieve greater control over the timing of particular operations.

If, on the other hand, our aim is to provide a general purpose language that is to be used to build software development environments, data base systems, operating systems, graphical window-based user interfaces, etc., we might then opt for the power and flexibility offered by an object-oriented language, especially if this can be achieved without sacrificing static type checking.

Finally, we might ask if there is some way of supporting both embedded systems and more complex general purpose systems without sacrificing either efficiency or expressive power. It should be possible also to implement object-oriented extensions to Ada in such a way that one pays the overhead of the object-oriented features only if these features are actually used. Both C++ and Objective-C provide examples where this aim is accomplished with the base language C.

6. CONCLUSIONS.

Our experience in using Ada to represent programs in a software reengineering environment suggests that the ability of Ada to support the design and implementation of reliable, modifiable, and efficient systems depends to a large extent on the nature of the data being manipulated by the system.

Ada appears best suited for handling data objects that can be allocated statically and whose information can be expressed in a rigid format. Such data items include numerical items, enumeration literals, record structures without variants, and fixed-length arrays. These are the kinds of data structures we would expect to use in embedded real-time systems.

Ada appears less successful, however, in handling data items that are created dynamically and that can assume a variety of formats. These include variant record objects, variable sized arrays, and pointers to other objects. Ada implementations of this type of system tend to be overly complex and even inefficient, compared to an implementation of the same system using an object-oriented language with inheritance and dynamic code binding.

We feel that serious attention should be given to the possibility of adding object-oriented inheritance and dynamic code binding to a future version of the Ada language, particularly if this can be accomplished without compromising Ada's ability to handle embedded systems efficiently.

References.

[EB 89]   Eddy, F. S. and P. C. Brown, Package Types: Extending Ada for Object-Oriented Development, position paper, General Electric Company, Corporate Research and Development, Schenectady, NY, July 1989, presented at the Informal Workshop on Support of Object-Oriented Programming in Ada, Woburn, MA, September 1989.

[Evans 83] Evans, A., K. J. Butler, G. Goos, W. Wulf, *DIANA Reference Manual*, Revision 3, Tartan Laboratories, Pittsburgh, PA, February 1983.

[Lamb 87] Lamb, D. A., Implementation Strategies for DIANA Attributes, *SIGPLAN Notices*, 22, 11, November 1987.

[Nestor 89] Nestor, J. R., J. M. Newcomer, P. Giannini, and D. L. Stone, *IDL: The Language and Its Implementation*, Englewood Cliffs, NJ, Prentice-Hall, 1989.

What does ADA bring to the building of test programs?

Michel GAUTHIER

University of Limoges

ABSTRACT

With Ada, using widely the exception handling, the block instruction, and generic iterators, a test component can be built in the form of a unique program. Such programs always terminate after visiting all properties and all relevant data. The Ada library unit structure ensures great improvability and versatility of the obtained test program. The method works also with unconstrained types, with limited types, and with generic components.

The impact of Ada is essentially new in our process of building. Old languages, either have no genericity tools, or have no abnormal conditions handling, and more often have none. Ada provides both, and programs can be constructed, suitably to get an answer like "we trust in that program, and every customer can control why".

Keywords and phrases

Ada, program testing, reuseability, genericity, exception handling.

1 ABOUT TEST PROGRAMS

Testing of programs is known as mandatory in computer programming. Of course, with reusable components, this rule takes the form of testing each component independently from the others (except those it imports, either considered as tested before, or simulated for the purpose of testing). Both are the same problem.

Testing is, at a high level, twofold. One aspect is the need of correctly defining what the component or program must do, the so-called "specification", with the necessary adaptations to put it in a form suitable for a program. The second aspect is reducing all possible data to a set, sufficiently large to correctly test, and sufficiently small to run in an acceptable time[1].

The precise form of specification will not be studied here. It will only be supposed that during the phases before programming (restricted sense: the language level of the whole process of solving the real problem), some specification was built, from which are extracted suitable properties for correct testing. Similarly, the set of all relevant data will not be defined, such as

---

[1] It is hard to define "acceptable time". In all cases, we consider 60 hours as always acceptable, as one may activate the test on friday afternoon, and get the results on monday morning.

162 M. Gauthier

to obtain the desired result. It will only be considered that such a reduced set is available. And this set will be used, *in Ada*, to build the so-called "test program".

Testing progresses to obtain as a result that the program or component is in some sense "correct", or that it fails. More generally speaking, it determines a set of properties and associated data, for which the component fails. Now, suppose that yesterday's result was failing for some properties and some data. It was deduced where the program was wrong. The program was modified, and testing was tried again. Too often, programmers tend to re-test with only bad data and associated properties, but, if they do so, they risk not to detect new bad data, introduced by recent modifications. Hence, *the full old test must be re-activated*. To achieve that goal, testing must take the form of "something" permanent, hence *in a file*, possibly greater than the preceding one, but *in no case smaller*. That "something" can be a set of data to read, a file of system commands to execute, and some other... All choices have finally the same power, but here we shall choose non-interactive programs, and the reasons will appear later. In all cases of testing components which handle files, more than one program will be necessary, and consequently the test will be a system commands file activating these, but our conclusions are the same.

How can the buiding of a test program be achieved in Ada?

2 TESTING ONE AXIOM

The specifications were assumed to be written in the form of axioms to be controlled. Then, these axioms must be handled to write them into a second form, namely that of procedures to verify *one* property with *one* item of data. As many procedures as needed are written, without caring about the entire number of items, and of how to choose them.

2.1 Elementary cases

For instance, consider the control of properties like the following, where N is of some integer type (say RELATIVE_DAY), and D of some type (say GREGORIAN_DATE) for the package of which a test is currently being built:

$$D + 0 = D$$
$$D + (N + 1) = (D + N) + 1$$

Such controls need very fine handling of and control over abnormal[1] situations, arising in Ada as *exception raising* in the component. Hence more accuracy is needed in specifying. For the first axiom, no exception can be raised. For the second axiom, the equality is to be taken in a strict sense: if the computation of either term terminates with no exception, then the second must do so, and their results must be the same. If either raises some exception (here, CONSTRAINT_ERROR), then the second must do the same, with the same exception. All that specification can be written as a procedure, which always terminates, and calls either PASS or FAILS[2], from some testing tools package:

---

[1] The word «abnormal» is usual, but not satisfactory, as many cases of use correspond to normal foreseeable situations, but outside the direct way of computation. We suggest to prefer «exceptionnal», or better to find an ad hoc precise term.
[2] We suppose the availability of some test handling package with at least PASS and FAILS procedures, each with one "in" parameter of type STRING.

```
procedure AXIOM_1 ( D : in GREGORIAN_DATE ;
                    N : in RELATIVE_DAY ) is
   DATUM : constant STRING := some_image_of_the_parameters ;
   A , B : GREGORIAN_DATE ;
begin
   A := D + ( N + 1 ) ;
   begin
      B := ( D + N ) + 1 ;
      if A = B then
         PASS ( DATUM & some_relevant_message ) ;
      else
         FAILS ( DATUM & some_relevant_message ) ;
      end if ;
   exception
    when CONSTRAINT_ERROR =>
         FAILS ( DATUM & some_relevant_message );
   end ;
exception
 when CONSTRAINT_ERROR =>
      begin
         B := ( D + N ) + 1 ;
         FAILS ( DATUM & some_relevant_message ) ;
      exception
       when CONSTRAINT_ERROR =>
         PASS ( DATUM & some_relevant_message ) ;
      end ;
end AXIOM_1 ;
```

In fact, exception handling is simplified if no integer addition can raise any exception. Here, the only integer addition is "N+1", and verify that T'BASE'LAST for any T is not a useful item for any test. If this assumption fails, then an extra effort is needed for this last value, probably leading to additionnal internal block(s) to separate exception handling for "N+1" and for "D+()". For the actual example, the assumption succeeds, and the condition is added, that T'BASE'LAST should not be used as a test item. We shall emphasize later about exceptions and their correct use.

All axioms must lead to such a procedure. How to achieve that goal is out of the scope of the paper, but certainly most specification formalisms can lead to our form. We only propose one among various forms to express properties. *The exceptions tools of Ada are essential to achieve the construct.*

2.2 Testing for limited types and unconstrained types

Unconstrained types and limited types (in the Ada sense) can also be treated in such a way, via the use of a functionnal programming style. When assignment is not available, two other ways are suitable to give another name[1] to some computed value of a limited type, the function result and the "in" subprogram parameter. The latter is often a good solution. Suppose that a test is needed for a component for formal calculus, with a limited private type EXPRESSION. Inside it, a partial test is required that a function SELECTOR has undistinguishable results for two parameters LEFT and RIGHT, both and the result being of type EXPRESSION. Then we shall build a function DISTINGUISHABLE, with an internal generic function like the following:

---

[1] At highest levels, assignment must be considered as a way to give another name to some value. Copy is only a way to implement it in some cases, but not in all.

```
generic
    type RESULT is limited private ;
    with function EQUALITY ( LEFT , RIGHT : RESULT )
                         return BOOLEAN ;
function RESULT_DISTINGUISHABLE ( LEFT , RIGHT : RESULT )
         return BOOLEAN ;
                            --◊◊--
function RESULT_DISTINGUISHABLE ( LEFT , RIGHT : RESULT )
         return BOOLEAN is
    local declarations are further in the text
begin
    return LEFT_TEST ( SELECTOR ( LEFT ) ) ;
exception
 when RESULT_ERROR =>
     begin
         return EXCPT_TEST ( SELECTOR ( RIGHT ) ) ;
     exception
      when RESULT_ERROR =>
         return TRUE ;
     end ;
end RESULT_DISTINGUISHABLE ;
```

The main interest of the internal functions is that the name of their parameters can be used for every purpose, while not having the assignment. We build them as follows, including another level of internal declaration of function:

```
function LEFT_TEST ( LEFT_RESULT : RESULT )
                     return BOOLEAN is
    -- we know that SELECTOR ( LEFT ) terminates
    function RIGHT_TEST ( RIGHT_RESULT : RESULT )
                          return BOOLEAN is
        -- we know that SELECTOR ( LEFT ) terminates
        -- we know that SELECTOR ( RIGHT ) terminates
    begin
        return EQUALITY ( LEFT_RESULT , RIGHT_RESULT ) ;
    end RIGHT_TEST ;
begin
    return  RIGHT_TEST ( SELECTOR ( RIGHT ) ) ;
exception
 when RESULT_ERROR =>
     return FALSE ;
end LEFT_TEST ;

function EXCPT_TEST ( RIGHT_RESULT : RESULT )
                      return BOOLEAN is
    -- we know that SELECTOR ( LEFT ) raises EXPRESSION_ERROR
    -- we know that SELECTOR ( RIGHT ) terminates
begin
    return FALSE ;
end EXCPT_TEST ;
```

2.3 Non-interactive testing of interactive subprograms

File handling for TEXT_IO package is also possible with the use of file redirection [LRM.14.3.2]. Note that, for this reason, the component for test handling cannot use in-out procedures without file parameter, but with explicit standard file parameter. For size reasons, we cannot elaborate on this.

2.4 A little more about exceptions

I argue here that Ada adresses the community of programmers to revisit the old programming theory in order to determine whether it is validated or its limits are detected and, if the latter case, improvements are necessary. Of course, old theory is widely validated for old programming languages, and for old capabilities of new languages, but not necessarily for new capabilities of new languages.

Exceptions are one of the features for which the question is raised. Is it possible to continue to consider that a subprogram succeeds or fails? More control is needed for greatest quality programs. Every subprogram has some exits, ordinarily more than one, each one with an associated precondition. Preconditions are naturally exclusive, but without a new view, they are seldom exhaustive as they would be. Among all possible exits, one is *syntactically* distinguished as "normal", and others are somewhat hidden, but they do exist[1]. In all cases, this implies that much more detailed assertions are needed about abnormal cases. Please note that the information is exactly the same when exiting with goto's, with status returning information, with aborts, and with exceptions, but only the latter is fully compatible with reuseability and with embedded software.

Some elementary rules arise from that view of exceptions. Particularly, no exception must be handled if the programmer did not determine exactly the set of syntactic points where that exception is possibly raised, and prove which of these points correspond to false assertions. Hence it must be proved that EXCPT_TEST, LEFT_TEST and RIGHT_TEST cannot raise EXPRESSION_ERROR, except during the execution of SELECTOR. In complex cases, this rule will lead to distinguish different exception raisings in the same expression, sometimes introducing new levels of subprograms and blocks.

3 ITERATING ON DATA

Quite independently of elementary controlling procedures, generic procedures must be defined to enumerate elements to use as parameters for these. They are ususaly called "iterators", and have a declaration like:

```
generic
    with procedure REPEAT ( ITEM : in TYPE_TO_ENUMERATE ) ;
procedure FOR_ALL_TYPE_TO_ENUMERATE ;
```

or:

```
generic
    with procedure REPEAT ( ITEM_1 : in TYPE_1 ;
                ... ... ...
                ITEM_N : in TYPE_N ) ;
procedure FOR_ALL_DATA_FOR_SOME_AXIOM ;
```

Such procedures are easy to write, as they often are in one, among a small number of styles:
• enumerate the full type, in cases where it is small, or composed of elements very different by their effects,

---

[1] We can deduce from that argument that MacCabe-like measures are underestimated of the whole number of possible exception raisings. Further, proving non-raising properties is a way to drastically reduce the static complexity of the program. But this is not the aim of the present paper...

• enumerate a set of independent elements, possibly structured as a unique array,
• less often, enumerate a list or a file, or some other sequential structure[1].

Sometimes, it is interesting to define more than one level of test, for example the first is quick for simple and systematic test inside the programming team, the second is appropriate for a once-a-day deeper test, and the third for great week-end test before final release. Assuming iteration on a discrete type (the following is reasonably reuseable as a generic component):

```
procedure FOR_ALL_TYPE_TO_ENUMERATE is
    SOME_VALUE : constant TYPE_TO_ENUMERATE := distinguished_value;
begin
    if TEST_LEVEL /= HIGH then
        REPEAT ( ITEM => SOME_VALUE ) ;
        if TEST_LEVEL = LOW then
            return ;
        end if ;
        if SOME_VALUE /= TYPE_TO_ENUMERATE ' FIRST then
            REPEAT ( ITEM => TYPE_TO_ENUMERATE ' FIRST ) ;
        end if ;
        if SOME_VALUE /= TYPE_TO_ENUMERATE ' LAST and then
            TYPE_TO_ENUMERATE ' FIRST / TYPE_TO_ENUMERATE ' LAST
        then
            REPEAT ( ITEM => TYPE_TO_ENUMERATE ' LAST ) ;
        end if ;
    else
        for K in TYPE_TO_ENUMERATE loop
            REPEAT ( ITEM => K ) ;
        end loop ;
    end if ;
end FOR_ALL_TYPE_TO_ENUMERATE ;
```

For multiple-parametered procedures, or for non-scalar types like dates, multiple iterators can be built systematically, as it was done for the above example:

```
generic
    with procedure REPEAT ( DATE : in GREGORIAN_DATE ;
                            NUMB : in RELATIVE_DAY ) ;
procedure FOR_ALL_AXIOM_1 ;

procedure FOR_ALL_AXIOM_1 is

    procedure ONE_DATE ( D : in GREGORIAN_DATE ) is

        procedure ONE_NUMBER ( N : in RELATIVE_DAY ) is
        begin
            REPEAT ( DATE => D , NUMB => N ) ;
        end ONE_NUMBER ;

        procedure ALL_NUMBERS is
            new FOR_ALL_NUMBERS ( REPEAT => ONE_NUMBER ) ;

    begin -- ONE_DATE
        ALL_NUMBERS ;
    end ONE_DATE ;
```

---

[1] Enumerating an array is not ordinarily useful, as a sequence of calls of the parameter "REPEAT" leads more simply to the same result.

```
procedure ALL_DATES is
    new FOR_ALL_DATES ( REPEAT => ONE_DATE ) ;

begin -- FOR_ALL_AXIOM_1
    ALL_DATES ;
end FOR_ALL_AXIOM_1 ;
```

It will not be discussed here how to obtain a correct set of data items. That is another job, which is only partially known. Ordinarily, one part is built from the formal specification, and classes of data arising from it. That set is completed by observing the body of the component, in order to ensure some properties like activating every instruction or obtaining all values of boolean expressions.

This construct is in no way difficult, but somewhat unusual. It strongly uses genericity, possibly further than allowed in cheap compilers, but among what people must require from them. *The genericity tools of Ada are important to achieve the construct*, but not essential as, in other languages, instead of genericity, subprograms can be used as parameters of other subprograms, and this is widely available.

4 FULL INTEGRATION

4.1 Non generic component

These iterator procedures can be instantiated with these elementary axioms procedures as parameters, and test programs are built essentially as the sequence of unique calls of these instantiations, as in the schema:

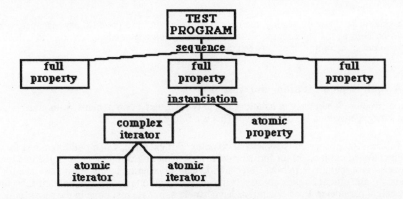

It is important in such constructs to get a great ability in modification, partly for properties to control, but essentielly for data to be enumerated. To achieve this, axiom procedures and iterators must be compiled as library units, each importing the component to test. The control procedures also import the general test tools package. Also instantiations are library units. If it is processed in that way, strongly independent components are obtained, in the three classes, axiom control, data iterator, instantiations. Modifying an axiom (currently for better exception handling) involves only recompiling of a body. Adding a data item can often be written in such a way that also only one body is recompiled, at the price of more (very small) components.

Hence, all the system is improvable at very low cost, but numerous units are constructed, really too many units for an unstructured library, and some organization is needed, like the following, found in the working directory:
• the specification of the component, and compiler output for it,
• a subdirectory, and also sublibrary, containing all testing units, and possibly the body of the component,
• the executable test program.
Of course, such an organization is environment-dependent.

4.2 Generic components

Testing generic components is a bit more complicated. First, the test program must take the form of a generic procedure, with at least the same generic parameters as the tested component. Additionnal parameters can be useful, such as IMAGE functions returning STRING or distinguished values. We did not actually determine which instantiations are suitable to get a good test. It is possible to instantiate on request, but systematic constructs are always better, and we have no solution to that problem.

All components of the non-generic construct would depend on the generic parameters in the generic case. So, the same form cannot be kept exactly. A partial solution is obtained by separing (in the Ada meaning) templates for data iterators, bodies for axiom controls, and full controls built by their instantiations. The difficulty arises from some dependencies (on generic templates) between separate elements, with possible incorrect treatment by the Ada library manager, as the LRM needs none and the case needs one.

With generic components testing, the need is found again for a good library manager, which would be able to manage components like those which are needed, and able to achieve a correct order of recompilations between them.

4.3 Actual implementation and cost

Such a structure is not easy to handle, especially for generic components, without a suitable library manager, which we do not have. This is a future work.

The full resulting program is somewhat complex. For example, when building a test for the aforementioned component for formal calculus, the resulting complexity involved two levels of generic subprogram definitions, three additionnal subprogram levels, for iterator and for its parameter, and other complex constructs like an instantiation inside a subprogram A, using A as an actual parameter. Four exceptions have handlers, but at most three in the same frame. It is not exotic programming, but of real difficulty.

The number of data items can be very large, espacially with multi-parametered properties. Whenever it is possible, it is always preferable to reduce that number. For instance, with the above example, it would be better to test:

$$D + 0 = D$$
$$D + 1 = NEXT (D)$$

for some function NEXT built in the test program for that unique purpose, but of course, not a

function of the controlled component. With one-parametered properties, one can sometimes consider the exhaustive set of data, which is the best solution whenever possible.
In the current state (at the date of the full paper), the real cost (compilation and execution) was not measured for such a process, and for various components to test, on various target machines, and with various compilers. We suppose that in many cases, night batch is suitable, but partial tests are in every case allowed, as long as nobody tries to assert it as a full one. The cost of computations should not be the only one considered, but the full cost for all software engineering tools for the whole project should be taken into account.

4.4 Relevance of the method

Can we really trust in the method? It is "well known" that a program is not a good solution to test another one. Let us modify the question to "what do test programs need in order to be better than human control?". Do you really trust in human verification for large data sets? It is a real problem, with no general solution. The answer is strongly dependent on the required quality. But good arguments exist for the method.

In most cases, a fail in the test conception will lead to a fail in the test activation. This is not a problem, as an extra effort is always necessary in that case, if the effort applies on both the test and the component. It can happen that the test and the component have complementary defaults resulting in no detected errors. Relevant methods have still to be raised, founded:
• on independance of the teams building both programs,
• on redundancy of properties and items, easy with automatic testing but heavy with human one,
• on the detection of weaknesses in construction and proofs, and subsequent controls[1].
Also, please keep in mind that safety is in no case reduced when adding controls, and that testing is not alone in the process, but always concurring with proofs and construction methods.

5 CONCLUSION

It is clear from the above explanations that Ada is appropriate to build test programs much more easily, and with greater impact on the quality of products. These are not really based on Ada, but on some of its features, namely powerful and safe reuseability, genericity, and versatile exception handling. The result program is complex, but not out of the know-how of good programmers, and it is an acceptable price to pay for improved safety.

One of the main characteristics of the method is the rather natural expression of everything needed, a single procedure for each property to control, a single iterator for the data associated with that control, an instantiation of the second with the first as a parameter, and the whole test is a sequence of all these instantiated controls. Each elementary component is well isolated and easy to maintain.

In its actual state, the method still needs too much know-how. It is complicated, and the ratio between component contruction and test construction is dissuasive. Sophistication is needed, with automatic —interactive?— construction tools, but this is a future work.

---

[1] For example, if there is a risk to make assumptions on the implementations and use them in the conception of a test, fundamentally different assumptions must be raised, and used also in an additional test. In all cases, at least one will work correctly. Hence, local weakness can improve the full process.

Of course, other languages seem to offer similar features. Eliminating those which have nothing similar to exception handling, eliminating those which have nothing to express iterators, I issue the challenge that very few other languages can do with such tests, and that whenever they can, the result is much more complicated and less natural than in Ada.

Ada can...

Insecurities in Ada

B A Wichmann
Division of Information Technology and Computing
National Physical Laboratory, TW11 0LW, UK

1 Introduction

The Ada programming language was designed to cover a very large application domain. Hence Ada is not ideal for many specific applications. For instance, in writing small, safety-critical software it would be technically better to use a language that has been specially designed for that area which enforces a programming style aimed at formal verification [5, 12]. However, the overheads in introducing yet another programming language in industry are very high so that in practice one is likely to be using Ada for such applications; and in any case, Ada compares favourably with other standard languages [4]. Hence the question arises as to what undesirable features Ada has which could cause an Ada program to behave in a manner which could not be reasonably anticipated by a responsible programmer. This paper attempts to identify such features (called 'insecurities' after a corresponding paper for Pascal [13]). Avoiding the pitfalls identified here should help to achieve high integrity Ada (i.e. Ada programs in which one can have a high degree of confidence which might be essential to certain applications). This topic is of substantial interest in the UK due to recent draft standards [9, 8].

While safety-critical software can be expected to be small and use a very disciplined approach, larger items of software in Ada can be expected to be critical in other respects. Good style is vital in any language and for Ada there are guidelines for this which it is reasonable to expect programmers to have followed [11]. In spite of following such guidelines, problems can arise with large Ada programs many of which are a consequence of scale. The proposals for subsets [3, 6] do not help since they lack the functionality to write large systems effectively. The Ada user needs to know where problems can arise so here we try to enumerate the potential insecurities which could arise with large programs as well as small ones.

The basic source material for this study is primarily the Ada Reference Manual (RM [7]), the Ada Rapporteur Group list of Language Issues, material in the Ada Evaluation Suite (AES) [2] and bugs lists in Ada compilers. The ARTEWG paper [1] provides similar material which has been checked against this report. The Safe Ada study [6] which indicates how to avoid erroneous execution is also relevant to this study.

The source of insecurities can be traced to three primary causes:

1. Uncertainties in the language definition. These are handled by the Ada Rapporteur Group which performs a vital role in cataloguing these issues and attempting to resolve them. Because of the work already undertaken, this area is well charted and understood.

2. Deliberate 'flexibility' in the language definition which can cause programs accepted by compilers to legally do unpredictable things. The Ada language was carefully designed so that implementations could be efficient in a variety of environments. This requires that some flexibility is given to the compiler-writer. Unfortunately, this flexibility can easily be a trap for the unwary. A new group call the Uniformity Rapporteur Group is handling issues under this heading.

3. Implementation faults. The primary check of compiler validation is assumed here. This check is a severe one, since the Ada Compiler Validation Capability (ACVC) is aggressive in its testing. Unfortunately, most Ada compilers lack 'maturity' and one sometimes gets the impression that they have learnt to pass the ACVC but little else! The Ada Evaluation Service (AES) is an interesting second level test, although it does not primarily handle issues of correctness.

In this paper we are primarily interested in insecurities which could cause programs to be unpredictable during execution. This is important because a substantial complexity in Ada is due to the 'static semantic checks' which determine the legality of an Ada program. If some of these checks are implemented incorrectly, in many cases a legal program may fail to compile (which is not dangerous) or sometimes an illegal program may compile but the meaning of it would not be seriously in doubt.

The classification given above cannot be applied too rigorously. For instance, an uncertainty in the language definition could well result in an implementation fault.

2   Risk Assessment

The question which this study addresses is that of the practical consequences of insecurities in the Ada language. For each aspect of Ada that is considered, the risk is assessed with perhaps a restriction to the class of programs at risk.

For instance, a feature might be quoted as 'medium risk for programs using tasking' or 'low risk' (implying all applications). Three levels of risk are used — low, medium and high. See [14] for full details.

The notion of risk is hard to quantify (for software) and it must be admitted here that the choice is a personal one. Two aspects must certainly be born in mind — the probability of it occurring in real programs and the effects if it does. Risk is the topic of a recent defence standard [10].

3   Uncertainties in the language definition

If anybody locates a potential uncertainty in the Ada reference manual, they are invited to write in to the Ada Joint Program Office giving details. Around 800 such issues have been catalogued up to early 1989. On the face of it, this large number of issues appears to indicate major problems with the language, since the comparable number of issues for ISO-Pascal is only about 60. There are a number of reasons for the large number with Ada:

1. The Ada reference manual invites people to write in. Other standards make no such provision.

2. The Ada language was standardized before many implementations were produced. This naturally gave rise to many queries from implementors.

3. The Ada language goes much further in specifying things than most other standards, and in consequence, new issues arise with Ada that are not relevant to other high-level language standards.

4. The Ada Joint Program Office has been successful in ensuring that only validated Ada compilers can be marketed effectively. This, combined with the stringent Ada test suite, has ensured that the language standard is effectively enforced.

5. The Ada policy of no extensions has meant that there is no 'escape' mechanism for implementors.

Even if the Ada standard were word perfect, my belief is that the above reasons would result in a significant number of Ada issues. Of course, the Ada standard is not perfect and hence the need to interpret the standard so that a revised version could be produced. It can be assumed that Ada 9X will at least include the agreed interpretations. Indeed, the Ada Rapporteur Group (ARG) is producing a document which amends the RM by including the agreed issues.

The Ada issues are processed by the ARG which is a subgroup of the ISO working group responsible for the Ada standard. The ARG also reports to the Ada Board which advises the US Department of Defense on Ada. By reporting to two bodies, the ARG decisions are effective both for the military standard and the ANSI standard (and hence the ISO standard).

4   Deliberate flexibility in the language definition

As indicated in the RM (1.6), there are two forms of flexibility which cause the form of insecurity that concerns us here: erroneous execution and incorrect order dependence. Also, there are non-deterministic aspects of the execution of Ada programs which can cause problems. These are usually regarded as portability issues rather than insecurities; a list of such features is taken from [11]. These are considered in turn.

4.1   Erroneous execution

The index of the RM indicates eight cases as follows:

1. due to an access to a deallocated object, RM 13.10.1.

2. due to an unchecked conversion violating properties of objects of the result type, RM 13.10.2.

3. due to assignment to a shared variable, RM 9.11.

4. due to changing of a discriminant value, RM 5.2, 6.2.

5. due to dependence on parameter passing mechanism, RM 6.2.

6. due to multiple address clauses for overlaid entities, RM 13.5.

7. due to suppression of an exception check, RM 13.5.

8. due to use of an undefined value RM 3.2.1.

All of these issues give serious cause for concern, mainly because a detailed analysis is necessary of a complete Ada program in order to determine the absence of such an insecurity. For further details, see [14].

4.2   Incorrect order dependence

Twelve forms of incorrect order dependence are listed in the index as follows:

1. assignment statement RM 5.2.

2. bounds of a range constraint RM 3.5.

3. component association of an array aggregate RM 4.3.2.

4. component association of an record aggregate RM 4.3.1.

5. component subtype indication RM 3.6.

6. default expression for a component RM 3.2.1.

7. default expression for a discriminant RM 3.2.1.

8. expression RM 4.5.

9. index constraint RM 3.6.

10. library unit RM 10.5.

11. parameter association RM 6.4.

12. prefix and discrete range of a slice RM 4.1.2.

Currently, all these issues are a minor risk since they depend upon side-effects in functions, except the order of elaboration of library units. The library unit issue is a high risk. The Uniformity Rapporteur Group is recommending that incorrect order dependence does not raise `PROGRAM_ERROR` which removes one uncertainity from the language.

4.3   Portability Issues

This paper is not primarily concerned with portability. One would expect some packages to be imported to the system. Inadequate re-testing during re-targeting of such software is always a danger. The references to the portability guide use the notation P d.d, where d.d refers to the section in the RM.

1. use of implementation-defined pragma, P 2.8.

2. use of an uninitialized value, P 3.2.1.

3. no assumption should be made as to whether `NUMERIC_ERROR` or `CONSTRAINT_ERROR` will be raised as a result of a range constraint, P 3.5.

4. values outside the range of safe numbers for floating point types should not be assumed, P 3.5.6

5. the raising of NUMERIC_ERROR for overflow with floating point should not be assumed, P 3.5.6.

6. for fixed point types, avoid the use of values which may not be in the range of model numbers, P 3.5.9.

7. the use of equality and non-equality for real operands needs substantial care, P 4.5.7.

8. the use of type conversions when the result is not determined, such as INTEGER(FLOAT(1.5)), P 4.6.

9. ensure adequate storage space for access types by specifying the collection size, P 4.8.

10. do not assume that the accuracy of the evaluation of static real expressions exceeds that of the target machine, P 4.9

11. do not assume that the pragma INLINE has any effect, P6.3.

12. do not assume when the termination of tasks in library units takes place, P 9.4.

13. do not use priorities to enforce synchronization, P 9.8.

14. do not assume that the abort statement is 'immediate', P 9.10.

15. do not use pragma SHARED, P 9.11.

16. with either an implicit or explicit raising of an exception, do not assume that locally updated global variables have been assigned, P 10.6.

17. if a statement can raise more than one exception, do not assume which particular one is raised, P 11.1.

18. address clauses must not be used to overlay data or to link an interrupt to more than one entry, P 13.5.

19. machine code should not be used, P 13.8.

20. pragma INTERFACE should not be used, P 13.9.

21. aliasing of files must not be used, P 14.1.

22. package LOW_LEVEL_IO must not be used, P 14.6.

Some of these are simple static checks and are therefore simple to perform, perhaps aided by a tool. Others, like the erroneous program executions issues, require a detailed analysis of the whole program which makes avoidance hard to guarantee.

5   Implementation faults

It is not easy to quantify the reliability of Ada compilers. One possible measure is the number of lines of source text that can be moved from one system to another per bug detected in the new system. In writing a large number of lines, the time taken will be long and the problems with the development are likely to mask any measurement of the bugs. Moving the code is different in this respect and hence the bug rate can be measured. For Pascal, the reasonable figure would be about 10,000 lines per bug located. It is thought that the rate for Ada is about ten times higher.

Various 'tricky' tests have shown major weaknesses in virtually all implementations. For instance, a test three years ago from CWI of floating point attributes, a recent test from SEI of UNCHECKED_CONVERSION and new tests from NPL of storage allocation all revealed major problems. Fortunately, these tests are widely distributed and vendors quickly correct their implementations.

An examination of the bug reports from two compilers indicated a roughly equal split between the compiler crashing, the compiler not compiling correct programs, and executing programs incorrectly. Obviously, the last case is the high-risk area.

One of the most troublesome areas for compilers is that of the code generator. A special program has been written at NPL to check this for Pascal compilers [15]. It automatically generates correct, self-checking programs which are arbitrarily complex. Although the current version only checks expressions, it has so far found faults in all compilers which perform any optimization. In view of the comparisons above, a similar Ada generator would find even more faults. The conclusion is that use of optimization is a high risk.

6   Conclusions

To obtain an Ada program in which one can have a high degree of confidence needs substantial care. Three forms of insecurity are identified and assessed in this report as follows:

1. Uncertainties in the language definition. The ISO Working Group is resolving problems here rapidly and effectively. There appears to be no

essential barrier to producing high integrity Ada programs due to the language definition.

2. 'Flexibility' in the language definition. An Ada implementor has quite a few options which can impact upon the integrity of the Ada program. For instance, the fact that parameters of composite types can be passed by copy or reference. In this respect, Ada is no different from FORTRAN in which a similar option on parameter passing exists.

3. Implementation faults. This is a serious concern at the moment. Users should ask for an evaluation of the compiler by the AES [2].

The main areas of high risk are detailed in the Appendix.

While it is true that the size of Ada contributes to the risk, several factors help to off-set the risk. For instance, the large and competitive market means that users can choose a compiler which is more appropriate for their application. Similarly, the growing number of users implies that good textbooks are available and that there is less risk of programmers being confused by an unfamiliar language.

6.1   Future Developments

Two Ada subsets have been designed to overcome many of the problems identified in this report [6, 3]. However, such subsets are not appropriate for large systems even when tools are available to ensure conformance with the subsets. Also, a subset program will typically be compiled with a compiler for the full language, thus encountering the implementation problems noted above.

Apart from the subsets noted above, the following developments should aid the construction of high integrity Ada:

1. The completion of the resolution of the Ada issues by the ARG.

2. The publication of recommended implementation strategies by the URG when the language allows divergent implementations.

3. The development (planned for completion at NPL this year) of a tool to locate code generation bugs in compilers [15].

4. The development of better validation techniques, such as that based upon an intermediate language called Low-Ada [16].

References

[1] Catalogue of Ada runtime implementation dependencies. ACM/SigAda/ARTEWG, December 1st 1987.

[2] BSI Ada evaluation service. Preliminary information sheet. October 1987.

[3] B A Carré and T J Jennings. SPARK - The SPADE Ada Kernel. University of Southampton. March 1988.

[4] W J Cullyer, S J Goodenough and B A Wichmann, "The Choice of Computer Languages in Safety-Critical Systems", (to be published in the Software Engineering Journal).

[5] I F Currie, NewSpeak - an unexceptional language. Software Engineering Journal. Vol 1, pp170-176. 1986.

[6] R Holzapfel and G Winterstein. Ada in Safety Critical Applications. Ada-Europe Conference 1988.

[7] J D Ichbiah et al. Reference Manual for the Ada programming language. ANSI/MIL-STD-1815A, 1983.

[8] IEC SC65A/WG9 "Software for computers in the application of industrial safety-related systems". 3rd draft, June 1989.

[9] Interim Defence Standard 00-55, "Requirements for the Procurement of Safety Critical Software in Defence Equipment", undated.

[10] Interim Defence standard 00-56, " Requirements for the Analysis of Safety Critical Hazards", undated.

[11] J Nissen and P Wallis. Portability and Style in Ada. CUP. 1984.

[12] SPADE Pascal, Program Validation Ltd. Southampton, 1987.

[13] J Welsh, W J Sneeringer and C A R Hoare, Ambiguities and insecurities in Pascal. Software - Practice and Experience. Vol 7, 1977.

[14] B A Wichmann. Insecurities in the Ada programming language. NPL Report DITC 137/89. January 1989.

[15] B A Wichmann and M Davies. Experience with a compiler testing tool. NPL Report DITC 138/89. March 1989.

[16] B A Wichmann. Low-Ada: an Ada validation tool. NPL Report DITC 144/89. August 1989.

A Summary of high risk areas

1. if UNCHECKED_DEALLOCATION is used,

2. if UNCHECKED_CONVERSION converts to an access type,

3. shared variables, if tasking is used,

4. changing discriminant values, assuming they are changed at all,

5. dependence upon the parameter mechanism,

6. use of the pragma SUPPRESS,

7. use of an undefined value,

8. order of elaboration of library units,

9. use of priorities for synchronization,

10. use of the abort statement,

11. state of locally updated global variables after an exception,

12. use of address clauses,

13. use of machine code,

14. use of the pragma INTERFACE,

15. use of LOW_LEVEL_IO,

16. use of optimization,

17. use of the pragma STORAGE_UNIT,

18. extra precision and range, if fixed point types are used,

19. use of representation specifications,

20. use of record types with unconstrained dynamic bounds,

21. dependence on preemptive scheduling,

22. to distinguish between NUMERIC_ERROR and CONSTRAINT_ERROR exceptions.

PART VI: Object Oriented Design

Graphic Interface Management in ADA

R. VIVO, M.A. JUAN, A. CRESPO

Universidad Politecnica de Valencia
Grupo de Automatica e Informatica Industrial
Spain

1. INTRODUCTION

Supervision and process control applications are the most common in the industrial world. In this context, programs interact with data acquisition and actuation devices, normally with real-time restrictions.

Traditionally, these tasks have been directly performed on the physical devices, or by means of control panels. Measures and operator inputs were managed via these panels.

Nowadays, the trend is towards the centralization of interaction in panels. In this way, access to information and operator response are faster, and thus, reliability is improved.

In computer-controlled systems, there must be a logical equivalent of the panel. Moreover, elements such as lights, numerical and analogical displays and other input-output devices should have a graphic equivalent in panel representation [YOU87].

The user-process communication will be carried out by a set of such panels, each of them representing a logical part of the process. A panel consists of a set of symbols, each one being the representation of a physical element.

As control applications become more complex, the design of the operator interface assumes greater importance. The best way to establish a good man-machine dialogue is throughout the use of interactive graphic techniques [FOL84].

As it is known, interactive graphic interfaces are extremely difficult and time-consuming to build, but in contrast they are easy to learn and to use, even by a beginner user [FOL74]. This leads to the need of a set of tools that help the developer in the task of building the user interface of an application.

User interface tools can be classified in two general groups: user-interface toolkits and user-interface management system (UIMS).

A toolkit is a library of interaction techniques, that can be used by an application to communicate with the operator. Different kinds of logical interaction devices allow machine independent designs [ERO87]. As a general rule, interactive graphic techniques are based on pick and locator logical devices, implemented with alphanumeric keyboard and mouse.

A UIMS is an integrated set of tools that help programmers create and manage many aspects of interfaces [MYE89]. Any UIMS must control two kinds of communication. One is the man-machine dialogue an the other, the communication with the application (in our case, the process control or supervision).

In order to describe the man-machine dialogue, several methods have been used: AITs [VAN88], state transition diagrams, context-free grammars, event languages, or object-oriented languages, like MacApp [SHM86].

Regarding communication with the application, UIMS can be classified depending on who controls the communication. Toolkits use internal control (application control), i.e., the application calls interface procedures when necessary.

UIMS's normally use external control (UIMS controls the execution). This can be acomplished through the use of shared memory or callback procedures whose names are passed by the application to the UIMS.

In this paper a model of communication between application and graphic interface system is described. This model constitutes a framework where man-machine dialogue can be included.

2. **OBJECT-ORIENTED DESIGN**

Prior to the graphic interface definition, an object-oriented design [GOL83] and implementation of the control process should be made. The output of this task would be a set of objects and the operations they can suffer and perform.

Those of such objects that are decided to have a graphic respresentation will be named OCV's (Object Control View). Besides, the following assumptions are made on them:

- It is necessary to add to every OCV a new method allowing to notify to the object that a user request has been issued.

- OCV state is defined by its attribute values, meaning measures and turnable parameters.

- The system provides a means to notify the graphic interface that an OCV attribute change happened (a daemon mechanism would be adequate).

- Those OCV's that can be modified by means of a user action, must provide the necessary methods to allow that.

The result of the design process is a class hierarchy described below:

SYMBOL: OCV parameterized graphic representation. Local man machine dialogue will be defined here with the help of a specification language, such as AITs.

SYMBOL CLASS: The objects of this class have a position, a set of generic graphic attributes and a list of pieces. In this class there are defined methods for symbol creation, drawing and deletion. There are also defined methods for pieces update and retrieval.

SYMBOL SUBCLASSES: As class variable, it has a list of pieces subclasses, needed to build a symbol instance. Here, symbol drawing methods are refined and specific attributes are added.

User-symbol interaction is defined specifically for each symbol subclass.

Instances of this subclass will become graphic representations bound to OCV's.

PIECE: Parameterized graphic lowest level unit (graphic token) which it is posible to address to, by means of a pick logical interaction device.

PIECE CLASS: Every object of this class has a reference to the symbol object that created it. It also contains generic graphic attributes. Definition of creation, deletion and drawing methods are needed.

PIECE SUBCLASSES: These subclasses refine drawing methods and add specific attributes.

Piece subclasses are supposed to be kept in a library, in order to achieve graphic representations reusability.

Instances of these subclasses will compose list of pieces of symbol instances.

CGI (Control Graphic Interface): In order to achieve modularity goals, it is necessary to consider the existence of an intermediate object that carries out any information flow between OCV's and their associate symbols.

This flow is driven by evaluation of a set of direct and inverse transformation functions. Direct functions take values in the OCV attributes domain and give visual-metric results. Inverse functions perform the opposite mapping.

CGI CLASS: Instances of this class will allow communication between OCV's and symbols. They contain references to both of them.

It has as attributes the transformation functions corresponding to the symbol-OCV connection.

Methods for updating symbol and notifying OCV are provided.

Figure 1 shows the anatomy of this design.

3. **DEVELOPING THE GRAPHICAL INTERFACE**

In a first step, OCV's are modified as said above and instantiated. In the following, these instances are supposed to be available.

With the help of a Symbol Editor, subclasses of Symbol class necessary to represent OCV's are built. Symbol layout and panel configuration are defined.

Object generation order is commented below:

1. For each OCV, an instance of CGI is created giving it transformation functions, OCV and the symbol subclass that represents this OCV.

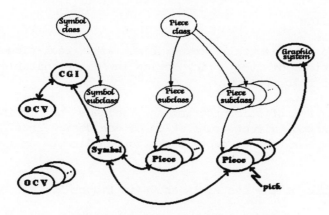

Figure 1. Object Oriented Design.

2. Symbol subclass instance creation is acomplished.

3. This produces the creation of one instance of every piece subclass included in the pieces classes list described in the symbol subclass.

4. NORMAL OPERATION

In a steady state, the two main actions to which the system reacts will be: user action in order to change process state, and graphic representation update due to a change in process state.

User Action: User selects a specific piece in the active panel. The piece notifies this fact to its symbol. This last one starts a dialogue with the user to determine the full requested action. With this information, CGI must be notified. CGI, in turn, applies inverse transformation functions and transmit to the OCV the requested action with the turnable parameters values.

Change in process state: OCV attributes modification must be notified to the associated CGI, either by direct call or by means of a daemon based mechanism. CGI applies direct transformation functions, obtaining visual metric parameters and passing them to the symbol updating method. The symbol determines which among its pieces must be modified and issues the adequate requests.

5. ADA DESIGN

In order to achieve full integration with real-time systems, implementation of the prior design in Ada is suitable. This is the goal of this section.

Due to the fact of this programming language not being purely object oriented, direct translation of the design into Ada is not posible. As a matter of fact, there is no direct equivalent of subclasses.

The structure of the system is shown in figure 2.

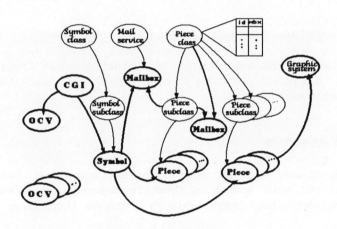

Figure 2. Ada design

In general terms, classes are implemented by means of types exported by Ada packages. For instance, PIECE is a type exported by the package PIECES. Subclasses of PIECE, such as DIAL.SHAPE, are types exported by packages that refine PIECES. Any subPiece inherits all the instance operations of PIECE.

When a subPiece enhances the Piece data structure, the subPiece is defined as a record with a Piece field and other fields for the rest of information.

```
    --PACKAGE PIECES CLASS--------------
    with MAIL_SERVICE; use MAIL_SERVICE;
    package PIECES is
        type PIECE is record
                    ID: IDENTIFIER;
                    RECEIVER_BOX: MAILBOX;
                    --other common attributes
        end record;
        procedure ATTEND( PICK: IDENTIFIER );
        procedure STORE( POBOX: MAILBOX; ID: out IDENTIFIER );
        --other procedures
    end PIECES;

--PACKAGE DIAL: SUBCLASS OF PIECE---
with GKS; use GKS;
with MAIL_SERVICE; use MAIL_SERVICE;
with PIECES; use PIECES;
package DIAL is
    type SHAPE is limited private;
    MY_MAILBOX: MAILBOX:= new POST_ADDRESS;
    procedure CREATE( ADIAL: out SHAPE; ID: out IDENTIFIER );
    procedure SET_RECEIVER( ADIAL: SHAPE; POBOX: MAILBOX );
    procedure DRAW( ADIAL: SHAPE; LARGE: FLOAT; COLOR: INTEGER );
    --other procedures
private
    type SHAPE_STRUCTURE;
    type SHAPE is access SHAPE_STRUCTURE;
    type SHAPE_STRUCTURE is record
            GENERAL: PIECE;
            SIZE: FLOAT;
            FOREGROUND_COLOR: INTEGER;
            --other attributes
            NEXT: SHAPE;
    end record;
end DIAL;
```

The same method should be applied for other classes.

CGIs are instances of a generic package. When the generic is instantiated, actual direct and inverse transformation functions are provided.

```
--GENERIC PACKAGE CONTROL-GRAPHIC INTERFACE--
with MOTOR; with SYM_MOTOR;
generic
 with function SYM2MOT(SLOPE:SYM_MOTOR.ANGLE) return MOTOR.SPEED;
 with function MOT2SYM(VALUE:MOTOR.SPEED) return SYM_MOTOR.ANGLE;
package CGI_MOTOR is
   --exportable procedures
end CGI_MOTOR;
```

Each symbol and OCV contain a task. When one of them needs to
establish communication, it executes an accept. The corresponding
CGI is polling on them by means of a conditional entry call.

Communication between a symbol and its pieces is implemented
through the use of mailboxes [BUR85]. There is a MailService
package that provides a MailBox task type. There is a mailbox
for each symbol and one for each piece subclass.

```
        package MAIL_SERVICE is
            task type POST_ADDRESS is
                entry RECEIVE(ID: in IDENTIFIER);
                entry COLLECT(ID: out IDENTIFIER);
            end POST_ADDRESS;
            type MAILBOX is access POST_ADDRESS;
        end MAIL_SERVICE;
```

Piece class keeps a list of pieces and their mailboxes (a class
variable). This list is updated whenever a new piece is created.

When a symbol is created, it instances and actives its pieces,
reporting them about the symbol mailbox. This mailbox is
included in each piece.

When the user, through the Graphic System, picks a piece, the
ATTEND procedure is invoked. This method looks for the mailbox
corresponding to that identifier and puts the id in the piece
subclass mailbox.

The piece subclass that owns that mailbox, collects the id and
put it into the mailbox of the symbol the picked piece belongs
to. That symbol collects this information and acts consequently
(starts interaction).

Note that the piece subclass knows that one of its instances has
been picked and a local echo can be produced without intervention
of the symbol. Higher levels of the man-machine dialogue rely on
the symbol.

The mechanism of mailboxes gives a practical solution to the problem of reciprocal invocation between packages.

6. CONCLUSIONS

A graphic interface system writen in Ada for process control applications has been presented.

The system has been designed using object oriented techniques and implemented with the special features of the Ada language. The main problems in matching both views and the solutions implemented have been detailed in the paper.

The tool developed is formed by a set of Ada tasks communicating through mailboxes.

In the paper a taxonomy of graphic elements has been built using an inheritance approach. As we say before, a symbol is composed of graphic tokens called pieces. Each piece is an instance of a piece subclass library. Communication between the graphical interface and the application is carried out by CGI's. Finally a description of the Ada code implementation has been proposed.

REFERENCES

[BAR82] J.G.P.Barnes. "Programming in Ada"
        Addison-Wesley, 1982.

[BUR85] A.Burns. "Concurrent programming in Ada"
        Cambridge University Press, 1985.

[ERO87] J.Ero, R.van Liere. "User Interface Management
        Systems".
        Advances in Computer Graphics III. Eurographic
        Seminars, 1987.

[FOL74] J.D.Foley, V.L.Wallace. "The Art of Natural
        Graphic Man-machine Conversation".
        Proc. of the IEEE, 1974.

[FOL84] J.D.Foley, A.van Dam. "Fundamentals of
        Interactive Computer Graphics".
        Addison-Wesley, 1984.

[GOL83] A.Goldberg, D.Robson. "Smalltalk-80"
         Addison-Wesley, 1983.

[MYE89] B.A.Myers. "User-Interface Tools: Introduction
         & Survey".
         IEEE Software, January 1989.

[SHM86] K.J.Shmucker. "MacApp: An Application Framework".
         Byte, August 1986.

[VAN88] J.van den Bos. "Abstract Interaction Tools:
         A Language for User Interface Management Systems".
         ACM Trans. on Programming Languages & Systems, Apr 1988.

[YOU87] R.L.Young. "An Object-Oriented Framework
         for Interactive Data Graphics"
         OOPSLA'87 ACM Press.

Lessons Learned:

Object-Oriented Methodologies and Ada

L. A. AMBROSE AND K. L. ROGERS

The MITRE Corporation

1. INTRODUCTION

1.1 Purpose of This Paper

This paper documents our experiences with object-oriented methodologies and Ada during the construction of a small (11K statements) system. This system attaches a commercial User Interface Management System (UIMS) to a network populated by communicating simulations of Space Station Freedom systems. It supplies requested data from various systems simulations to the UIMS, allowing the rapid prototyping of human-computer interfaces. It is labeled "HAE," for Human-Computer Interaction Laboratory (HCIL) Ada Executive.

In addition to supplying the necessary functionality to support prototyping, the HAE effort was used to investigate two areas of current interest in software engineering. One was object-oriented methodologies. We attempted to use an object-oriented approach to the development of the system design. For similar evaluation purposes, the Ada language was chosen as the implementation vehicle. The goal was to gain first-hand experience in the benefits and detriments of using the language which had been mandated for new software development for the Space Station Freedom Program (SSFP).

1.2 Background of the Prototype

The Operations Management System (OMS) Integration effort at the National Aeronautics and Space Administration's Johnson Space Center is an ongoing series of prototype demonstrations, focussing on establishing interoperability between Space Station Freedom system simulations in a networked environment. System simulations are hosted on the various nodes of the network. The OMS Integration effort represented a good source of realistic data which could serve as the basis for analysis of candidate SSFP human-computer displays.

Our prototype consists of two separate processes: BLOX®, a commercial UIMS from Template, which handles the display aspects of the prototype; and the HAE, which supplies the data from the network. These two processes communicate via a Digital Equipment Corporation VAX® VMS® operating system service known as mailboxes.

The HAE was developed using Ada. It offers its services to BLOX (or any user) via a series of procedure calls. The user may request 1) that data values be gathered periodically from the network, 2) that such values be returned to the user, 3) that the type and units of available data elements be supplied, and 4) that the HAE shut down.

2. OBJECT ORIENTED METHODOLOGIES

2.1 Overview

Object-oriented methodologies include object-oriented requirements analysis (OORA), design (OOD), and programming (OOP). This project attempted to take an object-oriented approach to the design phase and to examine the implications of that approach on the Ada implementation.

Two books on object-oriented methods were influential during this project (Cox, 1986; Booch, 1987[b]). Since the completion of this project, we participated in a class offered by EVB Software Engineering and taught by Ed Berard. It presented a specific approach to OORA (Berard, April 1989). This section is influenced by the understanding which we developed as a result of that classroom experience.

It is difficult to talk about design in a meaningful sense without acknowledging the implementation constraints, including the language. The influence of Ada on this project cannot be overstated. In the discussion that follows, the object-oriented approach is viewed in light of Ada as an implementation language.

2.2 Characteristics Of An Object-Oriented Methodology

There are four generally agreed upon characteristics of OOP: data abstraction, information hiding, dynamic binding, and inheritance (Bach, March/April 1989; Stroustrup, May 1988; Pascoe, August 1986). This definition of OOP is fairly widely held: much more controversial are the newer concepts of OOD and OORA. OORA, it can be argued, is independent of the implementation vehicle and can be used as a first step for any project, regardless of intended language and environment. A natural way of defining a problem is emphasized, with information hiding and data abstraction as key goals. The "hows" of inheritance and binding may be postponed. In contrast, OOD, like any design method, must reflect the realities of implementation. It must address the details of how the problem is to be solved, as will be elaborated in the following sections.

3. SUCCESSES IN APPLYING OBJECT-ORIENTED TECHNIQUES

Working from the Smalltalk model, we attempted to design objects which were complete in and of themselves. The goal was to encapsulate both methods (i.e. procedures) and data within each object, shielding the underlying implementation.

The object-oriented approach we used took advantage of *information hiding*, which allowed us to localize any required code changes. A case in point is a module that supplied the procedures to create, read from, and write to VAX VMS mailboxes. When the mailbox service was perceived as a source of problems, a second version of the module package body was created that employed external files as a communication mechanism. Later, when the mailbox problems were resolved, the original version was replaced. This was all done without changing the interface or perturbing the rest of the system.

We also achieved *reuse* of objects. This reuse resulted from the realization, during implementation, that a certain construct was already available for use. These objects included small, generic objects, such as a tree structure and a time stamp, and a large, application-specific object, the Master Measurement List, which contained all valid data elements for the Data Management System (DMS). This reuse showed us some of the power of objects.

We did not use a "master control task." Instead, we used tasks to implement objects, which resulted in a *loosely coupled system*. Knowing that this implementation decision had been made allowed the design to take the shape of independent objects, which could each be considered alone. This was perceived as a strength of the resulting system, making it easier to understand and change.

The *design was still visible* in the code after implementation, although some modifications were made in response to a growing understanding of the problem and the environment. This visibility might have contributed to ease of maintenance had the prototype a longer life span.

4. DIFFICULTIES IN APPLYING OBJECT-ORIENTED TECHNIQUES

4.1 Identifying Objects and Classes

In our experience, objects were hard to identify. Textbook preparation was not adequate to enable us to apply the technique effectively to our real world problem. For this type of application (where the physical world is rather remote), objects were less intuitive than they seemed in textbook examples involving factories and robots. The question "What is an object?" was a central concern, and the issue was compounded by the differing views offered by a top-down versus a bottom-up approach. Small objects were easy to see and high level objects were eventually chosen, but reconciling the two proved to be a sticking point. Our first step was to develop objects from the problem description. Several iterations were necessary as we attempted to define objects and their interrelationships.

One problem was that the bottom-up approach tends to push complexity up, while the top-down tends to simplify the high level while postponing complexity as a lower level detail. We used a top-down approach and identified the major top-level objects followed by a bottom-up approach to create low-level objects. The intervening levels that would integrate the high- and low-level objects were not identified, due to schedule pressure. As a consequence, the design was not broken down far enough. This effect pushed complexity further into the implementation. Large objects became large modules, incompatible with good coding practice.

The Berard method would have assisted us in the identification of objects. Objects, whenever identified, are documented in a specific format, called an Object/Class Specification, showing what each object supplies and requires. Each object is considered independently, with the recognition that objects will be of differing levels of complexity and problem-specificity. Considering each object in isolation avoids building in interdependencies and produces reusable specifications. Further, it is not necessary to have envisioned the entire system in order to start the specification process: each piece is recorded as it is identified, with the total solution arrived at gradually. Both top-down and bottom-up views of the design process can be incorporated and a design team may alternate between the two, gaining increased insight with each iteration.

4.2 Combining Ada and Object-Oriented Methodologies

Our reliance on the Smalltalk model, as presented by Cox, had profound consequences on the design process and its result. In retrospect, it is apparent that the Smalltalk model and the Ada language are not a good match.

First, Smalltalk is an environment, not just a language. It has an "ether" through which objects may communicate. Part of the solution is presented by the platform. The Ada language does not include an analogous "ether", so a language-based equivalent to the "ether" must also be constructed. Further, Smalltalk is an easily malleable system that offers run-time flexibility and late binding. Ada uses strong typing and compiler-enforced binding. Another difference between Ada and Smalltalk is how inheritance is achieved. Although Ada can be used to simulate inheritance, it does not provide the straightforward mechanisms provided by Smalltalk, a situation which is to be expected since Ada was designed to be methodology-independent (Stroustrup, May 1988).

We would have benefited from having a more detailed design technique, with some built-in recognition of Ada. The importance to design of the implementation vehicle became apparent: knowledge of tools and materials must affect the design or trouble will result.

Object-oriented design is clearly different for each language and the entire approach taken should reflect this fact. The following sections address specific areas of concern: encapsulation vs. strong typing; inheritance; and visibility.

The implementation phase revealed an incompatibility between our object-oriented approach using *encapsulation* and the *strong typing* of Ada. We initially continued the approach established in the design where each element was to be self-contained and would not reference code elsewhere in the system. The top-level objects were to be constructed of lower level objects and types were to be supplied by the object that logically defined or controlled them. Thus, a lower level object might supply a type at its interface (the formal parameters of its procedures) which the higher level object in turn might also need to supply to its users.

One mechanism to do this was to rename types in the higher-level object (package) specification. However, record components are not visible in subtypes defined on other packages' types. This made the types unusable, since assignment to parts of a record was necessary. Other solutions, such as derived types, existed, but time was short so we chose to have the user of the higher level object import its constituent lower level objects in order to access the types they supplied. A more involved approach would have been to have each object supply procedures which would allow individual component assignment. The use of access types might facilitate this structure, but these implications were not examined.

The Berard method of design directly confronts the issue of Ada typing and alters the Smalltalk paradigm to form an Ada-specific variation of object-oriented techniques. It is recognized that objects will not fully encapsulate sub-objects. If an object (or type), A, appears as part of the interface to a second object, B, then the user of B must deliberately import A. No attempt is made to conceal A within B. Had we been aware of the Berard method (and had it been formulated) during our design, we might have felt more comfortable with the visibility of sub-objects outside of their parent objects. Deliberate use of such visibility might have produced a cleaner solution.

The preceding section hints at the issue of *inheritance*. Ada does not support Smalltalk style inheritance, but an approximation can be achieved using generics. The disagreements about using Ada in the context of object-oriented methodologies frequently focus on this issue. Arguments range from strongly pro-Smalltalk positions, which hold that any deviation defeats the purpose, to pro-Ada stances, which ask if the concept is "object-oriented" or "inheritance oriented." The latter group feels that the benefits of inheritance can be achieved without precisely duplicating the mechanism.

We did not attempt to create an inheritance mechanism in Ada, primarily because we did not develop a design which required classes. However, had we been using Smalltalk, classes would probably have been a natural consequence of the implementation effort. Since Ada does not specify a design methodology, the developer of an Ada system must have an added awareness of object-oriented techniques in order to achieve the full range of benefits.

Visibility issues also interfered with object-oriented design as we were practicing it. Two packages cannot "see" each other (via an import statement), but it is natural to think that two objects can. This problem can be addressed in a tasking system via an agent task which the two communicating tasks use as an intermediary. At the time, we did not consider this solution: instead, we designed around the problem by eliminating some communication between objects. This emphasizes the importance to design of being familiar with the implementation vehicle.

4.3 Determining an Object-Oriented Development Life Cycle

OORA is a logical antecedent of OOD, while functional approaches to requirements analysis are more controversial preparation for OOD (Bailin, May 1989). However, structured analysis is a well-established method and OORA is still emerging as a technique. In this project, we initially wrote functional requirements, then developed a top-level object-oriented design. We were then requested to complete a structured analysis approach to the problem. We consequently developed data flow diagrams (DFDs), then moved forward again to an object-oriented design.

Berard argues strongly that the process of functional decomposition is antithetical to good object-oriented requirements analysis and design. While it gives an understanding of the problem, it may predispose one towards a particular type of solution: a functional one. Instead, requirements resulting from structured analysis should be transformed into object-oriented requirements.

To examine the life cycle further, object-oriented approaches work well with an iterative process of analyzing a little, designing a little, implementing a little, and testing a little. Interesting or difficult classes can be created and tested, with the resultant knowledge feeding back into the design process. Berard suggests that a recursive, parallel life cycle model is most appropriate for object-oriented development. The top level objects of a system are defined first, noting what each supplies and requires. If Ada is the implementation language, package specifications for the newly identified objects may be written, followed by the body of the code which uses them (the "main" program). Then the next level is considered and so forth, recursively, until the system is completed. The objects at each level are de-coupled, so parallel development is possible.

This parallel/recursive life cycle can provide more control points for monitoring the software process than a traditional waterfall approach. The software development process can be facilitated by holding frequent, short "Technical Exchange Meetings," instead of waiting for larger, less frequent milestones to identify and resolve problems.

4.4 Communicating an Object-Oriented Design

A design must be communicated before it can be successfully implemented. The customer must understand what is proposed, and team members must understand what they will build. Graphical techniques to support OOD are beginning to emerge, but at the point the HAE project was started, the chief technique was Booch diagrams (Booch, 1987[a]). In our experience, Booch diagrams were not appreciated by an audience that was unfamiliar with them. Even though we were convinced we had a sound design, the design reviewers were not comfortable approving the design when documented using Booch diagrams. Instead, they requested DFDs of the same design, which were much more positively received.

From the DFDs, we attempted to form objects by examining data stores and the processes which surrounded them. To indicate these new groupings, we drew lines around the items which were to be encapsulated into objects (Figure 1). The new boundaries revealed which data flows would become part of messages. When these boundaries were made into opaque shapes and their data flows transformed into active messages with parameters, the high level objects were in effect defined (Figure 2). These drawings, which we called Object/Method diagrams, proved to be a more effective tool for expressing objects than the Booch diagrams which had been used in the preliminary design review, possibly because of their evolution from DFDs.

One point of real interest to both the MITRE design team and the design reviewers was which objects execute methods on other objects. In our opinion, this information, showing how a system is composed of objects and how these objects interrelate, was important to understanding the design. The Object/Method diagrams show this clearly. The understanding of necessary package visibility, which such diagrams provided, simplified the eventual transformation into packages.

5. SUMMARY

Object-oriented methodologies are not a "silver bullet" for all software engineering problems, but they are a logical next step for software development, amenable to prototyping, and useful in achieving productivity gains. Although intuitive in many ways, these approaches are still difficult for first time users. Education and experience are necessary to realize their full benefits.

While requirements analysis may be implementation-independent, design is not. The design methodology must reflect the implementation vehicle: if Ada is to be used, the concepts of object-oriented design must be tailored accordingly. An integrated life cycle using object-oriented methodologies is a desirable goal, since it is smoother to move into object-oriented design from object-oriented requirements analysis than from functional analysis. However, communication is essential in the software development process. The entire design review team requires education on the design method being practiced.

The concepts of object-oriented methodologies are still being refined, particularly in association with Ada. Any long term project should use a flexible approach to take advantage of improved techniques as they become available.

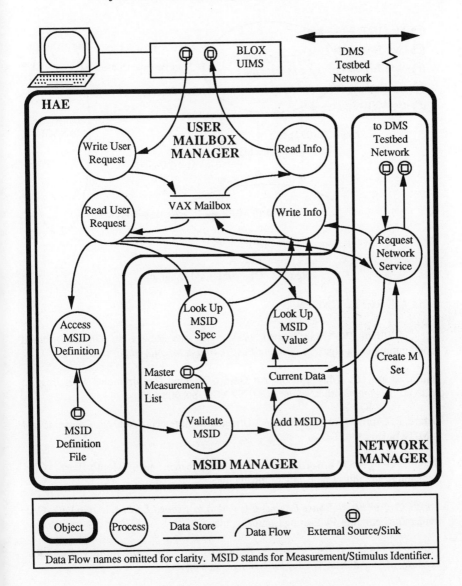

Figure 1. Data Flow Diagrams with Objects Identified

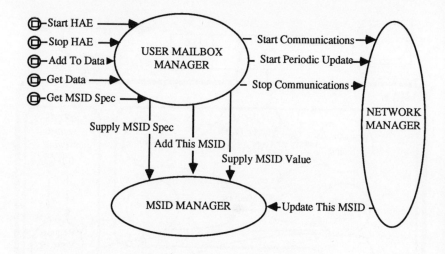

Figure 2. Object/Method Diagram

LIST OF REFERENCES

Bach, William W. (March/April 1989), "Is Ada Really an Object-Oriented Programming Language?," *Journal of Pascal, Ada & Modula-2*, pp. 18-25.

Bailin, Sidney C. (May 1989), "An Object-Oriented Requirements Specification Method," *Communications of the ACM*, XXXII:5, pp. 608-623.

Berard, E. (April 17-21, 1989), Object Oriented Requirements Analysis Course, taught at MITRE, Houston, Texas.

Booch, G. (1987[a]), *Software Components with Ada*, Menlo Park, CA: Benjamin/Cummings Publishing Company, Inc.

Booch, G. (1987[b]), *Software Engineering with Ada, Second Edition*, Menlo Park, CA: Benjamin/Cummings Publishing Company, Inc.

Cox, B. J. (1986), *Object Oriented Programming: An Evolutionary Approach*, Reading, MA: Addison-Wesley Publishing Company.

Pascoe, G. A. (August, 1986), "Elements of Object-Oriented Programming," *Byte*, pp. 139-144.

Stroustrup, Bjarne (May 1988), "What Is Object-Oriented Programming?," *IEEE Software*, V:3, pp. 10-20.

An ADA-OODed Application On-board a Submarine

Jean-Pierre Rousselot

Hervé Bonnaud

Direction Des Constructions Navales, CAPCA, 83800 Toulon Naval, France

Jean-Marc Lippens

Jacques Arnol

Syseca Temps Reel, 92213 Saint-Cloud Cedex, France.

1. INTRODUCTION

STROOD is an object-oriented design and development method for large, real-time ADA software, and has been chosen as the common method to be used by the software teams involved in the first-to-date French Navy Mission Critical Computer System using ADA.

First of all, the computer System and STROOD shall be introduced in the presentation. Then a description of the application of STROOD during the low-level software design shall be given. The description shall be illustrated by assessing the approach in terms of:

- technique,

- project management,

- quality.

2. THE COMPUTER SYSTEM

The Computer system is an Action and Information Organization (AIO) system which is part of the combat system to be installed in a newly-designed French submarine.

The responsibility for the AIO system is assumed by the CAPCA department of the DCAN (Direction des Constructions et Armes Navales) in Toulon (FRENCH NAVY). The task of software design and development has been granted to SYSECA.

The AIO System shall perform the following operational functions:

- acquire information from the sonar suite,

- correlate the information with that from the other sources (periscope, underwater telephone, satellite communications, etc.),

- elaborate and display the resulting tactical,

- evaluate the corresponding threat, and situation,

- propose actions to the Commanding Officer.

Such on-board systems generally use specific hardware in order to withstand the required environmental constraints and conditions. The hardware architecture in this case, therefore, consists of over a dozen signal and display processing units, based on 68K family processors, interconnected by two high-speed communications buses.

The software design and development is planned for 2.5 years, requiring an estimated 100,000 man-hours.

3. THE METHOD: STROOD

STROOD (Système Temps Réel Object Oriented Development) is a method of enforcing the OOD concept (as proposed by Grady BOOCH) by providing an approach which deals with real-time constraints.

STROOD perceives two main phases in the design process:

- an organization phase for problem solving, known as "working in problem space",

- a pre-implementation phase, known as "working in problem space".

The first phase is language-independent; its objectives are to facilitate identification of objects, to verify their relevance to the problem in hand and to initiate the first approach to system dynamics.

It is highly iterative and is initiated by the selection of objects which are assumed to be relevant. This relevance is then checked by "simulating" the dynamic behaviour of the resulting model of the system.

The first phase is broken into five steps:

1. identification of objects and main attributes,

2. identification of object methods,

3. description of active object behaviour (for "active" objects),

4.   establishment of inter-object visibility,

5.   establishment of inter-object dynamic relations, by preparing a chaining graph of the various object method invocations triggered by each class of system event (external or periodic).

The last step makes it possible to verify that selected objects correspond to system specifications by addressing the problem raised by the different perceptions existing in a real-time system. The end product of this iterative procedure is an object by object structure that gives a good idea of the future dynamics of the system.

After the number of iterations that the designer feels necessary to be performed have been completed for each of these five steps, the final outcome of the first phase is:

-    an individual description of each identified object (or class), plus

-    a general inter-object visibility diagram, plus

-    a chaining graph of object method invocations for each class of events.

The second phase is a traditional object oriented ADA design phase, and consists mainly of selecting the ADA-language representation of objects and classes described in the previous phase.

In this phase, STROOD provides the means of monitoring real-time system behaviour.

For the last step of the first phase (setting up object dynamic interactions), there is a corresponding step in the second phase (implementation of communication and synchronization mechanisms).

For each chaining graph there is a corresponding figure using the RJA BUHR conventions which describes the ADA task structures that will implement the graph.

The outputs of this second phase are:

-    the ADA package specifications for each object and class,

-    a diagram, using G. BOOCH's formalism, showing the static structure of the application,

-    a BUHR diagram for each chaining graph,

-    a skeleton outline of the application that can be exercised by simulating system prompts, and that will serve to validate the software structure, regarding its dynamic behaviour, before proceeding to low-level design and coding.

The combined process - problem space + solution space - is implemented recursively at increasingly low levels, and results in structures that are simple enough to be coded directly in the ADA language.

A new version of STROOD with tools called STROOD-MACADAM has been available since January 1990 and operates on any UNIX workstation.

4. APPLICATION OF STROOD

Three design phases have been identified for the application of STROOD in the AIO system:

- System Design: dividing of the Computer System into Top Level Computer Software Components (TLCSC's or *logiciels*), a *logiciel* being performed by a single processing unit.

- Software Design: dividing of the *logiciels* into Low Level Computer Software Components (LLCSC's or *modules*).

- Component Design: dividing of the *modules* into Units (or *composants*).

4.1 System Design
The system design had to deal with the following criteria:

- previously selected hardware architecture,

- constraining performance specifications, which imposed a balanced distribution of the CPU on the processing units and minimize the messages exchanged between the processing units,

- possibility of degraded modes with regard to processing unit failure(s).

A traditional approach has been taken for system Design, which seemed more appropriate for taking the above implementation constraints into account at an early stage, and which led to the definitions of the *logiciels* (one for each processing unit) and the elaboration of a dictionary describing the messages exchanged between the *logiciels* via the communications buses.

The functional specifications of each *logiciel* were then written using a SADT-like method. The ADA data type supporting the messages were also produced.

4.2 Software Design
The Software Design had to deal with the following criteria:

- evolution of the system/segment specifications,

- use of ADA as a programming language,

- newly designed hardware,

- host computer different from target computer.

STROOD was chosen for the Software Design because the corresponding division between its two phases (problem domain and solution domain) facilitated:

- the dialogue between the software designers and the operators (so that the end user could speak the same language as the "soft-man" and so that the evolution of the system specification could be more manageable),

- a simple validation of the selected software architecture (thus minimizing the risk arising from the use of a new programming language to be implemented in newly-designed hardware).

Once the *logiciels* had been designed, additional advantages were revealed:

Project Management
- The SADT formalism enables the smooth transition from analysis to design. The use of actigrams and datagrams for the specification of each *logiciel* greatly simplifies the identification of objects and their methods by facilitating synthesis between the functions to be produced and the data manipulated by these functions.

- The design time (problem + solution) for a *logiciel* varies from 4 to 6 months, depending on the complexity of the software and the experience of the designer. About one third of this design time is dedicated to "work in the problem space".

- Increased responsibility for the developers, who were implicated in the design tasks and who were allocated all or part of the responsibility in the solution-domain phase: a simple validation of the selected software architecture (thus minimizing the risk arising from the use of a new programming language to be implemented in newly-designed hardware).

- Preservation of the *module* concept as an homogeneous unit for function, development and documentation (each object defined by the solution-domain phase generally corresponds to a developing unit).

Technique
- Identification of re-usable objects: these objects have been identified during both of the STROOD phases, providing top-level objects (such as THE_BUS, for all communications within the system) as well as low-level objects (such as THE_CLOCK, for periodic task activation).

- Easy validation of the software architectures: using dynamic diagrams for functional validation and design "skeletons" for real-time validation.

The objective to be achieved by producing the "skeletons" are:

- software validation (functional and real time),

- identification and solution as early as possible of the problem areas of each *logiciel* e.g.:

    - specific inputs/outputs,
    - automatic re-configurations,
    - high parallelism,

-          a guarantee that the identified objects and their relations shall be preserved throughout development of the *logiciel*,

-          the realization of a model enabling modifications or evolutions in the *logiciel* to be quickly evaluated.

Only the first three objectives were considered in the software design phase.

We realized that in order for these objectives to be fulfilled, the designers had to carry out a rather detailed analysis outlining the analysis of each module, the closeness of which depended on the level of detail sought.

Due to some simple programming rules and to the development of small file processing tools, it was simple to use the documented "skeletons" in the source to obtain:

-          on one hand, the ADA code "skeleton", guaranteeing the longevity of the design,

-          on the other hand, the documentation of each module (outlined in the design phase).

We had therefore the following at the outcome of the design phase for each *logiciel:*

-          a design document in natural language,

-          a documented ADA source, implementing the "skeleton" and outlining all the modules of the *logiciel*,

-          an executable program validating the selected architecture.

4.3 Component Design
The Component Design has naturally been performed using STROOD: each object defined by the Software Design has been considered as a "problem", resulting in the following tasks:

-          if the object is sufficiently complex, lower layers can be defined during the problem-domain phase, which result in the implementation of ADA packages,

-          for less complex objects, the solution-domain tasks are easier: the development of the *module* simply follows the implementation of the object which has been initiated during the Software Design.

At the outcome of software design we have identified about sixty different objects for analysis, about ten of which have, after analysis, given rise to ADA (sub)-packages, thus resulting in a further level of abstraction.

The actual development of objects has not caused any particular technical problems, as the analysis and coding were prepared in the design phase and the tasks to be carried out correspond to traditional design tasks.

Project management
The major difference, in comparison with previous projects, is that the documentation of each *module* is entered directly at the development platform by the person responsible for the *module* (in source files).

The first people to use this solution were hindered due to the fact that it is difficult to separate the analysis phase from the coding phase during source documentation, since at first, the coding phase takes precedence at the expense of the analysis of the *module*.

This problem was solved by making a clear separation (in time) between the analysis and coding phases.

4.4 Quality
The method of quality control and assurance used by us (MACQUAL), based on the MAC CALL tasks, operates by using questionnaires which enable each control product to check that the criteria selected for the product are correctly satisfied.

Each phase of the life cycle, in particular the software design documents and the *module* documents, has its own set of questionnaires.

The method can therefore by easily adapted by updating the questionnaires relating to the products, this update being carried out by testing the first document produced in each of the two phases.

The time dedicated to testing (apart from the time taken to update questionnaires) was not altered by using STROOD.

5. CONCLUSION

Two years of practical experience allows us to say that:

-    a real-time application can be fully developed in ADA, to be implemented in a distributed architecture,

-    an OOD can be achieved in ADA,

-    a method is required to back up this approach, so that real time constraints can be taken into account as early as possible,

-    in particular, the production of design "skeletons" very early on in the product's life cycle allowed us to minimize the risks arising from the implementation on new hardware of, what is to us, a new programming language.

PART VII: Hierarchical Object Oriented Design

On the Translation of HOOD Nets into Ada

Raffaele Di Giovanni†

PRISMA Informatica, via Campo di Marte 4, 06100 Perugia, Italy

1. INTRODUCTION

HOOD (Hierarchical Object Oriented Design, [ESA 89]) is the standard ESA (European Space Agency) method for the architectural design phase of the software development life cycle. HOOD is a combination of Abstract Machines and Object-Oriented Design concepts and is oriented towards Ada program development.

HOOD has already been selected as the design method in several space programmes, such as Columbus and Hermes. In Columbus however the need has risen to increase the formality of a HOOD description.

A large part of the information associated to HOOD objects is given in Ada code or Ada pseudo-code. In this way, it is easy to keep the consistence between the two different phases of the software life-cycle, design and coding: the HOOD manual suggests to re-use the code or pseudo-code associated to a HOOD object as an initial framework of the final code. However, on the other hand, pseudo-code does not allow one to perform formal verification of properties of HOOD objects.

To solve this problem, the solution proposed in COLUMBUS has been to integrate a Formal Specification Technique (FST) into the HOOD method. Petri Nets (PN, [PETERSON 81]) have been selected as the formal technique to be integrated in the HOOD method. This choice is based both on technical and practical reasons. As a matter of fact, the suitability of PN to model in a natural way distributed concurrent systems keeps company with their graphical notation that allows a rapid understanding of this formal method also to non skilled users.

The use of a formal language like Petri Nets (PN) makes it possible to formally verify a large set of properties of HOOD objects. However, a new problem may arise. If Ada pseudo-code can no longer be used as the specification of a HOOD object, the consistency between design and

---

† This paper is based on a study made by the author while he was with Intecs sistemi S.p.A.

code may decrease.

In this paper we sketch a translation schema from HOOD nets to Ada code, so that no decrease in the aforementioned consistency is produced.

2. HOOD OVERVIEW

A HOOD object can be considered an instance of an Abstract Data Type. In fact an object is made of two main parts, a private *body* (containing the implementations of both data structures and operations which act on them) and a public *interface* (containing the declarations of the operations which other objects can use to act on its private data structures, its *resource*). The interface of an object can be divided into a *provided interface* (the functionalities provided to other objects) and a *required interface* (the functionalities of other objects used to implement its operations) The *use* relationship relates a user object with a used one.

For reasons of modularity, an object can be decomposed into several *child* objects. The *include* relationship relates the *parent* object to each *child* object.

An object may be either active (it has a proper control: requests which could lead the managed resource into an inconsistent state can be delayed) or passive (it is a mere collection of operations). The behaviour of an object is described into two classes of information items: the OBject Control Structure (OBCS) and the OPeration Control Structure (OPCS). An OBCS is associated to each active object and describes its control. An OPCS is associated to each operation and describes its implemented algorithm.

A HOOD system is a tree. The root of the tree is the *root* object, i.e. the object whose interface corresponds to the functionalities provided by the modelled software system. The leaves of the tree are *terminal* objects, i.e. those objects that are directly described, without any further decomposition. The branches of the tree are derived from the *include* relationship. This tree is called *design process tree*.

3. HOOD NETS

HOOD nets are a special class of Hierarchical Stochastic Predicate Transition Nets. There are two types of HOOD nets: *OBCS nets* and *OPCS nets*.

Each object of an HOOD system is associated to an OBCS net and to a set of OPCS nets, one for each exported operation. The OBCS net is at an higher abstraction level. Each transition of the OBCS net models an exported operation and is refined into the related OPCS net.

A passive object has no OBCS. As a consequence, its OBCS net merely consists of an *interface net*. An interface net is composed of a transition for each exported operation. Each transition is then connected with an input place and an output place. An interface net is depicted in the following figure.

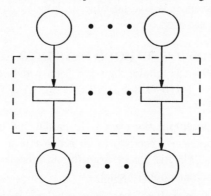

In addition to this interface net, the OBCS net of an active object also has a state machine net. This net describes the control of the active object. An active object can sequentialise conflicting concurrent operations on its internal resource, so that the resource is never moved into an inconsistent state. A resource can be decomposed into a set of sub-resources. In this case each sub-resource will be described by a state machine net.

The following figure shows the OBCS net of an active object. The object is a ten position buffer with the added constraint that to remove an element from the buffer one has to pay a ticket. In the net, the resource has been decomposed into two sub-resources, the ticket and the buffer. The current state of the resource is buffer empty and ticket not paid.

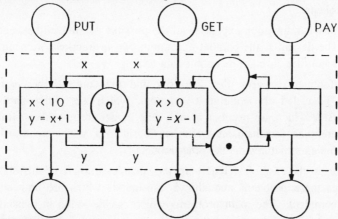

Each transition of an OBCS net can be refined into an OPCS net. Within an OPCS net, the resource management policy can be detailed (in case an operation uses a set of sub-resources, as the *get* operation in the previous figure, it is possible to highlight the allocation and deallocation events for each sub-resource). In addition, it is also possible to describe how the operations in the required interface are used.

4. THE TRANSLATION OF HOOD NETS INTO ADA

The problem of PN-Ada relationships has been widely dealt with in the literature [BRUNO 86a, BRUNO 86b, COLOM 86, MANDRIOLI 85, MURATA 89, VALETTE 88].

Some of the proposed solutions are only partial and others are too complex (and so not performance effective) to be acceptable in the Columbus context. The main problems directly comes from the differencies that exist between the Ada and the PN computational model.

The computational model of Ada is a standard "control-flow" model. The control-flow computational model (also called "von Neumann" model) has a global addressable memory and an instruction counter. The counter holds the address of the next instruction to be executed. The counter is implicitly or explicitly updated to provide the machine with a sequence of instructions to execute. The instruction under execution has free access to the global memory: inputs are read from and results are stored in the global memory.

The data-flow model [COMPUTER 82] has no counter and no global memory. Program data are distributed into several tokens which flow among the instructions. As soon as an instruction has received all its input data, it can be executed, regardless of the state of the other instructions of the program. After execution, output data are produced and sent to other instructions by means of output tokens.

A data-flow computation expresses all the possible parallelism between instructions. The default is the parallel execution: two instructions are sequentialised only if a conflict on input or output data arises.

The differences between the data-flow and the control-flow computational models have led to tentative translations which are either partial (some mechanisms which are peculiar of only one model are not taken into account) or too complex (mechanisms which are basic in a model are translated into very complex structures of the other model).

However, in the case of HOOD nets, the specific structure of this class of nets decreases these problems and allows translations which are both simple and almost complete. The main problems which can be found in translating from HOOD nets into Ada are related to the modelling of a parallel computation and of the resource management policy.

4.1. Modelling Parallel Computations
With HOOD nets a computation is intrinsically parallel while in Ada it is sequential. The mechanism used in Ada to express parallelism is the task construct. A parallel computation has to be expressed as a set of concurrent tasks. The necessary overhead for the task management is a constraint to the amount of expressible parallelism.

4.2. Modelling Resource Management Policies
In a nutshell, the problem is that sometimes, to decide if a request on the managed resource can be safely executed in the current state, we also need information on the current request. For instance, a memory manager must know how many blocks of memory are requested by a process to decide if the memory allocation request can be satisfied.

This information, which is external (i.e. *global*) to the resource manager, is easily handled in HOOD nets: any information on the incoming request can be associated to the colours of the tokens, and this colour can be freely examined in the logical formulae associated to the operation transitions.

This pre-analysis of the request queue is also feasible in a language like SR [ANDREWS 81]. On the contrary, it is not feasible in Ada. The basic mechanisms provided by the Ada language to handle request queues are the different classes of *select statements*. These mechanisms, however, are not powerful and flexible enough to implement management policies. This is mainly due to the fact that a strict FIFO policy is implemented to serve incoming requests on each entry point of a select statement, and request parameters can be read only after the request has been accepted (they cannot be used in the *condition* of the *select_alternative*).

The above means that a portion of the management policy has to be simulated through request queues and queue management procedures explicitly coded in Ada.

5. A TAXONOMY OF TRANSLATION SCHEMAS
The typical problem of a translation process when the differences between the source and the target languages are not negligible is the dichotomy automatic translation versus flexibility. An automatic translation is more convenient for the user and also more reliable (depending on the degree of trustability of the translator) but sometimes it is not flexible enough, because some choices have to be necessarily frozen.

The solution we propose to translate HOOD nets into Ada is to use some basic rules which produce a sort of *generic frameworks*. Then these frameworks have to be customised making some choices into a set of alternatives related to some specific features of the modelled system.

The basic rules are mainly due to the HOOD concepts inherited by the HOOD nets and, consequently, are closely related to the translation rules given in the HOOD reference manual [ESA 89]. These basic rules can be summarised as follows:

-    An OPCS net, which described an object operation, is translated into an Ada procedure or function;

-    When the OBCS net is more than a simple interface net, it is translated into an Ada task;

-    The set of nets related to an HOOD object (one OBCS net and an OPCS net for each provided operation) is translated into an Ada package.

In order to evaluate the possible translation alternatives for HOOD nets, the following main features are considered:

-    the implementation of the resource management policy;

-    the actual executor of the operation;

-    the desired degree of parallelism;

-    the kind of communication primitives.

These features are almost independent, but when constructing a translation schema the choice made for one feature may influence other choices. For example, if there is no management policy (i.e. the server is a passive entity) the executor of a requested operation must be the client itself; and if the executor is the client, there is no communication primitives selection problem: the request is a simple procedure call. Some other times, some choices are strongly suggested by cost/performance considerations. For example, if the client executes the operation usually there is no need to model the OBCS net with several control tasks to increase the parallelism.

For reasons of space, we are not going to describe these features in detail (an extended description can be found at the moment in an internal technical note [DI GIOVANNI 90]). A condensed table of the identified alternatives for each of the abovementioned features is presented here.

the resource management policy
    depending on the kind of resource we have three possible implementations:

-    a passive entity;
        when there is no resource or when the operations are all compatible;

-    an active entity with a management policy directly implemented by an Ada construct;
        when local information is enough to implement the policy;

- an active entity with wait queues explicitly implemented in Ada; when global information too is necessary to implement the management policy;[1]

the executor of the operation
  we have two choices:

- the server;
  when the resource is not heavily used and/or the operations are all incompatible and/or the operations are not time consuming;
- the client;
  in the opposite cases (when intermediate conditions arise, the programmer has to grade them);

the degree of parallelism
  for this feature it is not possible to identify a small number of alternatives; however we may distinguish between two cases:

- the fully sequential choice;
  the OPCS net is translated into an Ada procedure with no internal task; the OBCS net of an active object is translated into a single (control) task;
- the partially sequential choice;
  two tasks are demanded of the programmer:

  1 the identification of some independent threads of control in the OPCS net (they are related to time consuming requests to other objects): they are implemented as internal (service) tasks of the procedure which implements the OPCS net;

  2 the identification of some loosely related (i.e. seldom used together) sub-resources; each of these resources can be controlled by a different (control) task; another consideration when introducing several control tasks is that the operations on the resource should be time consuming;

the communication primitives
  we have three possible communication primitives:

- Remote Procedure Call;
  when the requested action is not time consuming or the results are indispensable to continue the computation;

---

[1] Actually the Ada select mechanism can deal with some limited global information, that is, the number of pending requests on each queue (while on the contrary the PN model has to be extended with inhibitor arcs to deal with zero tests). However, this feature does not significantly affect the following discussion.

- synchronous message passing;
  when the action is time consuming and other actions can be
  executed in the meantime;
- asynchronous message passing;
  when the action is time consuming but the results (if they exist)
  are not necessary in the nearest future.

5.1 A Simple Translation Schema

Again, due to space constraints, only a simple example will be shown
here. Consider the problem of the ten position buffer. This object provides two operations: put and get. The OBCS of this object is depicted in
the following figure. In this example the buffer is implemented through a
LIFO (Last In First Out) data structure (a stack): the control structures are
very simple but no parallelism is allowed. The OPCS of the two operations are very simple and are not taken into account here.

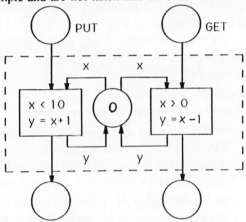

Following the table described above, the choices made are:

man. policy: the object is active but no global information is needed
               (put and get requests are always related to one position
               only, not specified in the request);

executor: the executor is the server;

parallelism: no parallelism is implemented;

com. prim.:   RPC is used.

The Ada implementation of this object is depicted in the next figure.
Comments have been included to identify the information which can be
extracted from the HOOD nets and the information which has to be
requested from the user during the translation activity.

```
package BUFFER_MAN is
   -- type of the resource (requested from the user)
   type MESSAGE is ...; -- some type;
   task CONTROLLER is
      -- entries of the control task (derived from
      -- the operation transitions)
      entry PUT (MSG: in MESSAGE);
      entry GET (MSG: out MESSAGE);
   end CONTROLLER;
end BUFFER_MAN;

package body BUFFER_MAN is
   -- declaration of the managed resource (requested from the user)
   BUFFER: array (0..9) of MESSAGE;

   task body CONTROLLER is
      -- declaration of the control variables (derived from
      -- the types of the OBCS places)
      INDEX: integer := 0;
   begin
      loop
         select
            -- check of the input guard (derived from the guards
            -- of the operation transitions)
            when INDEX < 10 =>
            accept PUT (MSG: in MESSAGE) do
               -- execution of the operation (requested from the user
               -- on the base of the framework derived from the OPCS
               -- net: in this example the OPCS net is empty)
               BUFFER (INDEX) := MSG;
               -- updating of the control variables (derived from
               -- the action of the operation transitions)
               INDEX := INDEX + 1;
            end;
         or
            when INDEX > 0 =>
            accept GET (MSG: out MESSAGE) do
               INDEX := INDEX - 1;
               MSG := BUFFER (INDEX);
            end;
         end select;
      end loop;
   end CONTROLLER;
end BUFFER_MAN;
```

6. REFERENCES

[ANDREWS 81]

Gregory R. Andrews "Synchronising Resources", ACM Transactions on Programming Languages and Systems, Vol.3, No.4, October 1981.

[BRUNO 86a]

G. Bruno and A. Balsamo "Petri Net Based Object-Oriented modelling of distributed systems", Proceeding of the Object-Oriented Programming Systems, Languages and Applications, Sigplan Notices, Vol. 21, No. 11, November 1986.

222   *R. Di Giovanni*

[BRUNO 86b]
G. Bruno and G. Marchetto "Process-Translatable Petri Nets for the Rapid Prototyping of Process Control Systems", IEEE Transactions on Software Engineering, vol.12, no.2, February 1986.

[COLOM 86]
J.M. Colom M. Silva and J.L. Villarroel "On Software Implementation of Petri Nets and Coloured Petri Nets Using High-Level Concurrent Languages", Seventh European Workshop on Application and Theory of Petri Nets, Oxford, July 1986.

[COMPUTER 82]
Special Issue on Data Flow Systems, Computer, Vol. 15, no. 2, February 1982.

[DI GIOVANNI 90]
R. Di Giovanni "Translating HOOD nets into ADA",Intecs Technical Note COL-INT-SDE-TN-011, 1990.

[ESA 89]
"HOOD reference manual", Issue 3.0, WME/89-173/JB, European Space Agency.

[MANDRIOLI 85]
D. Mandrioli, R. Zicari, C. Ghezzi and F. Tisato "Modeling the Ada Task System by Petri Nets", Computer Languages, Vol. 10, No. 1, 1985.

[MURATA 89]
T. Murata, B. Shenker and S.M. Shatz "Detection of Ada Static Deadlocks Using Petri Nets Invariants", IEEE Transactions on Software Engineering, Vol. 15, No. 3, March 1989.

[PETERSON 81]
James L. Peterson "Petri Net Theory and the Modeling of Systems", Prentice-Hall, 1981.

[VALETTE 88]
R. Valette and P. Vielcanet "HOOD Design Method and Control/Command Techniques for the Development of Realtime Software", Int. Symp. on Space Software Engineering: Columbus and Space Infrastructure, Torino, 1988.

Reducing the Risk of Using Ada On-Board the Columbus Manned Space Elements

S. R. Chandler

IPL, Eveleigh House, Grove Street, Bath BA1 5LR, England.

1.   INTRODUCTION

This paper reports on a software prototyping activity
which was commissioned by the European Space Agency
(ESA) as an exercise in risk reduction prior to the
development phase of the Columbus programme.

The Columbus programme comprises the development of a
free flying laboratory, a polar platform, and the
European component of the International Space Station
(Freedom).

MATRA-Espace, as prime contractor of the Columbus on-
board Data Management System, conducted this
prototyping activity as part of the Columbus pre-
development phase.   IPL and GSI-Tecsidel (a Spanish
company) contributed to this study providing
expertise on Ada and real-time operating systems.

Columbus is a major programme in the civil sector for
which Ada has been mandated as the language for
programming its on-board data systems.

In attempting to address the critical software
requirements for Columbus, the scope of this project
has included many of the topics currently under
debate as part of the Ada 9X process.

2.   THE SOFTWARE REPLACEABLE UNIT (SWRU) CONCEPT

ESA has specified a comprehensive set of software
requirements which are derived from the perceived
needs of a system with an operational life in excess
of 30 years.   The system will comprise heterogeneous
distributed processing nodes connected via a network
topology (Reference 1).

These software requirements cover issues such as:

-    language interoperability

-    dynamic configuration/reconfiguration management

- protection and security

- error management

- efficiency

- adaptability/extensibility

- software structure

The Columbus on-board software requirements have been addressed by ESA by means of a derived set of architectural requirements based on a Software Replaceable Unit concept (Reference 1).

A Software Replaceable Unit (SWRU) is defined as the smallest unit of software which can be exchanged.

A SWRU is classified as either on-line or off-line replaceable dependent upon its characteristics of exchange.

An off-line replaceable SWRU can only be exchanged when all node co-resident software is non-operational. This classification is usually reserved for basic operating system level software.

An on-line replaceable SWRU may be exchanged irrespective of its own operation state, but only when the node in which it resides is operational.

2.1   SWRU Characteristics

SWRUs exhibit the following characteristics:

- SWRUs shall communicate by means of a message passing mechanism supported by the execution environment.

- The execution environment shall ensure the integrity of data exchange between SWRUs.

- On-line replaceable SWRUs in an operational state shall be replaceable within one minute.

- SWRU internal data shall be stored separately such that its state is maintained during SWRU replacement.

- A SWRU shall be capable of independent initialisation from its state data.

- A SWRU shall be minimally bound to its execution environment.

- Any error detected by the execution environment shall be isolatable to an individual SWRU.

For any software to be considered compliant with Columbus on-board software requirements it must fully address both the general functional requirements and the derived SWRU architecture.

3.   PROJECT OVERVIEW

3.1   Project History

An earlier study commissioned by ESA (Reference 2 and 3) assessed how the Columbus software requirements could be met with Ada.

This study initially investigated the feasibility of using only Ada semantics as defined in the Ada Language Reference Manual (LRM).

The initial investigation raised many of the problems currently under debate within the scope of Ada 9X and the Ada RunTime Environment Working Group (ARTEWG), namely:

- absence of semantics to support distribution

- restricted use in a heterogeneous environment

- limited language interoperability

- dynamic reconfiguration complexity

- static binding

- ambiguities in the LRM leading to non-deterministic behaviour

The study concluded that a Distributed Operating System(DOS) that incorporated a multiprogramming Ada runtime system could meet the Columbus software requirements.

3.2   Objectives

The objectives of this software prototyping activity were to implement a three node loosely-coupled (LAN) distributed system based on the software architecture recommended in the above mentioned study.   The prototype could then be used to assess feasibility and suitability of the software architecture for use on-board the Columbus space elements.

In particular, the following issues were identified as being of interest:

-   Ada issues

        performance
        memory occupancy
        complexity
        design (HOOD) compatibility
        real-time performance
        reconfiguration
        distribution
        heterogeneity

-   The SWRU concept

        feasibility and compatibility with Ada static
        binding rules
        reconfiguration support
        design model
        performance
        fault-tolerance

-   DOS capability

        message passing performance
        transparency
        interface definition
        implementation requirements

By assessing the prototype system it is possible to generate review inputs to the Columbus software requirements.

Proceeding in this manner reduces the risk to the overall Columbus programme and permits a smooth and timely transition to the engineering phase.

3.3   Constraints

Several constraints were placed on the prototyping activity namely:

-   There should be no modifications to the Ada language to achieve the goals of the project.

-   The implementation should use a commercially available kernel executive (not necessarily an Ada kernel) to implement the fundamental services required by the DOS.

4.   PROJECT DETAILS

4.1   Hardware Infrastructure

A target hardware system was specified and procured such that the system would be representative of the Columbus hardware baseline.

The target hardware architecture comprises three identical processing nodes, networked by an Ethernet LAN. Each node contains a general purpose processor board based on the Intel iAPX386 and an intelligent Ethernet controller board which implements ISO OSI layers 1 to 4.

4.2   Software Infrastructure

The proposed prototype software architecture imposed many requirements on the services to be provided by the kernel executive. In particular, it should provide interfaces supporting:

-       Implicit Ada semantics support to ensure an efficient Ada tasking implementation.

-       Explicit task scheduling control to facilitate the implementation of the DOS services above those of the kernel.

-       Asynchronous   intertask   communication   to facilitate DOS implementation.

-       Ada multiprogramming to enable the DOS process model to encompass multitasking Ada programs in an efficient way.

The best conformance to the above requirements was found in a commercial product with an executive kernel that supported the first 3 interfaces mentioned above in a fully integrated way.

The compiler vendor provided access to proprietary information in order that an Ada multiprogramming interface could be implemented using existing kernel services. No changes were necessary to the kernel itself. Instead, enhancements were made to user accessible hooks in the kernel to manage not only task context but program context as well. Some changes were also necessary to components of the Ada runtime libraries to allow program context to be managed in this way.

The Ada multiprogramming interface supports the following services:

- Program start - start a program from its entry point.

- Program stop - stop a program and release its resources.

- Program suspend - suspend all the kernel tasks comprising a program.

- Program resume - resume all the kernel tasks comprising a program.

- Get Status - report the schedulable status of a program.

- Get identity - return the identity of the currently running program.

4.3   The DOS

The DOS was implemented as a mapper layer (Reference 7) above the kernel executive and multiprogramming interface.   It provides an unconventional process model wherein individual processes may themselves be multithreaded (ie. multitasking Ada programs).

It also supports a distributed interprocess communication mechanism that is transparent to the physical location of processes.   The DOS mapper was written in Ada.   Its interface was defined as an Ada package specification. However, processes are not directly linked to the DOS.   Instead there is an interfacing mechanism   that allows processes to be minimally bound to the service entry points of the DOS.   Minimal binding of processes to the DOS interface facilitates reconfiguration by eliminating the need for dynamic linkage.

4.4   The SWRU Design Model

At the design level, the SWRU is modelled as an Ada package, allowing static SWRU interface verification to be achieved by compilation.

The SWRU design model is particularly suited to the Columbus design methodology called Hierarchical Object Oriented Design (HOOD) since HOOD objects are modelled by means of Ada packages (Reference 4).

For reasons of minimal binding, reconfiguration and distribution, each SWRU package must conform to the rules governing Virtual Nodes (Reference 5). The HOOD method helps to enforce these rules by restricting object interfaces to the definition of provided and required operations with their associated parameters and types. The HOOD method has recently been updated to include Virtual Node Objects, thus ensuring design visibility of interfaces that will ultimately be supported by DOS message passing services and therefore be constrained by the semantics and timing of these services.

The semantics of SWRU replacement define a state model which each SWRU must conform to. The two operational SWRU states are:

- running - the SWRU is performing its designed function.

- suspended - the SWRU does not interact externally except to source or sink application specific checkpoint data under command of the SWRU management system.

4.5   The SWRU Implementation Model

The facilities of the DOS process model are used to implement the dynamic replacement characteristics of the SWRU. In this context, the physical entity representing a dynamic SWRU is implemented as a fully linked Ada program having no unresolved external references which maps uniformly onto a DOS managed process. Communication between SWRUs is supported by the DOS message passing primitives.

In section 4.4, the SWRU as a design object was represented by an Ada package. To convert it into an executable object, the package in question is encapsulated by a main Ada procedure. The package is also linked with dummy packages that have the same interface (specification) as its required services (other SWRUs). The main Ada procedure and dummy package bodies implement Remote Procedure Call (RPC) mechanisms above the DOS message passing mechanism. It is envisaged that this escapsulation process could be performed automatically in future.

4.6   SWRU Management

A functional representation of the SWRU Management hierarchy is shown in figure 1.

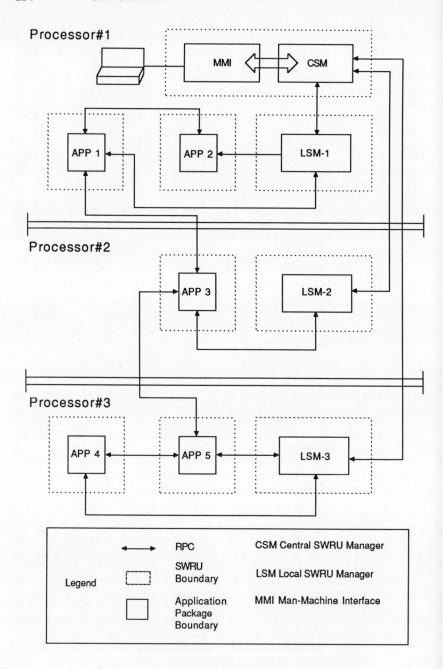

Figure 1 - Prototype Software Architecture

The Central SWRU Manager (CSM) provides the operations.

      create   SWRU
      delete   SWRU
      replace SWRU
      migrate SWRU

The CSM communicates with a Local SWRU Manager (LSM) on each node. The LSM provides the low level SWRU operations by interacting directly with the DOS facilities.

The CSM and LSM were designed as Ada packages, and converted to SWRUs in a similar manner to that described in section 4.5. The CSM and LSM are classified as off-line replaceable SWRUs.

5.   CONCLUSIONS

The overall objectives defined in section 3.2 have been met by the prototype implementation. Some of the key issues are highlighted here.

-    Distribution. Proposals to include semantics for distribution as part of Ada 9X will have considerable ramifications to the language. A suitable design methodology such as HOOD coupled with support for transparent distributed communication allow distributed systems to be constructed without enforcing explicit references to distribution within the Ada source code.

-    Design. Modelling the SWRU as an Ada package permits the use of HOOD, and the use of HOOD promotes conformance to SWRU binding rules. All software developed for the prototype was successfully designed using HOOD.

-    Reconfiguration. Dynamic reconfiguration and replacement of software components provide powerful mechanisms for error management, functional enhancement and software development. The different phases comprising each of the SWRU management operations are normally synchronised with a subject SWRU, thus ensuring the system remains consistent. However, under error conditions it is possible for the SWRU management to operate asynchronously to a faulty SWRU, relying on the DOS to maintain system consistency.

For normal SWRU replacement, the checkpointing of
SWRU state allows a logical SWRU warm restart to
be performed. Dynamic reconfiguration contravenes
the static binding rules of Ada, but provided
object interface definitions remain identical
(according to Ada recompilation rules), then
software replacement can successfully be
performed.   Interaction between the SWRU
development environment and the SWRU management
software is therefore essential to ensure this
interface consistency.   Where interfaces do
change, the Ada recompilation rules may be used
to define dependent sets of SWRUs to the SWRU
Management system. Replacement could then be
performed on the SWRU set as a whole.   Other
dependent sets of SWRUs may be derived from the
instances of a HOOD class object.

-    Fault Tolerance.   Error detection is performed
     both by the DOS and within the SWRUs themselves.
     Error reporting mechanisms could be used to
     initiate suitable recovery actions.   The SWRU
     boundary defines the limit of damage propagation
     and both hardware and software mechanisms may be
     used to provide suitable protection.   The SWRU
     granularity and therefore the granularity of
     error   detection   and   confinement   is   user
     configurable, affording maximum flexibility.
     Error recovery is achieved by SWRU management
     functions which may replace a faulted SWRU,
     perhaps checkpointing it if appropriate, or by
     re-distributing SWRUs that suffer a processor
     node failure.   Although not investigated as part
     of this activity, the SWRU concept could be used
     to support dynamic redundancy, perhaps having the
     same SWRU loaded into two different processor
     nodes, with one operational and the other in a
     warm standby state.

-    Ada.   All the prototype software was written in
     Ada, including the DOS mapper. The DOS interface
     was specified in Ada, but for reasons of
     efficiency the implementation of the body
     required additional semantics for asynchronous
     communication and scheduling control.   Standard
     interfaces providing these services (CIFO)
     (Reference 6) or language enhancement would
     therefore   facilitate   development   of   such
     software.

- Multiprogramming. Representing the physical SWRU as an Ada program permitted standard Ada compilation tools to be used to create SWRUs. Ada multiprogramming is a consequence of the requirement to support multiple SWRUs on a node. An efficient single scheduler model for multiprogramming was implemented as part of this prototyping activity and an interface to the multiprogramming services defined. Multiprogramming on an embedded target is currently being investigated by the ARTEWG.

In conclusion, this prototyping activity has confirmed the feasibility and power of combining Ada with the Software Replaceable Unit concept for Columbus.

This activity will therefore ensure a confident transition to the engineering phase of Columbus development.

6. ACKNOWLEDGEMENTS

The author thanks Mr R Allen of ESA and Mr J Antler of MBB-ERNO for their co-ordination and monitoring of this project and acknowledges Mr B Labreuille of MATRA Espace (Toulouse, France), Mr J Galera of GSI-Tecsidel (Barcelona, Spain), Mr D Iberson-Hurst of IPL (Bath, England) and the other members of the team for their contributions to this activity.

7. REFERENCES

1. European Space Agency, Columbus System Requirements, Reference COL-RQ-ESA-001 rev E., European Space Agency, April 1988.

2. D Bowen, S R Chandler, A Feasibility Study for the Support of Ada Applications Software within the Columbus Manned Space Station, IPL, Bath, 1988.

3. D Bowen, S R Chandler, the Support of Ada Applications Software within the Columbus Manned Space Station; Ada Expo '88 Conference Proceedings, 1988.

4. European Space Agency, HOOD Reference Manual, Issue 3, European Space Agency, September 1989.

234   *S.R. Chandler*

5. M Tedd, S Crespi-Reghizzi, A Natali, Ada for
    Multi-microprocessors, Cambridge University
    Press, 1985.

6. ACM Special Interest Group for Ada, A Catalogue
    of Interface Features and Options for the Ada
    Runtime Environment, Release 2.0, Ada Runtime
    Environment Working Group - Interfaces Subgroup,
    December 1987.

7. MATRA/TECSIDEL   SOFTBUS Final Report
    Reference 7032/87/NL/PP(SC).

8. MATRA/IPL/TECSIDEL DMS Test Bed Software
    Architecture - Final Report
    Reference COL-NA-TN-8341   December 1989.

Why not combine HOOD and Ada ?
An overview of several French Navy Projects

M. LAI

Cisi Ingénierie

Aix-Métropole, Pont des 3 Sautets

13100 Aix en Provence

France

Abstract : Since February 1987, Cisi Ingenierie has worked on several projects for the French Navy (Direction des Constructions Navales de Toulon). Most of them are scheduled to end in mid 1990. As Cisi Ingenierie was the prime contractor in developing the HOOD design method for the European Space Agency, it seemed a logical step to make this method available to its other clients. Furthermore, Cisi Ingenierie was amongst the first to use Ada as a programming language (1983). The purpose of this paper is to describe the problems we encountered using HOOD for design and Ada for coding. We do not intend to go into all the technical aspects in depth, firstly because much of the material is classified and secondly because it would be impossible in a paper of this length. We simply want to show the practical results of using HOOD and demonstrate its compatibility with Ada.

Keywords : Design Method , HOOD , Ada , Industrial Projects

1. INTRODUCTION

Although HOOD was developed only recently, is has already provided some interesting results when used on full-scale industrial projects. Using Ada for Naval projects is in itself highly original. The combined use of HOOD and Ada has effectively illustrated the advantages of using an object oriented design method prior to coding in Ada. By developing a project which incorporated artificial intelligence technology we were able to tackle the problem of interfacing the HOOD method with a methodology with a view to using an object oriented programming language.

The purpose of this article is to present the most important issues relating to the use of HOOD and Ada on three different naval projects.

These projects were all developed for the DCN in Toulon. The first one began in the first quarter of 1987, the second one in the first quarter of 1988 and the most recent in mid 1989. The final phases of these projects are staggered over 1990.

Only parts of these projects were developed on Cisi Ingenierie's premises in Aix en Provence. The rest was developed on the naval sites relating to the nature of the projects. This meant that a number of software services organizations were involved in both design and development. This article resumes the activities of the author in his various roles on these projects : software project manager for the DIVA project, member of the project team and project leader for the SEA project and finally advisory expert on methods for the PROTIS project. As a result, the issues presented here are restricted to the work the author was involved in only and do not pretend to put forward anything other than a personal viewpoint.

2.   PRESENTATION OF THE PROJECTS

2.1   Features of the projects

The DIVA project
The aim of this three year project was to define a potential on-board classification station. Project development took place within the GERDSM acoustic recognition group in the Brusc and was to culminate in a breadboard development which would allow the concepts chosen at the outset to be validated. Althought this software program is not the final operational version, Ada was chosen to meet the specifications relating to the quality of the software required, namely that it should be modular, portable and easy to extend, reuse and maintain over a long period of time. A specific feature of this project was that it involved two teams working in parallel. As the project advanced, one team of about ten specialist engineers provided technical specifications and programs written in FORTRAN, whilst the other team which was also composed of about ten engineers was responsible for developing an industrial standard version.

The project dealt with the following areas of activity : signal processing (visual and audio), the extraction of data from signal processing results, automatic interpretation systems and man machine interfaces (both dialogue and graphics). Most of the functions which were chosen are related to the state of the art in acoustic signature recognition.

The SEA Project
The main function of the SEA (Surveillance de l'Etat Acoustique/Acoustic condition surveillance) system is to assess whether or not the noise given out by a vessel exceeds the level necessary for discretion. The functional specifications and preliminary design were carried out at the CERTSM in Toulon. The subsequent development was handled by a

number of different sub-contractors (on a fixed-price basis with payment on results) who were each responsible for several HOOD objects resulting from the design phase. This project involved the same areas of activity as DIVA with the exception of the the interpretational aspects. SEA is considered to be a complex system due to the number of measuring points to be monitored and the degree of reliability required. We were responsible for the preliminary design. A team of five of our engineers handled the in-depth design and coding in Ada of three HOOD objects. The work took 18 months as scheduled.

The PROTIS Project

The PROTIS system was developed under the auspices of the CERDAN and aimed to identify the noise source responsible for a given acoustic fault, by means of a database combined with a signal acquisition and processing system. The PROTIS project was carried out by two different companies. The Cisi Ingenierie team was composed of 4 engineers working over a twelve month period. The programming languages used were C (for the signal acquisition and processing elements) and Common Lisp (SMECI) for attribution and diagnosis (expert system). HOOD was used for the overall design of the system. Once the objects which were to be coded in Lisp and which used the principle of inheritance between classes had been identified, they were designed using a specially developed extension of HOOD.

2.2 Hardware Architectures

The systems were all highly distributed (several computers linked up via a network). This feature had the great advantage of enabling us to resolve the design problems generally raised by such systems and find a suitable representation formalism. The various approaches used will be explained in the section on the use of HOOD.

Each application had its own specific computers. Thus some architectures contained array processors, standard scalar computers and symbolic computers for artificial intelligence technology as well as a specialised graphic computer.

The DIVA project used the following hardware : 1 VAX 785 , 2 Vax Stations , 2 Numérix , 1 Symbolics , 1 GOULD graphics station, 1 SYTER computer coupled with a PDP 11.

Several SUN workstations (4 to 5) were used for SEA together with a large number of remote processing modules (acquisition and FFT).

The PROTIS project also used SUN and HP workstations.

Each project included a functional specification phase in which SADT or a similar approach was used.

2.3   Block diagrams

In order to give a general outline of the projects concerned, the block diagrams below show
how each one can be broken down into functional modules.

Block diagram of DIVA

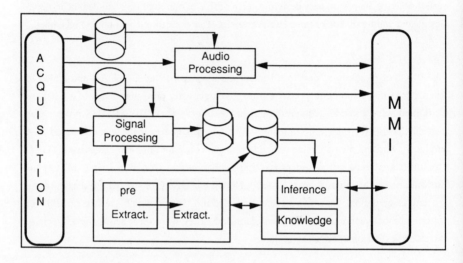

Block diagram of SEA

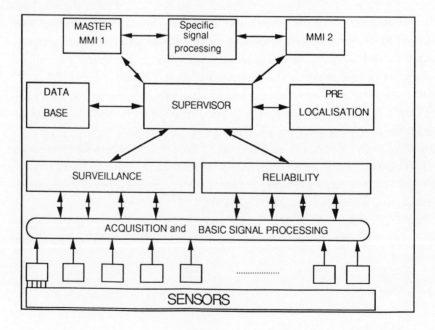

Block diagram of PROTIS

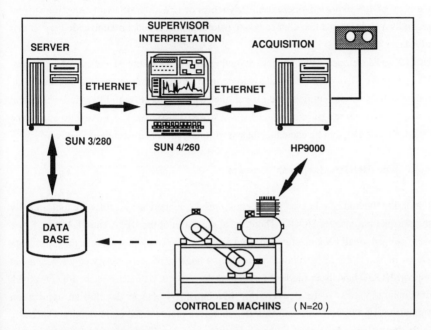

3.   THE HOOD METHOD

We do not think it necessary to review the HOOD method in detail here. Since its first presentation at the AFCET/ENST Ada conferences in Paris in december 1987 [2], the Ada community has become quite familiar with this method, so much so that in fact the combination of HOOD and Ada has become a European standard for major industrial projects.

However it would be helpful to give a brief summary of what the HOOD method is all about. HOOD uses a topdown approach to break down objects into a hierarchical structure, an object being an entity which groups together characteristics (or types in Ada terms) and operations. This decomposition produces a tree known as a design tree. Each node is a parent object. The objects beneath them are son objects ("include" relationship). At each level the decomposition, the son objects can use one another ("use" relationship) or use the objects used by the parent objects. The dynamic behaviour of an object is described in an object control structure which uses the same syntax as the Ada "tasking" instructions. These objects are said to be active as opposed to those which are said to be passive and do not have a behaviour of their own which is independant to the main control flow. There are two principal formalisms in HOOD for creating a design document : firstly a graphic program to represent the "include" and "use" relationships, the data flow and the specific features of the exported operations (asynchronous, with wait, with time limit), and secondly a standardised text element using natural language and a pseudo code very similar to Ada.

HOOD was developed with a view to designing large-scale technical and real time systems. It is particularly suitable when Ada is to be used in the coding phase, since it makes the modular division into entities even clearer, thereby enabling several different development teams to carry out the structural break-down work. It also makes it possible to handle the complexity of a system by enclosing data at various levels of structural break-down.

3.1   The HOOD Macintosh Support

If a design method is to be easily applied, it must be supported by a software tool. Initially this was not the case for HOOD. Therefore at the outset of the DIVA and SEA projects we were obliged to fall back on standard word processing software in which the diagrams were drawn in MacDraw or MacPaint. Since then, a number of software packages which can support HOOD have been marketed. As far as the projects we mention here are concerned, documentation was to be delivered on Macintosh. A plan to develop an application supporting HOOD format documentation therefore materialized quite rapidly, especially with the arrival of Apple's HyperCard software [3]. This tool, which is known as HyperHood [4], has gradually evolved and currently provides a satisfactory support for design phases using the HOOD method, in an integrated and homogeneous environment. It is worth noting that in addition to a graphical editor of tree-structured object diagrams, a predefined text description editor and a dictionary of data transiting between the objects, HyperHood also contains a base of Ada types which can be updated either manually, item by item, or automatically using a type file written in Ada or by means of the data in the dictionary. Consulting the base then becomes a process of navigation by clicking the elements which make up a given type.

Because HOOD has a number of different contexts for the use of a name, it is almost impossible to ensure the coherence or correct use of an entity "manually", when in fact the design phase produces a large number of names which have quite different meanings, although the written form is similar (STACKS , STACK , T_STACK for example may designate a package, a variable and a type respectively). Without some kind of tool, design reviews would rapidly have become search and spelling correction sessions and although it was often obvious that an incoherence was the result of carelessness, syntax nonetheless took over from semantics. The purpose of a tool is to reverse this trend and give the designer time to deal with more important issues.

3.2   Comments on the use of HOOD

Putting a new methodology into use usually gives rise to a certain number of reactions. A design phase does not naturally lend itself to rigorous definition and methods unlike languages, do not have compilers which make it possible to validate the conflicting interpretations of different members of the development teams and ensure correct application of a particular point of the method.

What is more, producing documentation, and one of the purposes of the deisgn phase is to do so, is not an obligation in itself. This is another striking difference between design and coding. A programmer will always do his utmost to run his program through a compiler, but a designer who comes up against a methodological problem could quite easily get round this by ignoring the part of the method which is causing the problem.

The point of these preliminary remarks is to remind the reader that it is not easy to formulate clear, objective criticisms of a design method and remain entirely technical when doing so. The human element is of primary importance. This means that the initial training, working context and motivation of the development teams should not be neglected as the advantages of using the method will largely depend on them.

All the comments on the HOOD method concern those definitions corresponding to the early versions of the reference manual, i.e. prior to version 3.0.

The DIVA development team took a five day Ada course and one day's initiation to HOOD. Throughout the design phases, the engineers could seek help from the software project manager for any problems relating to technical options, comprehension and application of HOOD or use of HyperHood. On this project each engineer was responsible for one complete part of the development (design, coding and partial integration). The way the project progressed led us to the conclusions that the HOOD training should have been longer (one week minimum), and that the time necessary to adapt to a design tool should not be underestimated. Even if the tool itself is straightforward, the context in which it is applied may not necessarily be so. The task was not made any easier by the fact that there were several versions of HyperHood in the course of the project. The object base in HyperHood includes 130 HOOD objects divided over a maximum depth of six levels.

On the SEA project design took place differently. The initial design phase was carried out in two stages by one team of engineers and was followed by a second development phase which included the in-depth system design, effected by a different team. The transition from one team to the next was by no means simple, but we shall come back to this point at a later stage. Level 0 was divided into 5 objects. The overall design generated approximately 40 objects not including the duplications required for the distributed version.

For PROTIS, the design set up was different again. After the functional specifications, two different teams carried out all the development work on their own premises. All members of the teams underwent a four day training course (3 days for Hood and 1 day for HyperHood). A further day was dedicated to a presentation of HyperHood++ [5] (an extension which takes account of the notion of class and inheritance between classes). A methodology expert supervised the design phase. The deadlines for this project were very short, which for certain members of the team justified the use of a word processor which they felt to be less restrictive than HyperHood.

Approximately twenty HOOD objects were required to present an initial software architecture to include distribution and the various UNIX processes used. The sub-contractors then introduced about seventy objects.

Preliminary design compared to in-depth design

The separation of these two phases had no particular effect on DIVA, whereas for PROTIS it could have influenced the time schedule although this was partly resolved by means of the communicating vessel principle. Any tasks not achieved during one phase, were carried out in the next. For a project such as SEA in which these phases were carried out by two different teams, it was obviously very important to define the limits of these phases very clearly. HOOD is not very explicit on this point and also tends to generate mini development cycles (one-level design, in-depth design, coding of interfaces and linking bodies). Under theses conditions, it is very difficult to make a contractual definition of where overall design ends and in-depth design begins.

Roughly speaking, everything relating to the external interfaces of the objects (object name, descriptions, constraints, provided and required interfaces (list of names), graphical representations and the "use" relationship) is overall design. Everything else (detailed data description (Ada types), description of an object's dynamic behaviour (OBCS) writing the pseudo-code for the operations (OBCS)) is in-depth design. The disadvantage of this definition is that it cannot be applied to sequential phases. In fact, in all HOOD objects, in-depth design can, and should be introduced before designing the sons .

Opinions are divided as to the definition of the pseudo-code which is similar to Ada (but not Ada). Some engineers judge it a waste of time, unless it can be made more efficient and readable. The lack of a compiler or translator to carry out part of the verification work is thought to be a considerable restriction. Others accept it and even over-use it. With the exception of the declarative part of the variables, the algorithms are not very far removed from the final code. Between the moment when the designer originally conceives of the system and the moment when this idea is represented in a programming language, all sorts of events may occur which are currently very difficult to account for in a method. This means that the engineers who have difficulty in expressing their ideas in the form of high level abstractions, whilst still using a syntax similar to that of Ada, tend to cling to the code as being the only tangible form of the original idea.

Distributed system design

One of the first issues a designer has to resolve during the overall system design, is how to include hardware constraints if the software is to be transposed onto a number of different machines working together via a network.

This was another point on which the three projects differed.

For DIVA, a HOOD object called "NETWORK" was created at the very first level of design. All the other brother objects use this object and there is no other relationship between them. This means that each object is designed as if it were to be completely installed on a particular machine (a machine can host several objects). The definition of "NETWORK" was restricted to communications via synchronous or asynchronous messages. Although this solution was easy to implement, it provided no formal presentation of the protocols of use between objects.

With regard to SEA, we chose to design a non-distributed software architecture and develop a breadboard in Ada which would run on one machine only. Then once the principles had been validated, work began to transform this non-distributed version into a distributed one. This approach is in theory very attractive since it means that all the machines will have a similar HOOD configuration, the only difference being the way in which the call operations are implemented. These may either be local or remote or impossible to activate. Our use of a set of Ada packages (PADS) [6], meant that remote objects could communicate (procedure calls with results sent back, removal of exceptions, rendez-vous). The major problem with this was that during the transformation stage, functional constraints and the need to optimize made us split the objects over several machines, which led to the creation of complex objects which were responsible for adressing the correct switch operation depending on the context.

The lessons learnt from these two projects were put to good use in PROTIS. From the outset, all the objects were designed for a particular machine. Each object was thus divided into several sons which were either local or virtual (body shaded). A HOOD object called "NETWORK" was also defined. A virtual object is obliged to use "NETWORK". A local receiver object also uses "NETWORK" in order to receive messages. In this form, the solution remains simple to implement (insofar as message transmission between objects is sufficient) yet there is still a clear formalization of the way in which one remote object may use another and the problem of object distribution is avoided.

Remarks on the "implemented by" clause and the "include" relationship

In the early days of the HOOD method, when there was no clause to distinguish between a detailed definition and an operation or OBCS, the definition of the upper levels was not very satisfactory. Because of the method's top-down approach, it was very difficult to express the complete behaviour and role of all the operations defined in "provided". The "implemented by" clause means that the definition of a parent operation can be carried over to a son (this is similar to a definition in "forward"). One of the advantages of this is that it allows the developer to keep the definition of the parent object interfaces and consequently fixes the use relationships between the brother objects. Some of the engineers instinctively took writing the "include" relationship in Ada to be the same as including packages in the "body" of the parent package. This effectively showed the visibility limits generated by the use relationship (installed using "with" clauses), but it also made it necessary to define the procedures relaying parent and daughter operations.

A semantic equivalent can be obtained by means of another Ada solution (use of the "renames" clause), without increasing running time, whereby the son objects are defined by independant packages and the parent package makes the "with" clauses for the son packages.

The use of "implemented_by" clauses makes it possible to structure the application with a succession of levels, whilst providing package interfaces at each level which are written in the code of the final application.

However this does not resolve the problem of having to fully define the interfaces at an early stage of the project, which means knowing the characteristics of the parameters to be passed onto the operations (types, modes, number). In the case of SEA (with over 600 types defined) this was no easy matter.

Another feature of the "implemented_by" clause is that it leads inexperienced engineers to believe that adopting a functional approach (the oi parent operation is divided up by the oj daughter operations) in itself justifies the creation of new HOOD objects. This of course is not in keeping with the method's object orientations.

Link between the "use" and "include" relationships

An Oi HOOD object can only use an Oj object if the latter is a brother (an object with the same parent). If an Oi parent uses an Oj parent which has an operation in "provided" and which is on one or more levels of break down and defined by an "implemented_by" clause, we can say in fact that Oi uses Oj.

There is no difficulty in implementing this situation in Ada. At design level however, even if it seems appropriate to limit arrow plotting in all directions, it would probably be better if the Ada implementation minimized the "with" relationships. This could be achieved automatically by means of a translator which would transform all calls to a parent object into calls to son "terminals" (if the "include" relationship is inserted using "with" relationships.

Passive objects vs active objects

HOOD definition allows a distinction between objects that modify the control flow and those that do not. The instinctive reaction to this is to use, Ada tasks for the implementation. The use of Ada to express the active object OBCS was well accepted by the team members and gave satisfactory results if certain points of method definition were clarified. For example, it is not necessary to declare an OBCS for each object (which certain engineers thought they had to do). Alternatively, the encapsulation of each task in packages at body level means that the distinction between active and passive objects is only useful when designing the terminal objects during the in-depth design phase.

The fact that HOOD has no graphical representation of a task (but an active object which can contain a number of OBCS split over the sons) considerably modified the developers' outlook.

Documentation : the design file

Defining standard document outlines is a relatively simple task which may nonetheless have serious consequences on the application of the method. Although HOOD is based on the work of G.BOOCH [7], it attributes greater importance to the form used for expressing text descriptions (ODS : object description skeleton) than to the way in which objects are created or the justification for creating them. These descriptions are not unrelated to the characteristics used prior to this in traditional developments (cross references, imported and exported entities, use of pseudo-code). "How" thus becomes far more significant than "why". Admittedly the connection with Ada is greatly simplified and it is quite possible to automatically generate an infrastructure in Ada using the text descriptions of the objects (which was not the case on any of the three projects and for which a similar process was defined in the most recent version of HOOD), but it is extremely difficult to get engineers to produce documentation relating to the writing and analysis of an informal strategy.

The benefits of using a graphical representation are no longer questioned. The linkup between the coding phase and Ada is an intereting phase of development (althought only when supported by an appropriate tool), but there are limits to this approach and the temptation to make the diagrams too explicit may also make them less readable, thereby losing the initial advantages of the technique. To our mind, the comparison between printed circuit design and the design of a software system effectively illustrates the scope of the domains to which a design method can be applied. The initial electronic diagram corresponds to the functional specifications (the position and exact constitution of the various elements is not yet determined). The synoptic diagram of the main components of the circuit (which should not be confused with any functional divisions which may have been provided with the theoretical diagram) and the plotting of the elements' position on the circuit correspond to the overall system design phase. Coding is represented by plotting the links between the different elements. There are no superfluous formalisms in printed circuit design.

If on one hand we can conclude that combining HOOD and Ada can be very beneficial, on the other we are obliged to note that there is a certain overlapping of the different phases of the software lifecycle which is not conducive to optimum development. Graphics enthusiasts look forward to the day when they will no longer have to program, whereas programming buffs aspire to systems which will automatically extract documentation from the source codes. For the moment, HOOD provides a happy medium, although it is perhaps a little too verbose on the text description side.

4. COMMENTS ON THE USE OF ADA

Ada was chosen for DIVA because our proposition with this bias coincided with a highly determined attitude on the part of those responsible for the project, and a great deal of motivation. Digital's Ada compiler in VMS was selected to support the development work.

As far as SEA was concerned, the project leaders were primarily motivated by the fact that the combined use of HOOD and Ada meant that the development could be sub-contracted to a number of companies. The customer's choice of Ada environment went in favour of the VADS 5.5. (Verdix Ada Development System). The main criterion for this was that the libraries supplied with the system made integration and interfacing with UNIX easier.

The DIVA development team went on a 3 day Ada initiation course. Only two of the ten engineers working on the project had any previous experience of developing in Ada. For SEA, the engineers responsible for handling breadboard development and software support, as well as some members of the project group took a four day course on Ada during which the VADS environment was studied in detail.

Almost 90 000 lines of code were written for DIVA, which corresponds to an average productivity per individual of 650 lines a month.

At the time of writing this paper, the coding phase of SEA has only just begun. In its current state the software environment already takes up 40 megabytes of disk space. Judging by the size of the design, there will be an estimated 60 000 lines of source code.

4.1 AP interfaces

On the DIVA project, the use of array processors driven by the VAX raised an interesting coding issue. As the procedures running on the array processors were to remain in FORTRAN, it was necessary to write an interface in Ada to allow driving, synchronization and communication between the NUMERIX processors and the VAX, whilst using the array processors' capacities to the full (in particular by efficient use of time sharing for processes carried out on the AP).

This was done by developing a monitor to handle all requests addressed to the AP. The latter uses the AST (asynchronous system trap) in VMS via the packages provided in Digital's Ada environment.

DIVAS's modularity and HOOD based structure means that the environments written in Ada are particularly well adapted to the client's operating requirements, i.e. the posssibility of incorporating new processes (signal or information processing) without making drastic changes to the rest of the system. These environments are built around an executive package which handles input requests, process attribution (distinguishing between basic processing and priorities) and synchronisation with the array processors.

4.2   Networks and The Unix/Ada Interface

With regard to DIVA the network interface was developed using Ada to write a layer of management for a mailbox system which uses the VMS input/output procedures (QIO) on a lower level. The "NETWORK" object is a generic unit with instances which allow type messages to be read and written on the network. This approach meant that the hardware configuration could be modified at any time during project development (addition of new Micro-Vax stations from the VS range) and processes could be carried over from one unit to another with very little modification.

For SEA, developing a network interface in UNIX was not quite so easy. As it was not possible to call non-inhibiting input/output procedures, we had to write a library program in C. The library program then had to be interfaced with PADS and ultimately it proved necessary to write a final layer of Ada to make PADS calls within the "bodies" of the remote objects.

4.3   Ada Types

The combined effect of separating the in-depth and overall design phases and having to include the large quantity of data used by the SEA system did nothing to simplify the coding and compiling of a large number of complex types. As these types were supplied by the client they were separated from the HOOD objects and consequently linking the two and using the types became more difficult for the development teams. The use of record with a variant containing parameterized types caused major problems which resulted in detrimental delays.

The use of large types was limited by use of the STORAGE_SIZE attribute.

4.4   Problems with the Ada Compiler

The use of the DEC compiler was entirely satisfactory. The VMS-dependant packages (tasking_services and starlet) proved very helpful, although they did not improve portability. With the exception of a few problems relating to the de-allocation of pointers in a program which has to run for thirty minutes and needs to allocate data blocks every minute, the Ada programming part of DIVA went very smoothly.

For SEA a preliminary breadboarding phase, carried out at the same time as the design served to highlight problems with the VERDIX compiler. Initially the breadboard was only supposed to execute a few scenarios in order to validate the design but gradually as the distributed version was developed and once the Ada types had been integrated, the breadboard became the structure for the final version. The modules developed by the sub-contractors then had to be integrated in this structure.

The generic function "unchecked_deallocation" does not work, which made it very dificult to free the space allocated for important data.

It was not possible to use a console with two sequential files for input/ouptut .

In order to interface certain procedures with C, we needed to know very precisely the size of the data provided by Ada. The use of the "size" attribute was not effective on certain non-constrained or variant type data.

5.   CONCLUSION

Choosing a new methodology like HOOD for projects of this kind was obviously taking a risk. The unfamiliarity of this method combined with the context in which it was applied, and the culture and lack of experience of some of the engineers all constituted difficulties to be overcome.   It is difficult to say what would have happened if HOOD had not been chosen. An ad-hoc documentation in natural language would probably have been used. Communication between clients, designers and developers remains a crucial issue. Although the documentation provided by HOOD is considered by some to be too cumbersome, it is nonetheless instrumental in the engineers' taking more precise design options at an earlier stage in proceedings than they would otherwise do. The other side of the coin is that the development teams have to work together much more : the age of isolated programming seems to have passed. However we still need tools which will relieve us of tasks which are much better done by a compiler.

As we expected the Ada factor was highly motivating for the developers. Even software engineers with no previous knowledge of the language can use it quite rapidly given a minimum of training. This of course is only possible if they are backed up by more experienced engineers and if the design phase has clearly outlined the project. Highly sophisticated problems in certain cases highlighted the weaknesses of one of the Ada compilers, but in theory these should have been corrected by the time this article is published. Nonetheless we were obliged to fall back on sytems engineers and Ada specialists.

In the meantime, HOOD has progressed and increased in accuracy. These three projects have provided us with valuable experience which will enable us to tackle future developments with greater confidence and greater knowledge of what is required. One of the next steps is to determine in relation to the market the tool which will best support HOOD on a workstation (SUN or VAX). Optimum use of this tool will then depend on a realistic estimation of the time required to learn how to handle it.

6 . ACKNOWLEGMENTS

These were all major projects in terms of budget, length and the number of people working on them. They gave us the opportunity to implement a methodology whilst using Ada. The wide variety of technologies was much appreciated. We would like to thank all the DCAN executive from the GERDSM, CERTSM and CERDAN who enabled us to participate in these projects. It is not possible to name all those who contributed to the development and worked towards the accomplishment of these projects but I am sure they will recognize themselves in this article. They may not have written it but they did play a very important role. Many thanks to them all.

7 . REFERENCES

[1]   HOOD Reference Manual version 3.0 ESA
[2]   Ada France Conference AFCET/ENST December 1987 Paris
        Ada France Conference December AFCET/ENST 1988 Brussels
        Ada Europe Conference June 89 Madrid Spain
[3]   HyperCard User Manual , Documentation Apple®
[4]   HyperHood Manuel d'utilisation et Manuel Methode, M. Lai , Cisi Ingénierie
        HyperCard + HOOD = HyperHood: M.Lai International Software Engineering
        Conference, Decembre 88 Toulouse France.
[5]   HyperHood ++ An object oriented design tool for developments in object oriented
        programming languages: M. Lai TOOL'S 89 , November 1989 Paris France.
[6]   PADS Packages Ada Distributed System Cisi Ingénierie Agence Aérospatiale
Toulouse
[7]   G.BOOCH
        Object Oriented design Ada letters vol 1 (3) March 1986
        Software Engineering with Ada   1983 et 1986 Menlo Park Benjamin/Cummings
        Software components with Ada , Rational The Benjamin/Cummings Publishing
        Company, Inc. 1987.

PART VIII: Language Issues

A New Exception Handling Mechanism for Ada

CHARLES J. ANTONELLI

Center for Information Technology Integration,
The University of Michigan, Ann Arbor, MI, USA.
Email: cja@citi.umich.edu.

RICHARD A. VOLZ

Department of Computer Science,
Texas A&M University, College Station, TX, USA.
Email: volz@cssun.tamu.edu.

Abstract

This paper describes a proposed new exception handling mechanism for Ada, which permits the propagation of exceptions from task bodies, provides for the resumption of execution in a signalling frame after the handling of an exception is complete, and solves the asynchronous transfer of control problem. The capabilities of the new mechanism are described, and an illustrative example is given.

1. Introduction

A new exception handling mechanism has been proposed in [Antonelli 89] for dealing with exceptional program conditions in an environment composed of multiple context objects*. This work extends the concept of exceptions and associated handlers to concurrent and parallel programs in which exceptions are signalled from one context object to another; consequently, the potential for asynchronous interference between a signalling and a handling task exists, and multiple exceptions may occur and must be resolved concurrently.

---

* Context objects are variously called processes or tasks; they represent scheduling units.

Ada's exception handling mechanism is modified in two phases. In the first, the existing exception mechanism is extended to allow exception propagation from a task body; interference to executing code is avoided through the conversion of such an exception to a kind of interrupt and the provision of an interrupt handler whose sole function is to await the arrival of such interrupts.

In the second phase, a new signal mechanism is added which augments Ada's exception handling termination model with a resumption model, and associates parameters with exceptions. The signalling mechanism supports three handler responses: resume, signal, and raise.

2. Motivation

To illustrate this work we show the addition of the new mechanism to Ada.

The basic problem motivating this work is the following:

(1)   The notification problem. Exceptions cannot propagate from a task body, causing tasks to terminate silently.

If permitting exceptions to cross task boundaries solves the notification problem, two further problems result:

(2)   The multiple notification problem. To which tasks should an exception be propagated, and how should this selection be determined?

(3)   The concurrent exception problem. Is it possible for an exception to arrive at a task that is not immediately able to handle it? Could a second exception be delivered to a task before the handling of the first is complete?

Three additional problems were found that hinder Ada's exception handling mechanism:

(4)   The forced abandonment problem. A frame* which raises an exception is always abandoned. Is it possible to allow other handler responses, such as resumption from the point of the exception?

(5)   The narrow bandwidth problem. No additional information accompanies a propagated exception. Is there a way to increase the bandwidth of information available to a handler in resolving an exception?

(6)   The unexpected exception problem. In Ada, an exception may propagate beyond the scope of its definition, and may propagate to invokers which are not expecting it.

While obtaining a solution to the notification problem is central to this work,

---

* In Ada, a frame is either a block, subprogram body, task body, or package body.

Section 5 discusses a solution to the asynchronous transfer of control problem afforded by the new mechanism.

3. Related Work

The recent and historical literature is divided into two classes: those that restrict an exception to the context object in which it occurs, and those that do not. Mechanisms of the former class predominate, and include PL/1 [Fike 70], Goodenough's proposal [Goodenough 75], Ada [RM 83], CHILL [Smedema et al. 83], CLU [Liskov & Snyder 79], Mesa [Mitchell et al. 79], and Yemini's proposal [Yemini 80].

Few mechanisms allow an exception to cross a context boundary. Levin proposed a mechanism [Levin 77] in which handlers may be attached to data objects shared by multiple contexts; when an exception arises involving the object, all contexts receive the exception. However, it is not clear how a handler may be kept from interfering with the context it serves, since it interrupts the context when the exception occurs. Also, resumption is always forced; this is difficult to do for an implicit exception such as "illegal instruction."

The UNIX operating system provides a signal handling mechanism [Ritchie & Thompson 78] which may be used to notify another process of a condition. However, the mechanism was not designed for exception handling, has many special cases, and permits unstructured and illegal access to data.

The Apollo DOMAIN operating system provides a dynamic fault handling mechanism [Apollo 86]. However, releasing handlers in an incorrect order results in the unexpected release of other handlers. While faults may be delivered to another process, this delivery is limited to the UNIX-style signal delivery mechanism; this results in a lack of uniformity in the overall mechanism.

Preliminary Ada [Preliminary RM 79] defined a FAILURE exception that could be raised in any task. This capability results in many problems, which are detailed in [Antonelli 89]. We observe that the FAILURE exception is not present in the current Ada definition [RM 83].

Cox and Gehani's Exceptional C [Cox & Gehani 89] allows an exception handler to retry execution of the current block a specified number of times, abandon the execution of the current block, or raise an exception in a surrounding block. Exceptional C also partially solves the unexpected exception problem by requiring each function to list in its header the exceptions it can propagate to its caller, and by converting an exception not listed there to the predefined exception Error. Exceptional C appears to solve the narrow bandwidth problem through parameters to exceptions, but this is not discussed in the paper. It is not clear if

Exceptional C's model includes exceptions implicitly signalled or raised by an implementation. It does not solve the notification and related problems since C has no language level units of concurrency.

4. The New Mechanism

It is convenient to present the solution to the unexpected exception problem first, since it is independent in nature from the rest of the mechanism, followed by the solution to the notification problem and then the solutions to the other problems.

4.1. The Unexpected Exception Problem

In Ada, since exceptions need not be declared in the specification of a frame, it is possible to propagate an exception to an invoker that is not prepared to handle it, in the sense that the possibility of propagating a given exception is not evident from an invoked frame's specification. It is also possible to propagate an exception beyond the scope of its definition (see Barnes [Barnes 84] pp. 141-142 for an example), and thus a handler for a given exception cannot always be written.

This unexpected exception propagation problem is solved by requiring that an exception must be specified by a frame which signals it by listing it in the frame specification. If the propagation of an unspecified exception is attempted, it is converted to the predefined exception UNSPECIFIED. This conversion guarantees that no exception is propagated for which its invoker is not prepared; this strengthens the separation of the levels of abstraction into which the program as a whole is divided. This implies an exception cannot be propagated from the scope of its definition, since an exception must be visible in order to be specified; instead, the exception is converted to UNSPECIFIED and propagated.

As an illustration, consider the following abstraction of a stack manipulation package:

```
1   package STACK is
2     STACK_OVERFLOW, STACK_UNDERFLOW: exception;
3     procedure PUSH(ITEM: in ITEM_TYPE)
4       raises STACK_OVERFLOW;
5     function POP
6       raises STACK_UNDERFLOW
7       return ITEM_TYPE;
8     function SIZE return INTEGER;
9   end STACK;
```

Line 4 in PUSH above guarantees that PUSH propagates only STACK_OVERFLOW or UNSPECIFIED. Programmers now know they need only write handlers for these two exceptions.

4.2. The Notification Problem

The solution to the basic notification problem involves the conversion of an exception which would otherwise silently complete a task to a kind of software interrupt. A special kind of task entry, called a raise entry, is defined and can be attached to such an interrupt. When an exception is propagated from a task body (called external propagation), an accept or select statement associated with the entry is executed.

For example, the specification

```
1   task EXCEPTION_HANDLER is
2     entry ERROR_ENTRY;
3     for ERROR_ENTRY use raise ERROR;
4   end EXCEPTION_HANDLER;
```

associates entry ERROR_ENTRY of task EXCEPTION_HANDLER with the exception ERROR; we say ERROR_ENTRY has been attached to ERROR. The form of the corresponding handler body is then as follows:

```
1   task body EXCEPTION_HANDLER is
2     -- declarations
3   begin
4     -- global initialization
5     loop
6       -- per-exception initialization
7       accept ERROR_ENTRY do
8         -- ERROR handling
9       end ERROR_ENTRY;
10      -- per-exception finalization
11    end loop;
12  end EXCEPTION_HANDLER;
```

Now consider the following task that is part of the same program containing EXCEPTION_HANDLER:

```
1   task CONTROL raises ERROR;
2   task body CONTROL is
3     -- declarations
4   begin
5     ...
```

```
6    raise ERROR;
7    ...
8    end CONTROL;
```

(An exception declaration declaring ERROR must be visible to both EXCEPTION_HANDLER and CONTROL.) When CONTROL line 6 is executed, exception ERROR is raised and causes the completion of CONTROL; the external propagation of ERROR is accomplished by converting it into a software interrupt and enqueuing it on task EXCEPTION_HANDLER's entry ERROR_ENTRY. Task EXCEPTION_HANDLER completes this rendezvous by executing its line 8.

In the absence of the new mechanism, CONTROL would have terminated silently. To achieve the functionality of the new mechanism, a periodic rendezvous with CONTROL by some other task could be employed [Knight & Urquhart 87], or an exception handler could be written for CONTROL that would rendezvous (via an entry call) with an exception handling task. Both are awkward and potentially wasteful of system resources.

4.3. The Multiple Notification Problem

As stated above there might either be no external raise handlers for a given exception, or more than one. This problem is solved by permitting several external handlers to attach themselves to a given exception; when propagated externally, all such handlers execute in an order not specified by the mechanism. If no external handler is attached to an exception at the time of its external propagation, then the predefined exception UNATTACHED is externally propagated. If no external handler is attached to UNATTACHED, then the entire program is terminated. This action is necessary to prevent the silent termination of task bodies.

4.4. The Concurrent Exception Problem

The solution to the notification problem also allows an exception to arrive at an external raise handler which is not waiting for it to arrive but rather is performing some execution of its own.

This problem is addressed by defining two classes of external raise handlers. Plain handlers, exemplified by EXCEPTION_HANDLER above, are invoked via a simple entry call; multiple calls are queued in FIFO order. Immediate handlers are introduced to solve the problem of encountering busy handlers in applications for which the associated delay cannot be tolerated. Immediate handlers, invoked via a (conceptual) conditional entry call, must be written according to a set of rules which ensure a handler will not be busy when an exception arrives.

For example, an immediate handler can execute neither entry calls nor accept, select, or delay statements. If these rules are violated, and it is determined during the conditional entry call that a handler is not ready to accept the call, a predefined exception BUSY is propagated externally. This provides a solution to the concurrent exception problem.

Finally, we must consider the problem of interactions between raise handlers and independently executing tasks in those cases where these other tasks cannot wait passively for an exception to be externally propagated. The raise point concept is introduced: a task periodically invokes an inlined function to check for the existence of an arrived exception at the task's companion handler (the external raise handler associated with the task). If so, this function raises an exception that may be used to abandon the current processing being performed by the task and continue its execution elsewhere within the task, or to cause the abandonment of the task and a concomitant release of system resources for the processing of more critical tasks. It has been shown [Antonelli 89] that raise points can be implemented very efficiently; see Section 5.2.

4.5. The Forced Abandonment Problem

The exception signalling mechanism is introduced to deal with the forced abandonment problem. When an exception is signalled, the signaller is suspended while the handler executes. Signalling an exception has the flavor of a procedure call, both when originally signalled and if signalled again by the handler. If a frame signals an exception for which no handler is provided by the programmer, then the predefined exception MISSING is propagated; this is because the simpler propagation semantics do not apply.

Signalled exceptions are handled via signal handlers, with a syntax similar to that of handlers for raised exceptions. A signal handler has direct access to all objects declared in its companion frame and may employ one of three different responses: resuming the signaller from the point of the exception; signalling an exception to another handler, suspending itself until that handler resumes it; or raising an exception and abandoning the signaller.

As a simple example, consider the following:

```
1   procedure SERVO is
2     ...
3   begin
4     loop
5       OUTPUT := CONT(CURR_POS,DESIRED_POS);
6       PUT(OUTPUT);
7     end loop;
```

```
8    exception
9    when signal UNSTABLE =>
10     STRATEGY := PID;
11     resume;
12   end SERVO;
```

CONT is a subprogram that calculates a control output for a servomotor based upon its current and desired position:

```
1    procedure CONT(CP,DP) signals UNSTABLE is
2    ...
3    begin
4    if STRATEGY = DEFAULT then
5      OUTPUT := DEFAULT_CTRL(CP,DP);
6    else
7      OUTPUT := PID_CTRL(CP,DP);
8    end if;
9    if OUTPUT > MAXIMUM then
10     signal UNSTABLE;
11   end if;
12   exception
13   when UNSTABLE =>
14     signal UNSTABLE;
15     OUTPUT := LAST_OUTPUT;
16     resume;
17   end CONT;
```

SERVO repetitively calls CONT and outputs the computed control value to the motor. CONT will signal UNSTABLE on line 10 if too large a value of OUTPUT is computed, causing the body of CONT to be suspended and the signal handler at lines 14-16 to run. This handler passes the exception on by signalling it again on line 14. This action suspends the handler and transfers control to the signal handler in SERVO at lines 10-11. The handler changes the control algorithm and directs CONT to continue via the resume statement on line 11.

An externally signalled exception is converted to a software interrupt. The semantics in this case are kept uniform with respect to the semantics for internally signalled exceptions. The same three handler responses — resume, signal, and raise — are defined for external signal handlers as for internal signal handlers, and the plain and immediate handler classes are also provided for externally signalled exceptions.

A detailed example of this part of the new mechanism is too large to be reproduced here; the reader is referred to Section 7.5 of [Antonelli 89].

4.6. The Narrow Bandwidth Problem

Signalled exceptions may be accompanied by parameters which are specified by the frame signalling the exception. Parameters may not accompany raised exceptions because locally declared variables passed as reference parameters may no longer exist by the time the handler executes, because the frame in which they were declared already has been abandoned and its storage therefore possibly reclaimed.

At the declaration and specification sites, a conventional formal parameter list, as defined for subprogram and task entry specifications, is attached to an exception declaration. At the signalling site, an actual parameter list conforming to the formal parameter specification must be given. At the handling site, the signal handler repeats the formal parameter list; the scope of these parameters covers the body of the handler.

For example, consider the previous SERVO example rewritten to use parameters to exceptions:

```
1   procedure SERVO is
2     ...
3   begin
4     loop
5       OUTPUT := CONT(CURR_POS, DESIRED_POS);
6       PUT(OUTPUT);
7     end loop;
8   exception
9     when signal UNSTABLE(STRATEGY: out STRATEGY_T) =>
10      STRATEGY := PID;
11      resume;
12  end SERVO;
```

The signal statement employed by CONT is now of the form:

```
signal UNSTABLE(STRATEGY);
```

Instead of depending on global variables, the communication between SERVO and CONT is now handled by the argument STRATEGY. The scope of the formal variable STRATEGY covers lines 9 through 11 above.

5. Asynchronous Control Transfer

The solution of the notification problem was the major goal of the work described in [Antonelli 89]. However, the mechanism can be used in solving the asynchronous control transfer problem.

5.1. Solution

This problem is introduced and an initial solution is proposed in [Katwijk & Toetenel 88] with a refined solution given in [Katwijk & Toetenel 89]. The problem to be solved concerns a system which is divided into mutually autonomous subsystems, one of which is responsible for rapidly sampling an analog signal. When the signal deviates from a prescribed norm, a different subsystem must be informed and this subsystem, normally performing other actions, must then stop what it is doing and attempt to correct the source of the fluctuation. After the attempt, this subsystem should return to its usual mode of operation; however, if the attempt was unsuccessful, another subsystem must first be informed.

Our solution is to signal an exception when the signal fluctuations exceed the constraints, and to provide an external raise handler for the second subsystem which interrupts the execution of the second subsystem by virtue of the handler's higher priority. If this attempt is successful, execution of the sampler and the second subsystem resumes, otherwise a different exception is raised.

Consider the following abstraction:

```
 1   type SAMPLE_T is new RECORD_TBD;
 2
 3   EMERGENCY, FAILED: exception;
 4   function SAMPLE return SAMPLE_T is separate;
 5   function SAMPLE_ERROR(SAMPLE: SAMPLE_T) return BOOLEAN
 6     is separate;
 7
 8   task SAMPLER signals EMERGENCY;
 9   task body SAMPLER is
10    RESULT: SAMPLE_T;
11   begin
12    loop
13      RESULT := SAMPLE;
14      if SAMPLE_ERROR(SAMPLE) then
15        signal EMERGENCY;
16      end if;
17      ...
18    end loop;
```

```
19  exception
20    when signal EMERGENCY =>
21      signal EMERGENCY;
22      resume;
23  end SAMPLER;
24
25  function OK return BOOLEAN is separate;
26
27  task LVL_X raises FAILED;
28  task body LVL_X is
29  begin
30    loop
31      -- normal mode processing
32    end loop;
33  exception
34    when external signal EMERGENCY =>  -- see below
35      -- emergency mode processing
36      if OK then
37        resume;
38      else
39        raise FAILED;
40  end LVL_X;
```

Here SAMPLER represents the signal sampling subsystem, and task LVL_X represents the second subsystem whose normal mode processing must be interrupted when the signal fluctuates.

Task SAMPLER signals EMERGENCY if the sample has fluctuated beyond its limits. This is an internal signal, and the internal handler at lines 20-22 then executes. Line 21 signals the same exception externally, causing the handler at lines 34-39 to be invoked.

Semantically, the handler of LVL_X behaves as though it were embedded in lines 7-9 of task body EXCEPTION_HANDLER seen in Section 4.2, with this task body embedded in the declarative region of LVL_X (that is, between lines 28 and 29). This construct is called a *demon handler* in [Antonelli 89] and is identified by the keyword "external" in line 34 above.

This invocation of the demon handler interrupts the execution of LVL_X because the demon runs at software interrupt priority. After attempting to correct the fluctuation, line 37 directs that the signaller be resumed if the attempt was successful; in that case the internal signal handler is resumed at line 22, and the handler subsequently resumes the sampler. If the attempt was not successful, line 39 raises the exception FAILED, which causes first SAMPLER and then

LVL_X to become completed, after which FAILED is externally propagated.

5.2. Analysis

The main difference between the new mechanism and others that have been proposed [Katwijk & Toetenel 88, Katwijk & Toetenel 89, RTAW 89] for Ada is that an executing task may effectively be interrupted by a priority-based mechanism. The demon handler runs in response to the arrival of an exception, interrupting the companion task, simply because the demon has a higher static priority. Problems dealing with interrupted Ada constructs, such as rendezvous in progress, waits for dependent task termination, delay statements and so forth, do not occur because these constructs are not abandoned but merely suspended while the handler runs. If the handler is constructed as an immediate handler, it executes immediately (that is, without waiting for synchronization points) and may make immediate changes to the companion task since it has visibility over the task's objects.

A characteristic of the new mechanism when utilizing it for asynchronous transfers of control is that the demon handler must interact with the companion task through shared variables; it has no direct control over the companion's flow of control. In fact, we claim it cannot have such control without being overly disruptive to the task. The indirect control it does have over the companion, in the form of the companion's execution of raise point code, constitutes polling. The reader may wonder if such a solution is adequate, in view of the great consumption of resources usually attributed to polling. Appendix A of [Antonelli 89] contains a calculation which shows that an Intel 80386 with a 20 mhz clock speed need spend far less than 0.1% of its time executing polling code in order to allow a newly detected incoming missile flying at 2000 mph to advance no more than 10 feet of linear distance after detection before routine processing is abandoned. For a more detailed treatment of this subject see also [Antonelli & Volz 90].

6. Conclusion

We have proposed a new exception handling mechanism for the Ada programming language. This new mechanism was designed to eliminate the notification problem by allowing exceptions to propagate from tasks. The major components of the mechanism were introduced. We reviewed the asynchronous transfer of control problem and examined three proposals for its solution. Finally, we illustrated how asynchronous control transfers may be programmed by means of the new mechanism.

7. Acknowledgement
We are pleased to acknowledge the comments made by the anonymous referees on the abstract of this paper.

References

[Antonelli 89]. Antonelli, Charles John, "Exception Handling in a Multi-Context Environment," Doctoral Dissertation, The University of Michigan, 1989.

[Antonelli & Volz 90]. Antonelli, Charles J. and Richard A. Volz, "Handling Exceptions in Real Time in Ada," submitted for publication.

[Apollo 86]. Apollo Computer Inc., "Programming With General System Calls," Update 1, Chelmsford MA, 1986.

[RTAW 89]. Asynchronous Transfer of Control Issues Group, Proposal RS-00001/00, Third International Workshop on Real-Time Ada Issues, Nemacolin Woodlands, Farmington, PA, June 1989.

[Barnes 84]. Barnes, J. G. P., *Programming in Ada,* Addison-Wesley, Second edition., 1984.

[Cox & Gehani 89]. Cox, Ingemar J. and Narain H. Gehani, "Exception Handling in Robotics," IEEE Computer, pp. 43-49, March 1989.

[Fike 70]. Fike, C. T., *PL/I for Scientific Programmers,* Prentice-Hall, Inc., 1970.

[Goodenough 75]. Goodenough, John B., "Exception Handling: Issues and a Proposed Notation," *Communications of the ACM*, vol. 18, no. 12, 1975.

[Katwijk & Toetenel 88]. Katwijk, Jan van and Hans Toetenel, "Asynchronous Transfer of Control in Ada," Proceedings of the Second International Workshop on Real-Time Ada Issues, Moretonhampstead, Devon, England, 1988.

[Katwijk & Toetenel 89]. Katwijk, Jan van and Hans Toetenel, "Language Extensions to Allow Rapid Mode Shifting in the Ada Programming Language," in *Ada: the design choice (Proceedings of the Ada-Europe International Conference)*, ed. Angel Alvarez, pp. 26-36, Madrid, June 1989.

[Knight & Urquhart 87]. Knight, John C. and John I. A. Urquhart, "On the Implementation and Use of Ada on Fault-Tolerant Distributed Systems," *Transactions on Software Engineering*, vol. SE-13, no. 5, 1987.

[Levin 77]. Levin, Roy, "Program Structures for Exceptional Condition Handling," Doctoral Dissertation, Carnegie-Mellon University, 1977.

[Liskov & Snyder 79]. Liskov, Barbara and Alan Snyder, "Exception Handling in CLU," *Transactions on Software Engineering*, vol. SE-5, no. 6, pp. 546-558, 1979.

[Mitchell et al. 79]. Mitchell, James G., William Maybury, and Richard Sweet, "Mesa Language Manual," CSL-79-3, Version 5.0, Xerox Palo Alto Research Center, 1979.

[Ritchie & Thompson 78]. Ritchie, D. M. and K. Thompson, "The UNIX Time-Sharing System," *Bell System Technical Journal*, vol. 57, no. 6, pp. 1905-1929, 1978.

[Smedema et al. 83]. Smedema, C. H., P. Medema, and M. Boasson, *The Programming Languages,* Prentice-Hall, Inc., 1983.

[Preliminary RM 79]. The United States Department of Defense, "Preliminary Ada Reference Manual," *ACM Special Interest Group on Programming Languages*, vol. 14, no. 6, part A, 1979.

[RM 83]. The United States Department of Defense, "Reference Manual for the Ada Programming Language," ANSI/MIL-STD-1815A-1983, 1983.

[Yemini 80]. Yemini, Shaula, "The Replacement Model for Modular Verifiable Exception Handling," Doctoral Dissertation, University of California, Los Angeles, 1980.

Ada for the Description of Wavefront Array Processors

KEVIN J. COGAN

Electronics Technology and Devices Laboratory
Fort Monmouth, New Jersey, USA

1. INTRODUCTION

1.1 VLSI Array Processors

VLSI array processors are inherently powerful machines offering considerable speedup over the processing of algorithms on sequential machines. Two types of array processors, systolic and wavefront, are representative of state-of-the-art architectures for Very Large Scale Integrated Circuit (VLSI) implementation for the efficient execution of parallel algorithms. A distinct difference between the two processors is that systolic arrays require a global clock which synchronizes the data transfer among all of the inter-communicating processing elements (PE's). Conversely, wavefront array processor operation is asynchronous whereby data transfer is accomplished by mutual convenience of pairs of communicating PE's. It will be shown that the Ada programming language has a powerful syntax to describe and simulate the abstraction of asynchronous communication for any two-dimensional array of concurrently executing PE's. A formal model was developed and tested using task types in an Ada program. A specially adapted graphics package was written in Ada to demonstrate the dynamics of parallelism and inter-PE communication for the wavefront processor using a known algorithm.

1.2 Motivation for an Ada Description

S.Y. Kung [1] developed a model for a VLSI wavefront array processor. He expressed the need for powerful algorithmic languages which could lead to hardware description and automatic compilation of such processors. There are compilation tools currently under development which portend to be capable of synthesizing machines in the VHSIC Hardware Description Language (VHDL) directly from software behavioral descriptions such as in Ada [2]. Based on Kung's model of the wavefront array processor, the author of this paper recognized that the Ada programming language could describe and simulate such a parallel processor through judicious use of the Ada task mechanism. Occam and other parallel languages have not been found to be suitable for such descriptions. Thus, if Ada can supply complete functional descriptions of complex hardware, the direct synthesis of micro-electronic hardware from software using silicon compilers may be achievable for a highly parallel and powerful class of machines.

2.   ADA TASK FEATURES

2.1   User and Server Task Definition

A principal feature of the Ada programming language is the ability to model parallel or concurrent processes. A concurrent process in Ada is described a **task.** Tasks are categorized as either pure servers, pure users, or a combination of the two. Pure servers accept requests from tasks which demand a service or an **entry** (a user task). The condition of requesting and accepting a service establishes a synchronization or handshake between two tasks. The synchronization and duration of the handshake is known as a rendezvous, during which the user task is suspended while the serving task is processing the request. The arrows in Figure 1 depict a task's rendezvous.

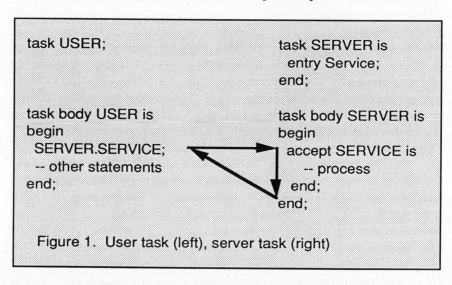

```
task USER;                      task SERVER is
                                  entry Service;
                                  end;

task body USER is               task body SERVER is
begin                           begin
   SERVER.SERVICE;                 accept SERVICE is
   -- other statements              -- process
end;                               end;
                                  end;
```

Figure 1. User task (left), server task (right)

2.2   Sequential Service vs. Random Service

The pure user has no entries whereas the server does. A task can both request (call an entry in another task) as well as serve (accept an entry call). A task can have zero or more entries. Characteristic of all entries is that each entry has its own queue which is a FIFO buffer. Thus a task with two entries has two queues. Depending on the logic of the task, two (or more) different entries from two different queues can be serviced sequentially or randomly with the use of the **select** statement as depicted in Figure 2.

```
task body SERVER is              task body SERVER
begin                           begin
  accept SERVICE_1 do             select
    -- process 1                    accept SERVICE_1 do
  end;                                -- process 2
  accept SERVICE_2 do               end;
    -- process 2                  or
  end;                              accept SERVICE_2 do
end;                                  -- process 2
                                    end;
                                  end select;
                                end;
```

Figure 2. Sequential service (left), random service (right).

2.3   Guards and Timed Entries

The select statement is robust enough to allow for random selection of an "open" accept statement, guard against one or more selections with a boolean condition, or timeout after a chosen **delay** statement if the user task is not available to rendezvous within a given timeframe. The timed entry call depicted in Figure 3 chooses a service, but if the service is not available in three seconds, the call is removed from the Service entry queue and the user task is free to do something else. This is a powerful construct for use in our model presented later. In addition to these features, Ada tasks have the ability to recover from faults, prioritize tasks, terminate and abort tasks, provide a loop for the iterative servicing of entries, impose synchronization without any additional process, and pass data as parameters to entries. A complete treatment of tasks is not possible here, but necessary components for an array processor description will be further elaborated later in the model.

```
select                          select
  when Available =>               Server. Service;
    accept Service_1 do         or
      -- statements               delay 3.0 * seconds;
    end;                          Do_Something_Else;
or                              end select;
    accept Service_2 do
      -- statements
    end;
end select;
```

Figure 3.   A guarded accept statement (left),
a timed entry call (right).

3.   WAVEFRONT ARRAY PROCESSORS

3.1   Asynchronous Processing

Synchronization, handshaking, buffers, and queues are inherent features of the Ada programming language which can serve to model the architecture of wavefront array processors. Ada tasks cannot provide the precise synchronization as would be required for a systolic array. But it is largely owing to the fact that wavefront arrays are asynchronous, data driven, and rely on the mutual convenience of two communicating PE's to pass data, that makes Ada a powerful algorithmic language for design and simulation of wavefront array processors.

3.2   Timing Model Requirements

Wavefront arrays require correct sequencing, not timing as in systolic arrays, to function properly. Information transfer between a PE and its nearest neighbors is by "mutual convenience", analogous to the rendezvous mechanism. The rendezvous is the simple transmission and acceptance of data when it is convenient between two tasks. Since there is no need to globally synchronize the wavefront array processor, the hardware implementation easily scales to very large arrays of PE's, where global timing becomes a difficult problem due to layout and skew. Thus Ada becomes a sufficiently capable langauge to describe and simulate the processor in a generic form with the use of the **task type**. Other technical characteristics of wavefront arrays are found in [1]. The reference further cites the need for parallel algorithms that are powerful, easy to understand, and compilable into a VLSI hardware description for implementation. The requirement for mutually convenient timing between pairs of PE's rather than all PE's simultaneously maps quite nicely to the Ada task mechanism. System, array, and PE architecture levels of description are also supported by the levels of abstraction available to the Ada language. Ada was designed to be readable, which supports the need to have an easily understood language to describe the wavefront array. Ada in fact may be the only suitable language to date to satisfy these stated requirements.

3.3   Wavefront Array Processor Architecture

In a wavefront array, PE's communicate with their nearest north, south, east, and west neighbor PE's. Array border PE's are special cases which communicate with either memory modules or I/O channels shown in Figure 4. An internal PE could thus be modeled as a processor which receives data when available from its west and north neighbors' output channels, processes it, and then passes data after the process to its south and east neighbors' input channels. This local communication with nearest neighbor PE's does not rely on global synchronization but rather on "as available" data for each local processor.

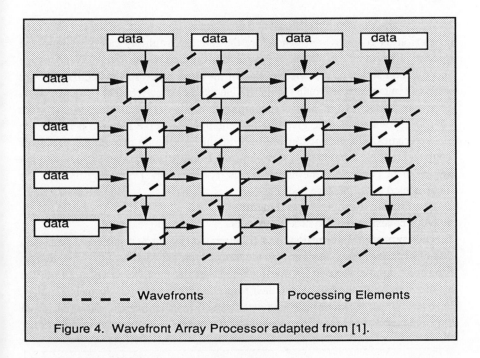

Figure 4. Wavefront Array Processor adapted from [1].

4. THE METHODOLOGICAL MODEL

4.1 Packaging the Array Processor

From a user's perspective, we would like perhaps to multiply two matrices, A and B. The user's view is at a high level of abstraction and thus if C is the expected resulting matrix, then one should expect to be able to write the statement   C := Multiply(A,B); which calls a function to perform the multiplication. Such a statement would be expressed in the control or main program, which is otherwise the user interface to the underlying implementation. In order to call such a function, a function library is presumed to be available to the calling environment and, for that matter a type called matrix, so that objects of this type can be called in the first place. In Ada, the encapsulation of types, functions, and procedures that are related are declared in a **package** specification. In this example, such a package can be expressed as follows:

```
package Array_Processor is
type Matrix is array (Positive range <>,
                      Positive range <>) of Integer;
function Multiply (A,B : Matrix) return Matrix;
end;
```

Here the matrix is two dimensional and there are no constraints on the range of each dimension as given by <>. Therefore the function Multiply can be generic and dynamically adapt to any size matrix multiplication desired. The package specification serves as the "visible" part of the array processor, much like the wire leads to a microelectronic chip - which define the user interface. The implementation details are "hidden" from the user in the **package body** and really are not the user's concern, provided that the given implementation meets the required performance characteristics. Thus function Multiply might be a single or multiple processor implementation. It could be a systolic, wavefront, or some other architecture not known or of concern to the user. In this model, a wavefront array processor is implemented in the package body.

4.2   Processing Elements as Tasks

Let each processing element in a wavefront array processor be represented by an Ada task. Let each input channel north and west be represented as an entry in each task. For each output channel from the south and east, let there be an **entry** call to the neighboring south and east task in their respective north and west channels. Further, for every entry, let there be a parameter passed representing the data transferred to/from neighboring PE's. Then each internal array PE is represented as in Figure 5.

```
task type PE is
    entry North(North_Data : Integer);
    entry West (West_Data : Integer);
end;

and the body of each task is implemented as

task body PE is
begin
  loop
    accept North (North_Data : Integer) do
      ND := North_Data;
    end;
    accept West(West_Data : Integer) do
      WD := West_Data;
    end;
    Compute;        -- perform the multiplication
    PE.West(WD)     -- transmit data from the west
    PE.North(ND);   -- transmit data from the north
  end loop;
end;
```

Figure 5.   A simplified task implementation for a PE.

4.3   Declaration of the Array Processor

Since this is a **task type**, we can declare any number of objects that will be identical to this PE model. For an economical hardware implementation, all PE's should be identical in design regardless of their array position in the processor. In Ada we can directly declare such an array. Thus a 4x4 array of PE's for a wavefront array processor could be declared as follows:

Processor : **array**(1..4,1..4) of PE;

or to adapt to any size AxB, then

Processor : **array**(A'Range(1), B'Range(2)) **of** PE;

where the result matrix C measures as the number of rows in A and columns in B as given by the 'Range attribute. Each processor of the wavefront array can thus be addressed as Processor(i,j), each with entries North and West.

4.4   Invalid Assumptions in the Model

This is a simplified model. It presumes that data can be immediately transmitted from the north and west processors and that data can be immediately received by the south and east processors. This is not the case in reality, nor should there be any dependency on the sequence of receiving or transmitting of data between processors. Refinement of the model is necessary in order to remove these assumptions and dependencies. It is also necessary that each Processor(i,j) know its position in the matrix, so that it is known if it should be able to receive and transmit data to neighbor PE's in the event that they do not exist. If each PE is identical in hardware implementation, then how it behaves as a function of position in the array must be under the control of its internal logic.

5.   REFINEMENTS TO THE MODEL

5.1   PE Function and Data Transmission

The model developed so far is inadequate to fully describe and later simulate an array processor. Chiefly, there are two areas that need to be refined - the PE logic as a function of its relative position in the array, and the sequencing of transmitting data. The latter concern could give rise to deadlock if not architected properly.

5.2   PE Identification

With regard to position in the array, it is necessary that each PE know its row and column, (i,j). This is not required for its own use, but so it knows which neighbor (i,j+1) the east or (i+1,j) to the south to call to pass data. Thus if a PE knows its own identity, it not only knows by what row and column to call its neighbor, but also if it has a neighbor at all, given the bounds of the two-dimensional array. To communicate a PE identification, the parent function Multiply broadcasts i and j to each spawned task to an entry call in the task as follows:

entry ID(I, J, Loop_Count : Positive);

The loop_count indicates how many times data will be passed to the task so that each PE will know when it has finished with its part of the algorithm. Now that a PE has its ID, it can know how it gets its data. There are four classes of PE's for this array processor model as follows:

(1) Processor(1,1) - the northwestern-most PE which gets both its North and West data from memory

(2) Processor(i,1), i /= 1 - all PE's in column 1 except (1,1) which get west data from memory and north data from PE's

(3) Processor(1,j), j /= 1 - all PE's in row 1 except (1,1) which get north data from memory and west data from PE's

(4) Processor(i,j), i and j /= 1 - all other PE's which get data only from other PE's

This logic was satisfied and written in the task body of all PE's, replacing the simple model in Figure 5 above. Thus all PE's are identical as required, but there logic dictates the communication paths for the reception of data during a rendezvous with a calling task.

5.3   Preventing Deadlock Using Timed Entries

The data transmission model can not remain simplistic either, as the entry calls PE.West and PE.North indicate in Figure 5. Both timing and sequencing analysis revealed that deadlock was a distinct possibility if there was not a way to alternate calls to east and south neighbors, if for other reasons, those neighbors were not prepared to rendezvous. This is analogous to trying to make a phone call to two parties, both of whom are initially busy. The caller could try to call Party 1 until that call was completed before attempting to call Party 2. The problem with this scheme, as related to Figure 5, is that Party 2 may be busy for a shorter interval, in which case the caller could have made use of Party 2's information earlier. The "timed entry" call shown in Figure 6 circumvents this dilemma and enhances the array processor model.

```
loop
    select
        Processor(I, J+1).West(WD);
    or
        delay 0.005;
    end select;

    select
        Processor(I+1, J). North(ND);
    or
        delay 0.005;
    end select;
end loop;
```

Figure 6. Modified data transmission scheme.

This scheme itself is simplistic, but it demonstrates that the calling task is willing to try to call its j+1 neighbor for 0.005 seconds, and if unsuccessful, tries to call its i+1 neighbor also for 0.005 seconds. With additional logic the loop statement would continue until both task entries were called. The solution to the problem also demonstrates the powerful syntax and facilities of the Ada task mechanism to portray the abstraction at hand.

6.   GRAPHICS TO SUPPORT SIMULATION

With an adequate model now developed, it would be interesting to observe the inter-communication of PE's and the intermediate stages of computation during execution of the algorithm. A reusable graphics package was utilized [4] and a display task was written which could map the C matrix as a two-dimensional array of nodes interconnected by arcs which would represent the Kung hardware model in Figure 4. For each node, when both north and west data have been received, the product of the two values are displayed graphically on the node. As data is transmitted to neighbors, the arcs blink to signify that a rendezvous has occurred. Observation of the simulator using graphics support reveals the advance of the wavefront in time as it proceeds from the northwest to the southeast as intended. When the algorithm is complete, the final value displayed in each node is the C matrix as a result of AxB.

7.   FUTURE MODEL ENHANCEMENTS

Future enhancements to the model are not only possible, but undoubtedly would be required before committing the design to hardware. Two areas of enhancement, fault tolerance and prognostics, deserve mention. A fault tolerant array processor must be capable of detecting PE's which are not available in the array either because of catastrophic failure or because of a localized "stuck at" fault. The detection is possible to model in Ada from the viewpoint of the calling PE. The use of the task attribute 'Callable indicates a called task which for unknown reasons is not available for a rendezvous. The calling task could notify its supervisor which would be capable of wiring in a spare PE by spawning a new task from the task type and giving it the same identity as the failed PE. Spare PE's on the chip or wafer in hardware would be prepared for this backup mission. A suitable schema for data recovery is also possible. Prognostics is also an important aspect of future systems. Presuming the program supervisor can manage fault tolerance, then close monitoring of failure rates and the use of spare PE's gives rise to the prediction of when the processor will have exhausted its potential to map in backup PE's. Though not complete in every aspect of prognostics, prediction analysis of global system failure can be reported from the monitored data.

8.   CONCLUSION

It has been demonstrated that Ada can be used as a powerful description and simulation language for parallel processing in emerging technologies such as wavefront array processors. The Ada task has a rich syntax to handle timing, local synchronization, and data transfer in an interconnected array of processing elements. Software descriptions for direct synthesis to microelectronic hardware may be possible as a result. Simulation aids the designer in conceptualizing refinements to the model such as deadlock and extensions to the model for fault tolerance and prognostics.

REFERENCES

[1] Kung, S.Y. et.al., Wavefront Array Processors - Concept to Implementation, Computer (IEEE), July 1987.
[2] Warshawsky, E.H. et. al., Synthesizing Ada's Ideal Machine Mate, VLSI Systems Design (IEEE), October 1988.
[3] Kung, S.Y., VLSI Array Processors, Prentice Hall, 1988.
[4] Cogan, K.J., System Simulation in Ada for the Project Manager, Proceedings, 7th National (USA) Conference on Ada Technology, 1989.
[5] Barnes, J.G.P., Programming in Ada, Addison-Wesley, 1984.

Hard Deadline Scheduling Using Ada

OLE SØRENSEN

DDC International A/S

1 INTRODUCTION

Embedded real-time systems frequently contain jobs with hard deadlines for their execution. Failure to meet a deadline reduces the value of the job execution, possibly to the extent of jeopardizing the mission of the system [Car-84].

Ada is designed for embedded real-time systems. However, the experience of using Ada in such applications has shown that the traditional implementation of Ada tasking makes it hard if not impossible to guarantee that deadlines are met. Due to this deficiency, a lot of applications have been written using the sequential part of Ada together with a general process kernel.

This paper describes how a new scheduling scheme for Ada tasking has made it possible to write embedded real-time systems with hard deadlines in full Ada. The scheduling scheme has been designed to meet the requirements of the Rate Monotonic Algorithm, to which a brief introduction is given.

In order to investigate the priority inversion problem in Ada and to evaluate the Hard Deadline Scheduling (HDS) run-time system from DDC International A/S, Denmark, a servo for a flexible pneumatic cylinder has been implemented at the Royal Institute of Technology, Stockholm [Blo-90]. The application and the found results are described in this paper.

2 RATE MONOTONIC ALGORITHM

The Rate Monotonic Algorithm was originally developed in 1973, by Liu and Layland in 1973 [Liu-73]. Given a set of periodic and independent tasks, the Rate Monotonic Algorithm assigns a fixed priority to each task, assigning a higher priority to a task with a shorter period.

The algorithm guarantees that all deadlines will be met if the utilization is below the bound calculated below:

$$Bound = u + \ln(2/(1+u))$$

where u is the utilization of highest priority task.

Note that the worst case bound equals $\ln(2)$ = 69%.

If the processor requirements of each task is known, the worst case bound can be substantially higher. In fact, the algorithm is typically able to schedule periodic task sets with processor utilization of 85% to 90%, see [Sha-86].

More recent work at the Carnegie Mellon University has refined the Rate Monotonic Algorithm to handle aperiodic, sporadic and dependent tasks. A description of the extended algorithms can be found in [Sha-88].

Compared to more ad hoc methods for achieving that deadlines are not missed, e.g. dividing the application into small time slots, there are many advantages of using this algorithm:

- Reduction of the integration and test time

- Reduction in maintenance costs

- Increase in reusability

- High system performance

- In overload situations, deadlines are missed in reverse order of priority

In order to use the algorithm, no uncontrolled priority inversion must take place in the application.

Uncontrolled priority inversion is defined as the situation where a higher priority task is blocked for an unlimited period of time by a lower priority task.

A typical example of uncontrolled priority inversion is the situation where a high priority task waits for a resource currently held by a low priority task, while a medium priority task is executing. The high priority task will be blocked as long as any medium priority task is eligible to execute.

3 LIMITATIONS IN TRADITIONAL ADA TASKING IMPLEMENTATIONS

Ada was specifically designed for embedded real-time systems and it is ironic that the traditional tasking implementations does not allow scheduling algorithms as the Rate Monotonic to be applied.

This is caused by the following problems:

- Entry queues are FIFO ordered, not priority ordered.

- If several select alternatives can be selected, one of them is selected arbitrarily.

- Uncontrolled priority inversion.

The use of FIFO entry queues and the arbitrary selection among tasks in open select statements may be appropriate for non real-time systems since it prevents starvation.

However, in embedded real-time systems, FIFO entry queues imply that high priority tasks may wait unnecessarily for lower priority tasks to be handled by the called task.

The arbitrary selection in select statements may lead to uncontrolled priority inversion and makes the behaviour of the application indeterministic, which is a very poor characteristic of an embedded system.

In traditional Ada tasking implementations, uncontrolled priority inversion may also take place when a high priority task has called an entry of a task currently engaged in a rendezvouz with a low priority task. The high priority task will be blocked as long as any medium priority tasks are eligible to execute. See Figure 1.

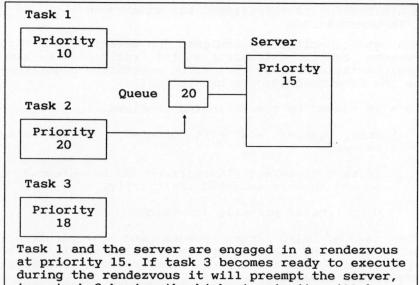

Task 1 and the server are engaged in a rendezvous at priority 15. If task 3 becomes ready to execute during the rendezvous it will preempt the server, i.e. task 2 having the highest priority will be blocked as long as task 3 executes, i.e. for an unbounded amount of time.

Figure 1. Priority Inversion.

Below the changes made to the Ada tasking kernel in order to meet the requirements of the Rate Monotonic Algorithm, are explained.

4 IMPLEMENTATION OF HARD DEADLINE ADA TASKING KERNEL

In order to support rate monotonic scheduling, the implemented tasking kernel has the following features:

- Priority based entry queues, not FIFO.

- In select statements, the highest priority task waiting for an open select alternative is chosen.

- Priority inheritance has been implemented in order to remove uncontrolled priority inversion.

Priority inheritance means that whenever a high priority task is blocked by a low priority task, e.g. when calling an entry, the blocking task inherits the priority of the high priority task. In the situation shown in Figure 1, the server task inherits the

priority of task 2 and will execute although task 3 is
ready execute.

The priority inheritance has been implemented in a
recursive manner, i.e. if a task is blocked by a lower
priority task which again is blocked by another task
etc. the high priority is inherited by all blocked
tasks.

Priority inheritance has been implemented in the
following cases:

- When a task is waiting in an entry queue, the
  called task inherits the priority.

- When a task is engaged in a rendezvous waiting
  for the rendezvous to complete. This is
  traditional Ada.

- When a task is waiting on a semaphore in the
  run-time system, the owner of the semaphore
  inherits the priority.

A special test developed at the Carnegie Mellon
University to test the capabilities of an Ada tasking
kernel to meet hard deadlines has been run using the
standard kernel and the implemented hard deadline
kernel.

The result proved that hard deadlines were missed at
an average utilization around 50% using the standard
kernel, compared to an average utilization around 90%
using the hard deadline kernel.

5 EXAMPLE

The HDS Tasking Kernel has been used in the
implementation of a servo for a flexible pneumatic
cylinder [Blo-90].

The servo should be able to position the piston within
the range of the stroke, which is 0.7 meters, with an
accuracy of 1 hundredth of a millimeter.

The positioning of the piston is managed by
controlling the amount of air in the chambers of the
cylinder, using two proportional valves. The feedback
input to the servo is the position of the piston, see
Figure 2.

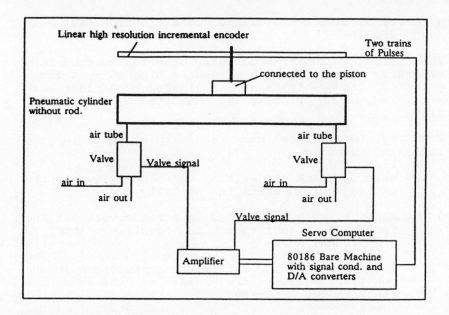

Figure 2. Application Overview

5.1 Description of the Tasks in the Servo

The servo has been implemented with six tasks. The tasks and their communication are shown in Figure 3 The values in the circles refer to the task priorities. The rectangles in each task denote the entries.

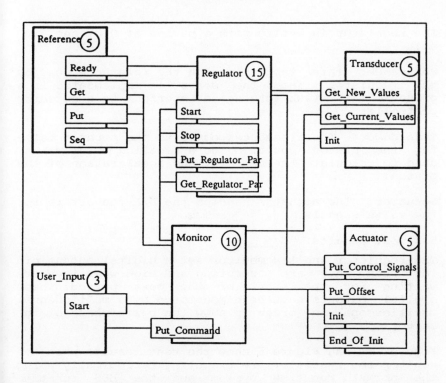

Figure 3. Task Overwiev.

Monitor: Used by an operator to start and stop the regulator and to monitor the excecution. When the regulator has been started the monitor is cyclic with a period of 0.1 sec (10 Hz).

User_Input: Reads the operator input and transmits it to the monitor.

Regulator: The regulator is the heart of the servo. The regulator starts a sample with a read of the current transducer and reference values. The control signals for the valves are then calculated and transmitted to the Actuator task.

The regulator is cyclic with a period of 0.01 sec (100 Hz).

Reference: This task maintains the reference used by the regulator. When the servo is implemented in a product this task acts as an interface to a superior controller.

Transducer: The transducer converts the counter value for the piston position to a floating point value, used to calculate the velocity and acceleration of the piston.

Actuator: The actuator handles the D/A-converters for the valve signals.

5.2 Test Results

The regulator and the monitor set a digital output pin low when they are executing and high when they are waiting for the start of the next period. These digital outputs have been monitored by a multichannel oscilloscope in order to show the performance of the servo.

Figure 4 and Figure 5 show the test results when the monitor and regulator are executing periodically using the normal run-time system and the HDS run-time system, respectively. In this test the monitor displays the piston position to the operator.

When using the normal run-time system the regulator task misses its deadline when the monitor is updating the piston position.

When using the HDS run-time system the priority inheritance ensures that the regulator process always meets it deadline.

In order to maintain the periodicy of the regulator when using the normal run-time system, the sampling frequency had to be reduced from 100 Hz to 50 Hz, while the sampling frequency could be increased to 125 Hz before deadlines were missed using the HDS run-time system.

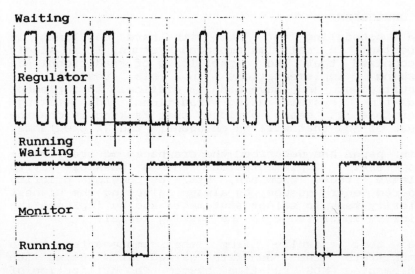

Figure 4. Periodic Performance with Normal Run-Time System.

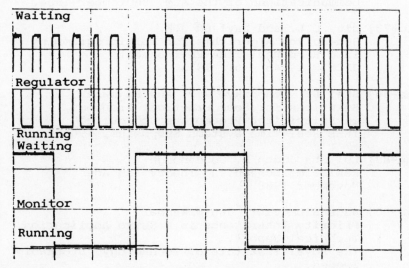

Figure 5. Periodic Performance with HDS Run-Time System.

6 CONCLUSION

The scheduling of jobs with hard deadlines is important in real-time embedded systems. It is widely recognized that the capabilities of traditional Ada tasking implementations in this respect are insufficient and have made it difficult to implement real-time systems using traditional Ada tasking. Therefore it seems obvious that tasking is one the areas of Ada that will be changed in the 9X programme.

This paper has described the drawbacks of traditional Ada tasking implementations and a possible way to releave these problems, viz. by having priority ordered entry queues, by always selecting the highest priority task in select statements and by implementing priority inheritance in the tasking kernel.

The test results from the implemented servo demonstrate the benefits gained from using the implemented HDS run-time system. The utilization of the hardware is increased and a more deterministic system behaviour is obtained.

REFERENCES

[Car-84] Carlow, G. D.
         Architecture of the Space Shuttle
         Primary Avionics Software System
         Communications of the ACM, September 1984.

[Liu-73] Liu, C.L. and Layland J.W.
         Scheduling Algorithms for Multiprogramming
         in a Hard Real-Time Environment
         JACM20(1):46 - 61, 1973.

[Sha-86] Sha, L., Lehoczky, J.P. and Rajkumar, R.
         Solutions for Some Practical Problems
         in Prioritized Preemptive Scheduling
         IEEE Real-Time Systems Symposium, 1986.

[Sha-88] Lui Sha, John B. Goodenough
         Real-Time Scheduling Theory and Ada
         November 1988.

[Blo-90] Hans Blomqvist, Jan Wikander
         Priority Inheritance in a Servo Application,
         Technical Report.
         The Royal Institute of Technology, Stockholm,
         Sweden.
         TRITA-MAE-1990-5, ISSN 0282-0048

PART IX: Distribution

Ada as a Tool: Experiences and Results

A. M. LEVY, J. VAN KATWIJK, A.J. VAN DE GOOR

Delft University of Technology, Delft, The Netherlands

1. INTRODUCTION

Software for a modern programming system typically comprises a set of objects which may be distributed over a distributed architecture, such as a network of microprocessors. Designing software for reliable and safe systems for such architectures is a difficult and error-prone task, regardless of the programming language being used to express the design. This even holds when using Ada as the implementation language.

The increase in size and complexity of software projects over recent years has made the support of Software Development Environments (SDEs) indispensable. Such SDEs are intended to provide assistance in the development of large systems, by supporting tools, and databases for the storage of project-related data. It is generally believed that properly equipped and applied SDE's allow improved software quality and productivity, particularly as they integrate automated support for more and more of the products, activities and practices of the software development process (Henderson (1987) and Henderson (1989)).

At Delft University of Technology we have been involved in Ada for several years. One of our objectives is to provide a methodology for constructing Ada programs for potentially distributed targets, together with automated support for this methodology. In Levy et al. (1989a) we discuss our proposed methodology in some detail, in Levy et al. (1989b) we discuss the architecture of a support environment.

The basic objectives of the project, reported in this paper, are: (i) to investigate the Ada language as a designing and prototyping tool; (ii) to investigate the Ada language as an implementation language; (iii) to identify the stages in the life cycle which must be supported by additional tools in a SDE system; (iv) to define the requirements to these tools; (v) to evaluate some drawbacks concerning the Ada language we have met during the design process.

We start the paper with a brief discussion of the problems when using Ada as a language for writing distributed applications, we then give a brief description of the methodology and the architecture of our envisaged support environment. Next, we discuss our experiences with the design and implementation of two applications, a distributed file system, and a generalized distributed resource manager. We conclude the paper with some conclusions and directions for future research.

2. THE PROBLEM

The Ada language provides support for modularity, real-time programming and exception handling. The (proper) use of the various language features enforces a strict programming discipline with the intention of making programs more readable, reliable, portable and modular.

It is well known that the Ada language has some drawbacks as an implementation language for distributed applications. One of the most well known drawbacks is that unrestricted use of tasking requires memory areas to be shared between tasks. Writing distributed applications enforces a limited and controlled use of such features. Furthermore, is the interpretation of time in distributed systems, especially in handling timed entry calls and timed accept statements over different nodes in the system is known to present difficulties.

On the other hand, the language contains quite some features that make it a language worthwhile to attempt to use it in such applications: (i) it provides packaging support, providing a suitable means for data encapsulation and information hiding; (ii) it provides separate compilation support, incorporating consistency checking over separately compiled modules; (iii) it provides support for concurrency and process interaction.

Distributed systems impose additional problems, in particular the exploitation of the computing power of all available processor units. Writing a distributed system that optimally uses the available computing power of all nodes, is therefore a hard and tedious task. A single programming language (even the Ada language) cannot be the only tool used in the development process. Particular activities that need to be supported, but that are beyond the expressive power of the Ada language, are:
(i) modeling the system;
(ii) building the system using a library of reusable components;
(iii) simulating and profiling the system.

We believe that, in order to support such activities , a support system should be available. The support system should assist the designer in making deci-sions in the design process, such as an allocation strategy, load balancing and object grain size. Furthermore, the environment should allow rapid sys-tem building, such that changes can be made quickly whenever some of the requirements above are not fullfilled.

3. DESIGN AND SUPPORT
In this section we describe the methodology and some features of the SEPDS support system, a *S*upport *E*nvironment for *P*rototyping *D*istributed *S*ystems.

3.1 The EDFG Modeling Concept
The EDFG (Extended Data Flow Graph) modeling approach is a trade-off between the strictly formal models that were used in e.g. Jard et al. (1988) and Nord and Pfenning (1989), and the informal icon-oriented models de-scribed in e.g. Buhr et al. (1989). In this subsection we briefly describe the basic features of our modeling approach.

We propose a top-down development. In our approach a prototype initially represents the system at a high level of abstraction. The objects in this prototype, encoded as EDFG's, encapsulate complex structures of data and computations. In a refinement process, these objects are refined in terms of other subgraphs, each representing an object in greater detail. The process is repeated until either the desired level of detail is achieved or until all actors have become primitive data flow graphs.

An EDFG is a bipartite directed graph in which two types of node exist, actors and links. *Actors* describe operations, *links* receive data from a (single) actor and transmit values to one or more actors using connecting arcs, called edges. A node (either an actor or a link) is enabled for execution when the appropriate input arcs contain tokens. A node that is enabled consumes tokens from its input arcs; it produces tokens on its output arcs. The set of input links to an actor defines the *input firing semantic sets* (IFS), and the set of output links define the *output firing semantic set* (OFS). We define an actor a in the EDFG as a 5-tuple

$$a = \{(\delta(a), PRE(a), POST(a), FUN(a), TYPE(a))\}$$

To use EDFGs as a performance analysis tool, it is necessary to associate with each event the time it takes for the event to execute. $\delta(a)$ refers to the execution time associated with the actor a. $\delta(a)$ may be constant for any firing of the actor, it may, however, depend on specific data values used by the actor. It therefore can be used to model (real-time) systems which take a finite amount of time to complete their execution.

PRE(a) specifies the conditions which need to be satisfied for the actor *a* to be enabled. This precondition is expressed as an arbitrary logic function over the IFS and OFS and allows to model situations where the IFS for an actor *a* is variable.

POST(a) refers to the post-conditions resulting from firing the actor. It specifies how the tokens are distributed over the output links of the actor after firing is complete. This field enables modeling those situations where tokens move only to a subset of links belonging to the OFS of a given actor. The logic function, implementing the field POST, is similar to the one implementing the field PRE.

FUN(a) defines the function carried out by this actor;

TYPE specifies whether or not an actor is a primitive graph. It is used to allow a description of a system at different levels of abstraction. If the actor represents a non-primitive EDFG component, then it has an inner structure associated with it. It can then be refined into a set of subgraphs. If an actor is non-primitive, then

$$\exists n, n > 1 \ such \ that \ a_i = (a_{i1}, a_{i2}, ..., a_{in})$$

Furthermore, any a_{ij}, where $a_{ij}, 0 < j \leq n$, can be nonprimitive itself, in which case this a_{ij} can be further refined, allowing a multilevel description of a complex system.

The basic advantage of using the functions *PRE* and *POST* is that we can introduce *state* links $l_i, l_i \in IFS$, which preserve their token when the actor is fired. During the refinement process such a *state link* can be replicated allowing more than one actor to use a state component which is held by the same *state link*. This concept allows encapsulation of the actor, links, and state links into an independent object, in which the state links represent some internal state of the actor, and the other links define the interface with the other actors.

The EDFG approach is discussed in detail in Levy et al. (1989a).

3.2 Architecture of the SEPDS system
The SEPDS system is designed to support the systematic construction, prototyping, and simulation of distributed systems in terms of EDFG's. Furthermore, it provides assistance in mapping the remaining nodes onto Ada program texts.

General requirements for distributed systems are difficult to determine, and their feasibility is hard to establish without constructing an executable model. Distributed systems impose additional problems of exploiting the computing power of the available processor units, therefore a support system should assist the designer in making decision about allocation strategy, load balancing and object grain size. In order to provide the required support, our SEPDS system consists of three main subsystems.

(i) A *User Interface* (UI) - provides tools for convenient interface with the designer, programmer or customer (not further discussed here);
(ii) A *Prototyping Tools Subsystem* (PTS) - provides all the tools for top-down refinement and modification of the prototype;
(iii) A *Simulator* - provides the tools for simulating, executing, debugging and profiling the prototype.

The Prototyping tools subsystem

The primary purpose of the prototyping tools subsystem is to provide a set of tools with which EDFG's can be constructed and decomposed and for which tools are available to rapidly construct prototypes of the system to be built. The subsystem consists of two basic parts : (1) an EDFG modeler and (2) a Template manager. The EDFG modeler provides tools for building and maintaining an Extended Data Flow Graph such as:
(i) A *Graph Editor* (GE) which helps the programmer in drawing and editing the model. It furthermore provides assistance during the partitioning process, saving, displaying, and maintaining the dependency traces between the actors.
(ii) An *EDFG Top-Down Modeler* (TDM) which builds the model under directions of the programmer. It assists the designer to decompose a single actor or a part of EDFG model into a set of simpler actors and provides assistance in connecting them via the primitive actors.
(iii) An *Actor Base Manager* (ABM) which maintains a data base of actors which can be used during the editing process. During the design process the programmer can obtain a list of the actors, available according to some classification Through the Graph Editor, he can retrieve the relevant actors, modify them, delete some actors, etc. in order to simplify the modeling process.

The template manager comprises the tools for maintaining the software base and building an executable prototype. The software base provides reusable software components for realizing a given EDFG model. One of the major problems is to achieve a systematical classification (Prieto-Diaz and Freeman (1987)) of the templates (Ada generics in our case) in order to achieve a reasonable level of reusability. A second problem is to provide Ada generic templates for the various actors and to link the actors and generics together. We are building two tools that support in the construction of Ada code.

(i) A template library manager, which maintains templates in an object-based database. We are looking for knowledge based systems to support the process of identifying reusable templates and connecting these templates to each other.

(ii) A prototype builder, which supports in retrieving the templates from the template library manager, and which supports the construction of stubs.

If a template does not exist or cannot be constructed, the relevant actor should be decomposed into a set of simpler actors. Finally, if the template library does not contain generic modules to implement the required functionality, the user is asked to implement the actor himself. An example of a resulting actor, encoded in Ada is presented in section 4.1.

The simulation subsystem

In an actual implementation, rare events (such as disordering of messages on a link) are unlikely to appear. Validation of a prototype requires some investigation of error handling in erroneous situations, however. Analyzing the possible behaviour of the prototype requires some kind of experimentation. In such situations, simulation is much more powerful than implementing a prototype. Simulation makes it possible to control parameters and to observe a distributed system in a way much better than would be possible on a implemented system. For instance, parameters such as *time* cannot be tampered with on an implemented system. Global time is an abstraction that may not be found in a really distributed system, but many distributed properties are stated with an implicit global time in mind, and simulation makes it possible to produce this global time.

The basic goal of the Simulator is to analyze performance of distributed systems. It is assumed that an existing application is already partitioned and the result is a distributed EDFG prototype that implements the same functionality as its sequential ancestor. If the distributed prototype runs faster and scales effectively to the number of available processors, the job of parallelization is essentially complete. However, in the majority of the cases the prototype does not run efficiently in parallel and does not effectively use the processors that are available. At that time a really difficult task begins, the program must be modified or redesigned entirely to take advantage of the available distributed hardware. The purpose of the Simulator subsystem is to provide a set of tools with which such tuning is possible.

The SEPDS Simulator subsystem contains three parts, a *debugger*, a *tracer* and a *profiler*. The debugger allows a designer to observe the behavior of an implementation. It has facilities (borrowed from the local Ada compiler) for initiating execution of an prototype and displaying results or trace information.

Using the information implicitly built in the EDFG prototype, the SEPDS profiler is able to execute each actor separately without modifying the prototype or linking any intrusive software. The SEPDS profiler consists of a kernel and profiling utilities. The kernel resembles an operating system kernel, with a two level scheduler and a set of primitives. The object scheduler dispatches the objects for executing. The scheduling discipline is specified by the designer to define the order of object execution. The allocation scheme specifies a mapping between the objects in the prototype and the available processors. During the profiling process, the designer can change both parameters, whenever appropriate. According to the allocation scheme and scheduling discipline the scheduler picks up the current object and sends it to the actor scheduler. For each object a set of actors, ready for execution is identified. The actor scheduler executes these actors according to the target EDFG and calls the appropriate primitives for moving or sending the tokens from the input channels to the output channels relevant to the EDFG.

After an actor has been fired, the profiling data for that actor is recorded. There are several kind of profiles concerning the design process:
(i) the parallelism profile, which shows the available parallelism in the current prototype;
(ii) the actor profile, which shows the execution and the frequency of execution of the actors;
(iii) the synchronization profile, which shows the time needed for synchronization between the objects;
(iv) the communication profile which shows the overhead concerning the communication through the communication medium;

Based on data of these profiles, the user is able to tune the parameters in his design and to rerun the simulation in order to investigate improvements.

4. EXPERIENCES
In order to validate our approach, we performed some experiments. The first

experiment, described extensively in Levy et al.(1989d) relates to distributing the Minix filesystem; the second experiment which is described extensively in Levy et al. (1989c), concerns the distribution of a general resource manager on a set of computersystems.

4.1 An implementation of the Minix filesystem As an exercise, we re-implemented the Minix filesystem in Ada, using our design and modeling approach. We made this choice for two reasons: (i) it is a traditional filesystem; (ii) it has been designed as an independent (C) program.

The goal of the experiment was to investigate our design method as a whole and to implement a complete program, in order to investigate the use of Ada in distributed applications.

As an example, we present the inode manager as it resulted from the design.

```
task body INODE_MANAGER  is
    . . .
begin
  loop
    select
      accept GET_INODE(DEV:  in DEV_NR; NUMB:  in INODE_NR;
                           RIP:  out INODE_NR)  do
        - Search the inode table both for (DEV, NUMB)
        - and a free slot.
        I_HANDLER(RIP).LOCK;
                         - synchronization with the handler
        - perform the necessary actions with the inode
        I_HANDLER(RIP).UNLOCK;
                         - release the handler
      end GET_INODE;
    or
      accept PUT_INODE(RIP:  in INODE_NR)  do
        I_HANDLER(RIP).LOCK;
                         - synchronization with the handler
        I_PUT(RIP);    - call the internal procedure
        I_HANDLER(RIP).UNLOCK;
                         - release the handler
      end PUT_INODE;
    or
        . . .
TASK BODY I_HANDLER  is
```

```
    FL: BOOLEAN;                    – locking flag
begin
  loop
    select
    accept ACQ_INODE(RIP: in INODE_NR; FLOCK: in BOOLEAN;
                INO: out INODE_STRUCT) do
    FL := FLOCK;
    – Grant the inode data
    end ACQ_INODE;
    if FL = TRUE then      – Lock is necessary
        accept REL_INODE(RIP: in INODE_NR;
                INO: in INODE_STRUCT) do
        INODE(RIP) := INO;
        end REL_INODE;
    end if;
  or
    accept LOCK do
        bf accept UNLOCK;
    end LOCK;
    . . .
```

Particular problems we experienced with constructing the resulting Ada programs are basically well known:
(i) inconsistencies with the Ada tasking model;
(ii) implementation problems.

The problems with the tasking model are more important than the implementation problems. They include:
(i) Incompleteness of the Ada virtual machine. The file system needs information about the tasks interacting with it. Such information is the task life cycle, parent or child task attributes, access control information for the task, etc. In traditional systems, the operating system kernel supplies such information through system or procedure calls. Using the Ada tasking model rather than a special kernel as the basis for a multitasking system, it is not clear how to obtain the necessary information. One often gets the feeling that the file system is developed over an incomplete virtual machine.
(ii) Interaction between tasks. Designing a server based on a "dispatcher-driver" approach, we clash with a "forwarding" problem. The dispatcher must pass the request to the selected driver to increase the parallelism into the server. Such forwarding is not in accordance with the synchronous nature of the rendezvous mechanism.

The second category of problems primarily consists of problems with the "C" language, bitwise operators and data manipulation. Due to space constraints we restrict the discussion to a single example, indicating the mapping of inodes to Ada records.

```
WORD:  constant := 2;                    – Storage unit is byte
–
– Represent inode type as a record
–
type INODETYPE  is record
    I_TYPE: INT16  range 0..15;          – Inode type(file type)
    I_UID_BIT: BOOLEAN;                  – UID bit
    I_GID_BIT: BOOLEAN;                  – GID bit
    I_RWX0: INT16  range 0..7;           – RWX field 1
    I_RWX1: INT16  range 0..7;           – RWX field 2
    I_RWX2: INT16  range 0..7;           – RWX field 3
end record;
–
– Define inode type fields representation
–
for INODETYPE  use record
    I_RWX2 at 0 * WORD  range 0..2;
    I_RWX1 at 0 * WORD  range 3..5;
    I_RWX0 at 0 * WORD  range 6..8;
    I_GID_BIT at 0 * WORD  range 10..10;
    I_UID_BIT at 0 * WORD  range 11..11;
    I_TYPE at 0 * WORD  range 12..15;
```

The Ada file server has been configured with two driver tasks for each level and an additional network handling package. The resulting fileserver is considerably slower than the original C Minix fileserver. Generally speaking, performance of a single computer implementation is about one third of the original C server. The main reason is the overhead with task interaction, the number of tasks in the system is far too large. Especially, the tasks dealing with inodes interact heavily.

4.2 A distributed resource manager
The second experiment we want to describe is the design of a general distributed resource manager, using prototyping and simulation. The emphasis in this experiment has been on simulation of the system, taking the number of available CPU's as a parameter.

According to the EDFG approach, a distributed system is described as a set of communicating EDFGs, where each EDFG represents an object which belongs to a class called *server*, or to a class called *client*. The distributed system consists of N client processes separated in K groups (N > K), where processes in the same group are treated equally. For each resource one may specify the number of processes that may simultaneously access that resource. Processes in different groups have exclusive access to that resource.

A server object called *Resource Controller* (RC), schedules the processes in the system according to the above requirements. The processes interact with this Resource Controller via two kinds of requests. *Acq*, a request for acquiring the resource and *Rel*, a request for releasing the resource.

A distributed version of a Resource Controller has been designed using the prototype SEPDS environment. During the design, the server object has been partitioned in two steps:
(i) according to the kind of user requests (Acq and Rel), as a result we obtain two kinds of servers - RC.Acq and RC.Rel;
(ii) according to the number of the available resource units (NUNITS). As a result we obtain a number of Acq and Rel servers - $RC.Acq_i$ and $RC.Rel_i$, where $1 < i \leq NUNITS$.

The resulting distributed system consists of a set of user processes (UPs), a set of Rel servers and a set of Acq servers. The choice of a partioning of the Acq server is influenced by the basic synchronization overhead, due to the distributed mutual access requirements. On a balanced system with more than one server, the speed up is - as can be expected due to the synchronization overhead - not linear with the number of additional CPU's.

In our experiences, through EDFG modeling a system can be decomposed into a set of objects, where the objects communicate with each other by message passing. Furthermore, each object can be refined and partitioned. This requires a coordination among objects which becomes an important issue for simulating distributed systems. The resulting EDFG is easily mapped onto the Ada language. The communication actors can be mapped directly onto entry calls and accept statements. The function associated with an actor is implemented as a subprogram, different objects are implemented as different tasks or packages.

5. RESULTS AND CONCLUSIONS
The basic results of using the SEPDS approach in an Ada environment can be summarized as follows:

(i) the approach is tied in with the EDFG model, it depends on the SEPDS;
(ii) SEPDS is a system for rapid prototyping, therefore the purpose of the profiling tool is to assist the designer in taking decisions about the level of partitioning, the allocation scheme, the task granularity, etc. It cannot be used as a very precise profiling tool and for correct timing measurement.
(iii) The Ada language has some drawbacks (as discussed earlier). Nevertheless, we believe that the language is better suited for this purpose than other languages. Especially the possibility of creating libraries of reusable generic components proved to be very useful.

Currently, we have some tools ready in our envisaged support environment, and we are gaining experience in modeling Ada constructs for the implementation of a large set of basic actors.

REFERENCES

R. Buhr, G. Karam, C. Hayes, and C. Woodside (1987). Software CAD: A revolutionary approach. *IEEE Trans. Software Eng.*, SE-15, March 1989.

R. Prieto-Diaz and P. Freeman (1987). Classifying Software for Reusability. *IEEE Software*, 4(1), January 1987.

P. Henderson (1987) Editor. *Proceedings of the first SIGSOFT/SIGPLAN Software Engineering Symposium on Practical Software Development Environments*, ACM SIGPLAN Notices, January 1987.

P. Henderson (1989) Editor. *Proceedings of the second SIGSOFT/SIGPLAN Software Engineering Symposium on Practical Software Development Environments*, ACM SIGPLAN Notices, February 1989.

C. Jard, J. Monin, and R. Groz (1988). Development of Veda, a prototyping tool for distributed algorithms. *IEEE Trans. Software Eng,*, SE-14(3), March 1988.

A. Levy, H. Corporaal, and J. van Katwijk (1989a). Simulation and top-down development of distributed systems. *Submitted for publication.*

A. Levy, J. van Katwijk, G. Pavlides, and F. Tolsma (1989b). SEPDS: A support environment for prototyping distributed systems. Accepted for *First International Conference on System Integration*, New Jersey USA, April 1990.

A. Levy, J. van Katwijk, G. Pavlides, and A. Kostov (1989c). Profiling the Synchronization Overhead in a class of distributed systems. *Submitted for publication.*

A. Levy and G. Pavlides (1989d). An Ada based distributed file system. *Submitted for publication.*

R. Nord and F. Pfenning (1989). The Ergo attribute system. In Henderson (1989).

Ada in Use: Experiencing Design and Implementation of a Portable Man Machine Interface

Luigi Vedani

Flavio Cassinari

Andrea Di Maio

TXT Ingegneria Informatica S.p.A, Vin Socrate 41, 20128 Milano, Italy.

Abstract

This paper describes an experience of design and implementation of a Man-Machine Interface (MMI) for a Command, Control, Communication and Intelligence System (C3I) conforming to industrial standards. This was one of the first large industrial Ada projects developed in TXT and we decided to exploit a major technology transfer from European research projects we were involved in. The design methodology was based on the Virtual Node approach, combined with an extensive use of Ada as PDL and object oriented design techniques. A first implementation of the system was done for VAX under VMS; then the system was retargetted to a Unix-based minicomputer. The paper presents the main issues concerning design, implementation and porting experiences.

1. The application

MMI is a menu-driven screen-oriented interface for VT100-like terminals. Its "look and feel" conforms to CCITT standards that reserves different screen areas for command input, data entry and monitoring.

MMI is a fairly complex application, mixing compiler and data entry techniques with communication handling and screen-oriented terminal management. and it consists of two parts: a development environment with a Form Description Language to describe data entry forms, a compiler and a form library manager; and a runtime environment, consisting of a form driver, a command handler and communication facilities. A significant aspect of the runtime environment is that it is structured in several processes with different lifespans: some of them are activated upon bootstrapping, e.g. network communication management, whereas others (such as user interaction handlers) run upon login.

We will mainly point out the design and the implementation of the runtime environment, as it presents the most interesting topics for our purposes.

The main attributes of the runtime environment were:

☐   *ROBUSTNESS*: MMI operates in real-time (compared to the human interaction with the system), must be reliable and must prevent unauthorized accesses to the system. Ada strong typing, exception handling and tasking offered us effective means to enforce these features.

☐   *PORTABILITY and CHANGEABILITY*: possible requirement modifications had to be taken into account together with the need for retargetting the runtime environment during the development of the system.

☐   *EARLY PROTOTYPING*: uncertainty about functional requirements and the target environment led us to prototype the most part of the system quite early in the lifecycle.

2. The design phase

During the design we had to choose a methodology that helped us in developing for portability.

The traditional approach to design such a system is *multiprogramming* : the system is designed as a set of communicating Ada programs, each one mapped onto a single operating system process, which we will call Physical Node (PN). Unfortunately it implies major disadvantages for both robustness and portability.

First of all, interface checking between different subsystems supported by high-level languages (and in particular by Ada) is lost if they communicate or synchronize using operating system primitives.

Actually the interprocess communication (IPC) primitives provided by most of the operating system can exchange only simple data types, such as integers and characters [Bach 86] [Leffler 89] [VMS 84]. Therefore the usual solution is to define a common package replicated in different Ada programs that declare message types. The compiler ensures that the format of the message is the same even in different memory spaces, because the types are the same: "UNCHECKED_CONVERSION" may then be used to and from message strings to be passed using operating system primitives.

A second problem concerns synchronization in the communication protocol supporting task-to-task communication.

Usually operating systems provide a variety of communication and synchronization primitives: synchronous, asynchronous, blocking, non-blocking, and so on. This requires a considerable initial effort in selecting a subset of these primitives and understanding the assumptions they imply. Moreover, each operating system has its own features so it is nearly impossible to define a 'common interface' generic enough to permit full portability on different kinds of systems.

A third problem of the multiprogramming approach is low configuration flexibility.

The allocation of subsystems to (Ada) programs is made too early during the design process, whereas it would be useful to guarantee a certain degree of flexibility in order to allow cheap reconfiguration of subsystems, due to load balancing, functional changes, etc. Another consequence is decreased portability: if the system is to be ported onto different machines, major parts have to be reimplemented.

Because of such constraints we selected a *monoprogramming* approach by adapting the novel *Ada Virtual Node* method [Atkinson et al. 88] whose most important feature is that it supports the development of the whole application in a single (multitasking) Ada program, thus enforcing Ada mechanisms for communication and synchronization. The AVN method is based on the identification, during the design of the system, of different "logical nodes" with potentially different requirements in terms of computing resources, life-span, functionalities and so on. Such disjoint nodes (Virtual Nodes) are expressed by proper abstractions featuring high internal cohesion and low node coupling.

Virtual Nodes can be completely defined in terms of Ada concepts. In the most general case they are the transitive closure of a procedure in an Ada library; the units of such closure must be compliant with a set of composition rules which provide the Virtual Node with the required properties.

In order to be such, Virtual Nodes must possess certain functional properties. The first is complete encapsulation of internal state, that can be accessed through a proper interface. Another property is the lack of reference to shared objects among Virtual Nodes; the third property is that each Virtual Node must have its own thread of control.

These properties are enforced by proprietary tools that classify library units and check conformance to the above rules.

Communication between Virtual Nodes is constrained to happen via *remote entry calls*; remote entries are those declared in a task contained in an interface package provided by a Virtual Node. Such entry calls can be called by other Virtual Nodes if the interface package is visible to them ("withed"). The communication protocol is then the Ada rendezvous model.

Since Virtual Nodes are functional abstractions they do not require any immediate mapping onto Physical Nodes. Therefore the whole application can be designed as a single Ada program made of many communicating Virtual Nodes, where the synchronization and communication mechanism used is Ada tasking.

The mapping activity can be delayed to a *configuration phase* that follows the design and the implementation of the Virtual Nodes library. After this configuration phase, that is supported by an automatic source level transformation tool, each set of Virtual Nodes allocated to a Physical Node is transformed into a separate Ada program: the remote entry calls that happen to cross the boundaries of a Physical Node are (automatically) translated into calls to primitives provided by a standard interface that implement an interprocess communication protocol semantically coherent to the Ada rendezvous on a given execution environment.

Strong type checking is enforced at the boundaries of communicating subsystems, and a single interprocess communication scheme with well defined semantics (i.e. the Ada rendezvous) is used. Porting from one system to another just requires reimplementation of a simple software layer handling the remote rendezvous implementation.

In our project the first effort was to recognize self-containined components of the system and the services offer and require. We divided the runtime environment in 'terminal controller' components like a Unix shell and 'application services' waiting for messages (commands, data, etc.) from the terminal shells and talking with local or remote applications. Each component had its own control thread and the communication interface was easily defined as a set of remote entries.

Early prototyping was made easier: a first version configured as a single Ada program was usable quite early after design phase to assess and validate many functional aspects of the system. Debugging of this version was eased by Ada debuggers, that can handle in a straightforward way multitasking programs. After the implementation phase, the program was configured onto several Physical Nodes according to load balancing, efficiency, life-span and so on.

This methodology is theoretically sound and proved to be effective on some case studies, but this might be the first time it is used in an industrial context.

It is interesting to notice that many of the properties of Virtual Nodes are those required by *object-oriented* design methods [Booch 87] [Meyer 88], which therefore are good candidate for Virtual Node based developments.

In our application, Virtual Nodes were well specified in terms of Booch diagrams, PDL text and natural language descriptions.

Our revised design standard combines now the Booch design methodology, the use of Ada as PDL and the Ada Virtual Node approach.

3. Some problems

The AVN approach is based on some basic assumptions. The first one is that the underlying operating system correctly interacts with the compiler-supplied Ada run time support (RTS): this is essential when designing the remote rendezvous protocol (see above). Unfortunately it is possible that something do no behave as expected. This depends on the implementation strategy chosen by the compiler producer. If each Ada task is implemented as an operating system process no problem should arise, but at present all the compiler producers map a (multitasking) Ada program onto a single executable image linked with the Ada RTS. In this case Ada tasking may conflict with the operating system. Several scenarios are possible depending on the RTS scheduling techniques: in the most cases, when the operating system schedules the process, the RTS chooses a task to be executed, but if this task performs a "blocking" system call, like a suspensive receive on a mailbox, all the tasks in the program might be blocked; unfortunately topic of task blocking is not explicitly tackled by the LRM and therefore let to implementation strategies.

Usually program blocking should not happen performing standard calls as in LRM Section 14 for Text Input Output operations on standard input or standard output, but unfortunately this is not the behaviour of all compilers. Therefore careful attention had to be paid in the implementation of the remote rendezvous protocol; nevertheless such concerns were limited to a minor portion of the system thanks to the adopted approach.

Another problem in the design phase was found to be the extensive use of the Ada PDL. It involves too much detail, and some premature decisions have to be taken in the early phases of the project. In this sense the design may result too "rigid" and implementation dependent features may lead to unnecessary iterations of the design process.

4. The implementation

During this phase, we introduced new staff that did not participate in the design phase. The main input for these people was the PDL-based design document. They built the Virtual Node library in a short time, performing program testing and evaluation of the single program configuration on a VAX under VMS. The design team, in the meanwhile, coped with low-level aspects of the system like interprocess communication on the target computer and terminal handling for the final configuration. As mentioned above, because of the PDL, premature decisions forced us to do some slight changes in the interfaces; nevertheless none of these problems obliged us to change components outside certain Virtual Nodes. In fact the Virtual Nodes plus the object-oriented design techniques enhanced modularity and information hiding of the software system: the most relevant changes were the addition of default parameters to interface procedures.

Last but not least we experienced all the usual disadvantages of the use of Ada on today's computer systems; requirements are greater than with other programming languages. The hardware must be oversized and sometimes the only solution is to increase the number of workstations available for the implementors team, with increasing costs in hardware and software -also considering the higher cost of Ada compilers and support environments.

The costs needed for the start-up of an Ada software factory and for the training of people are surely the main reasons for the relatively little use of Ada in the non defense application areas.

5. Retargetting experience

Upon request of our customer we retargetted MMI from the VAX/VMS implementation to a Unix one. Critical aspects in the MMI systems were interprocess communication and terminal I/O management. Therefore the main activity was to understand the new compiler and the interaction of this one with the Unix operating system. We prepared several benchmarks, emulating load and interaction of our software with the operating system and stressing it by performing contemporary terminal I/O and message sending and receiving from queues.

We ran these benchmarks on different Unix systems, both BSD and System V, using different compilers, namely: Alsys Ada and VADS Ada Development System on Sun workstations, DEC-Ada on a VAX/VMS, Motorola System V/68 Ada Host Development System on a Motorola workstation.

As far as terminal I/O is concerned, we experienced different and somewhat surprising situations.

One compiler at a first glance seemed to be input-blocking, but setting up the terminal in 'cbreak' mode magically unblocked the program (no reference was found in the manuals). For people not familiar with UNIX jargon, 'cbreak' mode [Thomas 86] is the setting of UNIX terminal driver that enables (program) availablility of characters typed on the keyboard as soon as a key is struck and not upon striking of a line terminator, e.g. the "return" key.

Another compiler needed the insertion of a C library procedure call as the first statement of the "main" procedure, setting up a tricky I/O decoupling using the UNIX "ioctl" system call.

The case of IPC services, mainly sockets and mailboxes, was even less clear. In one case we had a severe blocking problem calling IPC routines of a System V implementation. In the example below the RTS scheduler serviced only the task calling **function** NOBLOCK, and preempting the other one:

```
procedure STARVING_SOMEONE is
    ....
function NOBLOCK return INTEGER;
pragma INTERFACE(C, NOBLOCK);
------------------------------
--significant part of the C code:
--   #include < sys/ipc.h>
--   int
--   noblock()
--   { .....
--       /* read from a message queue with nowait option,
--          more explanations for non UNIXists on [Thomas 86]*/
--       status = msgrcv(id, msgbuf, size, 0, IPC_NOWAIT);
--       return(status);
--   }
------------------------------
    ....
task body GREEDY is
begin
accept START;
  loop
    exit when (NOBLOCK > 0);
  end loop;
```

```
    RECEIVED_SOMETHING;
  end GREEDY;
    ....
  task body STARVED is
  begin
  accept START;
    loop
      DO_SOMETHING_ELSE;
    end loop;
  end STARVED;
  - -main- - - - - - - - - - - - - - - - - - - - - - - - - -
  begin
    GREEDY.START;
    STARVED.START;
  end STARVING_SOMEONE;
```

The "NOBLOCK" routine performs via a C interface a non-blocking system call (msgrcv) reading a message from a message queue. The "GREEDY" task spinloops calling "NOBLOCK", then does something else. The "STARVED" task never receives the control because the Ada RTS of that implementation (that means: the compiler plus the RTS plus the operating system) services only "GREEDY". The same behaviour occured swapping the synchronization ".START" entry call.

We had to solve the starvation as follows:

```
  task body GREEDY is
  begin
  accept START;
    loop
      exit when (NOBLOCK > 0);
      - - the following statement, as side effect,
      - - force task rescheduling so RTS feeds the starved task:
      delay 0.1;
    end loop;
    RECEIVED_SOMETHING;
  end GREEDY;
```

We were a lot disappointed in discovering that using such a standard programming language with proper validation procedures drives programmers, in the practical use, to invent somewhat tricky calls or to bypass standard definitions (LRM Section 14 in the example above), writing their own I/O packages.

It seems that there are sometimes some incompatibilities between vendor supplied RTS and the underlying operating system of the host computer, such as if compiler vendors straightforwardly port bare-machine RTS onto general purpose operating system, without carrying out proper investigations about their interaction.

After sorting out all these detailed problems, thanks to the Virtual Node approach and the implied configuration flexibility, the main activity was to group Virtual Nodes into the actual communicating programs (i.e. Physical Nodes) that have to run separately on the target Unix machine as separate processes. Once implemented the remote rendezvous protocol for the specific target, we just configured the Virtual Nodes according to the life-span requirements: Virtual Nodes implementing non-stop activities were allocated to certain Physical Nodes, whereas Virtual Nodes managing single MMI sessions were allocated to other Physical Nodes, to be executed upon user login.

Other work about retargetting is in progress, and we have confidence that our MMI, after a tuning phase, will be available on almost all the compilers we benchmarked.

6. Conclusions

The experience made during this project confirmed that practical use of Ada in the development of system software is not a trivial task. The design methodology chosen may lead the designer to accept unconscious assumptions about the behaviour of the compiler, but unfortunately Ada compiler implementations differ, thus interactions between Ada tasking implementation and operating system features are to be evaluated in the early phases of the lifecycle.

As the use of Ada for "host based" applications, i.e. those applications running on the top of a multitasking operating system, increases, the Ada LRM should include a section defining the correct behaviour of an Ada program interacting with the host operating system.

Moreover we think that Ada 9X should take this topic into account, extending the standard definition and the validation suite.

We suggest the following possible improvements:

- Ada bindings for operating system, at least like POSIX Ada Binding P1003.5 when released [POSIX 89], should be included in the language standard.

- Different validation suites for cross and for host-based compilers.

- Define a standard interface for the Ada RTS so that programmers can freely handle tasking behaviour in critical cases.

- More commitment should be asked to the compiler producers to enrich documentation about runtime executives for Ada.

The Ada Virtual Node approach proved to be an effective way of writing retargettable applications with early prototyping requirements, and provided the only effective means to write multitasking applications for computers like VAXes and UNIX-based workstations, given the current status of commercial compilers and host-based RTS.

The final remarkable hint is that the use of Ada as PDL during the system design can lead in a quite natural way to a sensible increase of productivity.

References

[Atkinson et al. 88]

C. Atkinson, T. Moreton, A. Natali: Ada for distributed systems.
Cambridge University Press, 1988

[Booch 87]

G. Booch: Software engineering with Ada.
The Benjamin/Cummings Publishing Company Inc., 1987

[Bach 86]

M. Bach: The design of the UNIX Operating System.
Prentice Hall, 1986

[Leffler 89]

S. J. Leffler, M. K. McKusick, M. J. Karels, J. S. Quarterman: The design and
Implementation of the 4.3BSD UNIX Operating System
Addison Wesley, 1985

[Meyer 88]

B. Meyer: Object-oriented software construction.
Prentice Hall, 1988

[POSIX 89]

POSIX Ada Binding, P1003.5 Draft 2.2
IEEE-CS, May 1989

[Thomas 86]

R. Thomas, L. R. Rogers, J. L. Yates: Advanced programmer's guide to UNIX
System V
Osborne McGraw Hill, 1986

[VMS 84]

L. J. Kenah, S. F. Bate: VAX/VMS Internals and Data Structures.
Digital Equipment Corporation Press 1984

TOWARDS SUPPORTING DISTRIBUTED SYSTEMS IN ADA 9X

A.B. GARGARO
Computer Sciences Corporation
Moorestown, New Jersey, USA

S.J. GOLDSACK
Department of Computing
Imperial College London, UK

R.A. VOLZ
Department of Computer Science
Texas A&M University, USA

A.J. WELLINGS
Department of Computer Science
University of York, UK

ABSTRACT

The Ada programming language was designed to provide support for a wide range of safety-critical applications within a unified language framework, but it is now commonly accepted that the language has failed to achieve all its stated design goals. A major impediment has been the lack of language support for distributed fault-tolerant program execution.

In this paper we propose language changes to Ada which will facilitate the programming of fault-tolerant distributed real-time applications. These changes support partitioning and configuration/reconfiguration. We propose a two-tier execution model for an Ada program. One tier is concerned with partitions; it specifies the functionality of the system. The other tier provides the configuration facility; it is responsible for creating partitions, allocating them to logical processors, and reallocating as required.

1. INTRODUCTION

There is increasing use of computers that are embedded in some wider engineering application. These systems all have several common characteristics: they must respond to externally generated input stimuli within a finite and specified period; they must be extremely reliable and/or safe; they are often geographically distributed over both a local and a wide area; they may contain a very large and complex software component; they may contain processing elements which are subject to cost/size/weight constraints.

Developing software to control safety-critical applications requires programming abstractions that are unavailable in many of today's programming languages. The Ada programming language was designed to provide support for such applications within a unified language framework, but it is now commonly accepted that the language has failed to achieve all its stated design goals. Ada (as defined by ANSI/MIL-STD 1815 A), with an appropriate project support environment, has successfully addressed many of the software engineering issues associated with the production of large real-time software. It has failed, however, to satisfy applications requiring the use of multiple computers or parallel-intensive computation.

A particular concern is the language's lack of support for reliable distributed processing — although there is much continuing debate within the Ada community as to how that support should be provided. The goal of the reported work is to enable the fault tolerant programming of real-time distributed systems in a manner which is portable across Ada implementations. To achieve this, language facilities to support both *partitioning* and *configuring* must be designed. Partitioning can be defined as the structuring of Ada source code to support distributed, degraded modes, and fault-tolerant execution. Configuring can be defined as the physical allocation of a partitioned Ada program across a distributed target system.

The authors submit that partitioning and configuring are distinct activities in the design and implementation of programs and should be clearly separated. We therefore propose a two-tier execution model for an Ada program. One tier is concerned with partitions; it specifies the functionality of the system. The other tier provides the configuration facility; it is responsible for creating partitions, allocating them to logical processors, and reallocating as required. The language facilities that are developed in the reported work support this model.

2. PARTITIONING A PROGRAM

It is assumed that programs are decomposed by some design methodology into units. These units are variously known as: guardians(6), resources(1), or in the Ada community virtual nodes(2, 3, 4, 7). In this paper they will be called *partitions*.

In this proposal a partition is identified by a new library unit called a *partition*. Strictly speaking the partition library unit is the external interface to the partition; the whole partition being all the library units in the transitive closure of the context clause of the partition library unit (together with any associated subunits). As partitions can only be referenced via the partition library unit, the term partition will be used to indicate both the partition library unit and the whole partition. Figure 1 shows a partition consisting of the partition library unit and three other library units.

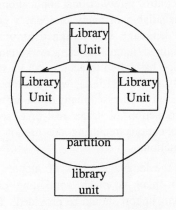

Figure 1: An Ada Partition

Clearly in following the transitive closure of partition X another partition Y may appear in a context clause. In this case that branch of the closure on partition X is concluded, as Y represents the start of another partition which is called by X.

If a library unit appears in two or more partitions then each partition has a *separate* instance of the library unit. For example if a library package, L, appears in the context clause of two partitions then two distinct instances of the package L are created. Any types declared in package L are also distinct in the two instances. This is a departure from the current Ada language standard where it is only possible to have one instance of a library package. The departure is justified to allow instances of the same partition (type) to be created by the configuration tier of the program (i.e., partition types).

In order for two or more partitions to communicate they must be able to share common type declarations. These type declarations are declared in another new type of library unit called a *public* unit. If two or more partitions name the same public library unit in their context clauses then that library unit is *shared* among the partitions.

Public library units can also be used to provide common services on all logical processors in a manner which is transparent to the application programmer. For example the traditional complex number package would be provided as a public unit.

Communication between partitions occurs by one partition calling the interface of another partition (which is declared by the partition library unit). Partitions are declared as anonymous types with an associated access type declaration. Consequently, the creation of an instance of a partition requires the action of an allocator. This is considered in Section 3.1. The important point is that a partition can only be accessed from another partition using an access variable to its partition library unit.

2.1. Public Library Units

Public library units are equivalent to invariant-state packages. A public library unit is identified by the new keyword **public** and has a specification and a body. The interface to a public unit can contain:

- types (but not access types),
- task types and task access types,
- static constants,
- subprograms,
- generic subprograms,
- packages (but they inherit the restrictions of the public unit),
- generic packages,
- generic instantiations,
- private types,
- exceptions,
- renames,
- pragmas.

The body to a public unit must have a well-defined state. This precludes the use of variables shared among the subprograms and tasks of the public because the public unit must be capable of existing at all sites in the distributed systems. It follows that context clauses for public units can only name other public units.

2.2. Partition Library Units

Partitions have a specification, a body and an initialisation part. A partition (type) can only be declared as an access type to an anonymous type. This is for two reasons:

1) references to partitions are required during reconfiguration (they will need to be passed across the distributed system at run-time)

2) an explicit access declaration cannot be an Ada library unit.

The following example illustrates how a partition (type) is declared:

```
with ...;
partition SERVER is
  -- server interface;
end SERVER;

with ...;
partition body SERVER is
  -- server body
begin
  -- initialisation section
end SERVER;
```

The notation is conceptually equivalent to:

```
with ...;
partition type SERVER_TYPE is
  -- server interface;
end SERVER_TYPE;

with ...;
partition body SERVER_TYPE is
  -- server body
begin
  -- initialisation section
end SERVER_TYPE;
type SERVER is access SERVER_TYPE;
```

Because instances of partitions can only be referenced by access variables the SERVER_TYPE cannot be explicitly named. Later where the type name is required, the new attribute 'PARTITION is used. This can be applied to any access partition type, but no partition object can be declared from the anonymous partition type.

Partition Specification

The callable interface to a partition is defined by the specification of the associated partition library unit. Potentially this interface may be called by a partition on a remote processing site. Therefore, certain restrictions are imposed on the entities that can be defined. In particular, variables and types are not allowed. Variables are not allowed because their access would require the machine of one logical processor to access the local memory of another. Types are not allowed because two or more instances of the partition would imply that the visible types would be distinct between instances. This would lead to the need for dynamic type checking. For example consider the following illustrative code.

```
partition X is
  type X1 is ..;
  procedure EXAMPLE(Z: X1);
end X;
  ...
A: X;
B: X;

-- create two instances of X accessed by A and B in
-- the configuration tier
-- A.X1 is not the same type as B.X1
T1: A.X1;
T2: B.X1; -- T1 and T2 do not have the same type

A.EXAMPLE(T1); -- legal
A:= B; -- legal, A now references a different instance
A.EXAMPLE(T1); -- illegal
```

Therefore, to avoid the need for dynamic typing, types are not allowed in the specification of a partition; they must be defined in a public unit.

A further restriction is that task types are not allowed in the specification of a partition; this is because the body of the task can have access to the internal state of the partition body. Consequently, a remotely created object could access memory located on a different logical processor. A similar argument disallows generic units.

The following list identifies those entities that can be declared in a partition specification: subprograms — as long as their parameter types are declared in a public unit or are of access partition type, tasks — as long as the parameter types to their entries are declared in a public unit or are of access partition type, packages — as long as the specifications inherit the partition specification restrictions. representation specifications, renames, some pragmas — although INLINE should be disallowed.

Partitions may include any other library units in their context clauses *except* nodes (see Section 3).

Initialisation Parameters to Partitions

Partitions can declare initialisation parameters in the specification part of their declaration. The types of these parameters are the same as those that can appear in the parameters to the visible procedures, functions and entries. Only *in* parameters are allowed.

Incomplete partition declaration

An incomplete partition declaration can be placed into the library.

Conformant partitions

A partition can be declared to have the same specification as another partition as shown in the following example.

   partition FULL_FUNCTION_SERVER **is**

   ...

   end FULL_FUNCTION_SERVER;

   partition body FULL_FUNCTION_SERVER **is**

   ...

   end FULL_FUNCTION_SERVER;

   partition DEGRADED_SERVER **is**
      FULL_FUNCTION_SERVER'PARTITION;

   partition body DEGRADED_SERVER **is**

   ...

   end DEGRADED__SERVER;

Note the use of the attribute 'PARTITION is required to name the anonymous partition type.

The above two partitions are called conformant partitions. They have the same type and therefore an access pointer to a FULL_FUNCTION_SERVER can be used to point to a DEGRADED_SERVER. Conformant partitions are useful for programming degenerate modes, alternative implementation modes (e.g., simulations), and diverse programming techniques (e.g., N-version programming).

Accessing the services provided by another partition

In order for partition A to access the services of another partition, B, it is necessary for A to name B's partition library unit in one of its context clauses. This only allows visibility of the partition type, and therefore an instance of that partition must be visible to the partition A. However, since partitions are unable to create other partitions (see section 3), a pointer to B must be passed to A at run-time. This will be done by the configuration software.

3. CONFIGURING A PROGRAM

A node is a new type of library unit; the term node is also used to indicate the transitive closure of the library units named in the node library unit context clauses. Its purpose is to collect together instances of partitions for execution on a single physical resource in the target architecture. Restricting instances of partitions to be created within node library units maintains a clear separation between the configuring (and reconfiguring) components of the application and the partitions themselves. A node has the following format:

```
with ....;
node X is
  -- node interface
end X;


with ....;
node body X is
  -- code which defines the configuration
  -- and which reconfigures when necessary
end X;
```

In a similar manner to partitions these declarations declare the access types from an anonymous node type. The attribute 'NODE is defined to allow the anonymous node type to be named in an allocator. A node can name any other library unit in its context clauses (e.g., other nodes, partitions, publics, packages). As with partitions, packages shared between nodes are replicated in each node.

3.1. Partition creation within nodes

Partitions can be created within nodes (and therefore at the same site) by declaring access variables and then creating instances of the partitions using allocators. For example:

```
with DEGRADED_SERVER;
node body X is
  -- an uninitialised partition access variable
  DS1  : DEGRADED_SERVER;

  -- an array type of 10 degraded servers access variables
  type ADS_T is array(1..10) of DEGRADED_SERVER;

  -- an array of 10 access pointers
  ADS1: ADS_T;
```

```
-- an instance of a degraded server
DS2 : DEGRADED_SERVER :=
  new DEGRADED_SERVER'PARTITION;

-- an array of 10 degraded servers
ADS2: ADS_T :=
  (1..10 => new DEGRADED_SERVER'PARTITION);

begin
  -- the following creates an instance of a degraded server
  DS1 := new DEGRADED_SERVER'PARTITION;

  -- the following creates 10 degraded servers
  ADS1 :=
    (1 .. 10 => new DEGRADED_SERVER'PARTITION);
end X;
```

Pointers to partitions can be passed to other partitions in the same node and to other nodes via the node interfaces.

3.2. Nodes and their creation

The restrictions that are placed on the interface to a node are exactly those that are placed on partition interfaces. Nodes can have initialisation parameters, and conformant nodes can be declared. Generic nodes have yet to be considered.

Any node can create another node. Node creation is achieved using an allocator. A parameter to the allocator indicates the logical processor on which the node is to be created. Only a single node can be created on one logical processor; multiple nodes per logical processor are not supported.

One node, called the *distinguished node* is created automatically by the environment.

4. SYSTEM ELABORATION AND TERMINATION

Separate load modules for each node type are created by the distributed Ada development environment. Each module is loaded onto one or more processors in the target architecture; each processor only has one load module. System start up follows but instead of the main procedure being called, the distinguished node is started by the underlying run-time support systems. The distinguished node then elaborates by the normal Ada elaboration rules. It then begins to execute. During its elaboration or execution it creates instances of its local partitions. It also creates one or more nodes indicating on which processor the node should be created. The run-time support system for the distinguished node will send a request to the run-time support system on the target logical processor indicated that the node should be created and should begin its elaboration. The thread of control in the distinguished node which requested the creation is blocked until the node has elaborated. If creation or elaboration of the required node fails (either because it does not contain a copy of the requested node, or because of an exception in the node's elaboration), then an exception is raised in the distinguished node. A successful elaboration returns the access pointer of the created node to the distinguished node. The created node may of course create other nodes and local partitions in a similar manner.

As partitions and nodes are library units, all tasks which they create will be local to the library — no task hierarchies can be distributed across the network, although task hierarchies can exist within a partition. The distributed system will terminate when all library tasks are prepared to terminate. It is beyond the scope of this paper to discuss termination in detail, however the rules for termination are the same as those presented by Hutcheon and Wellings for York Distributed Ada(5).

5. A SIMPLE EXAMPLE

The following example illustrates how a program can be partitioned and configured. A client partition (CP) reads some data from a file server partition (FSP) and outputs the data via a printer partition (PP). The file server partition uses the service of the disk partition(DP). The logical structure of the system consists of the following linked partition instances, shown in Figure 2.

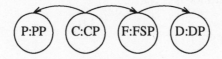

Figure 2: A simple Client/Server System

First, the partition types for the disk and the printer are declared.

```
with DISK_PUBLIC_TYPES;
partition DP is
  -- interface to the disk partition including
  procedure READ_BLOCK(..);
end DP;
partition body DP is ... end DP;
```

```
with PRINTER_PUBLIC_TYPES;
partition PP is
  -- interface to the printer partition including
  procedure PRINT(..);
end PP;
partition body PP is ... end PP;
```

Now the file server partition type is declared. It contains an access variable for the disk partition and declares a parameter which indicates the disk partition to be used:

```
with DP, FILE_SERVER_PUBLIC_TYPES;
partition FSP(D: DP); is
  -- interface to the file server including
  procedure GET_FILE(...);
end FSP;


with DISK_PUBLIC_TYPES;
partition body FSP(D: DP) is
  MY_DP : DP;
  -- procedure GET_FILE calls MY_DP.READ_BLOCK;
begin
    MY_DP := D;
end FSP;
```

Finally the client partition is declared.

```
with FSP, PP
partition CP(F: FSP; P : PP);


with FILE_SERVER_PUBLIC_TYPES;
partition body CP(F: FSP; P : PP) is
  MY_FS : FSP := F;
  MY_P : PP := P;

  task CLIENT;
  task body CLIENT is
  begin
    ...
    MY_FS.GET_FILE(...)
    MY_P.PRINT(...);
    ...
  end CLIENT;
```

```
begin
  ...
end CP;
```

The partitions now need to be created and allocated to processing resources in the physical architecture. It is assumed that there are two processors (MACHINE_A and MACHINE_B) and that the client and printer are to be created on MACHINE_A and the file server and disk partition on MACHINE_B. Two nodes are required: local and remote. Assuming the remote node contains the file server and the local node contains the client, then the remote node must pass the file server access variable to the local node.

```
with FSP;
node REMOTE is
  function MY_FS return FSP;
end REMOTE;

with DP;
node body REMOTE is

  D: DP := new DP'PARTITION;
  FS : FSP := new FSP'PARTITION(D);
  function MY_FS is
  begin
    return FS;
  end MY_FS;

begin
  ...
end REMOTE;

node LOCAL;

with CP, PP, REMOTE;
node body LOCAL is

R : REMOTE := new REMOTE'NODE(MACHINE_B);
P : PP := new PP'PARTITION;
C : CP := new CP'PARTITION(R.MY_FS, P);
begin
  ...
end LOCAL;
```

The local node is labelled as the distinguished node (possibly via a flag to the

Ada compiler) and therefore an instance is created by the environment node on MACHINE_A (at run-time).

6. CONCLUSIONS AND FUTURE WORK

This paper has presented some extensions to Ada which are designed to support the requirements for distributed fault tolerant programming. It has concentrated on a two-tiered model for partitioning and configuring an Ada program. The reference semantics for partitions and nodes enables them to be used for reconfiguring a distributed application in response to processor failure, mode changes, etc.

Although we believe that partitions and nodes provide the basis for fault-tolerant distributed programming in Ada 9X, there is still much to consider before the proposal is complete. In particular, attention must be given to:

- the role of public library units and the exact interface to partitions and nodes
- generic partitions and nodes
- standard Ada packages such as TEXT_IO, CALENDAR, and SYSTEM
- multiprogramming
- heterogeneous systems
- the integration with other 9X issues such as asynchronous transfer of control, scheduling, finalisation sections to packages etc.

Facilitating fault-tolerant programming in Ada 9X is a major challenge to the Ada language design team. Ideally this should be achievable with minimal changes to the Ada language standard, however, we believe that this is not the case. We hope that this paper will help keep distribution and fault tolerance as an important agenda topic of the language requirements process.

Acknowledgements

The ideas expressed in this paper are extensions of those developed at the 3rd International Real-Time Ada Issues Workshop. The authors would like to thank Kent Power for his help in developing some of the initial concepts.

References

1. G.R. Andrews and R.A. Olsson, "The Evolution of the SR Language", *Distributed Computing* **1**(3), pp. 133-49 (1986).

2. C. Atkinson, T. Moreton and A. Natali, *Ada for Distributed Systems*, Ada Companion Series, Cambridge University Press (1988).

3. A. Gargaro and C. Romvary, "Synthesizing Software Development Using Ada", pp. 256-265 in *Ada: The Design Choice, Proceedings Ada-Europe*

Conference, Madrid, ed. A. Alvarez, Cambridge University Press (1989).

4.   A.D. Hutcheon and A.J. Wellings, "The Virtual Node Approach to Designing Distributed Ada Programs", *Ada User* **9**(Supplement), pp. 35-42 (December 1988).

5.   A.D. Hutcheon and A.J. Wellings, "Elaboration and Termination of Distributed Ada Programs", pp. 195-204 in *Ada: The Design Choice, Proceedings Ada-Europe Conference, Madrid*, ed. A. Alvarez, Cambridge University Press (1989).

6.   B. Liskov and R. Scheifler, "Guardians and Actions: Linguistic Support for Robust, Distributed Programs", *ACM Transactions on Programming Languages and Systems* **5**(3), pp. 381-404 (July 1983).

7.   R.A. Volz, "Virtual Nodes and Units of Distribution for Distributed Ada", *Proceedings of the 3nd International Workshop on Real Time Ada Issues, ACM Ada Letters, Ada Letters* (1989).

PART X: Ada Application Case Studies

The Ada Prototype Project of the

Defense Logistics Agency

David J. Carney

Institute for Defense Analyses
Alexandria, VA USA

1. BACKGROUND

The Defense Logistics Agency (DLA) is the major provider of logistics support for the U.S. Department of Defense (DoD). The mission of DLA is to provide support throughout the DoD for a broad range of items such as materiel, weapons system components, contract administration services, and other administrative functions. In 1984-85, DLA began a 20-year long modernization program, the Logistics Systems Modernization Program (LSMP). As part of this program, DLA mandated that its computer systems would in the future be based on an open architecture plan consisting of large mainframes, medium-sized machines, and personal computers (PCs). Such a system clearly would be served by software that was portable and reusable. Therefore, DLA at the same time began a short-term project to determine the feasibility of Ada as the language for system software and for Automated Data Processing (ADP). This project, the DLA Ada Prototype Project, has lasted from 1986 to the present. It is performed by personnel at the DLA Systems Automation Center (DSAC) in Columbus, Ohio. To aid in implementing this project, DLA requested that the Institute for Defense Analyses (IDA) assist as technical advisor. In addition, TeleSoft Inc. was chosen to assist in the training of the Ada programmers. This paper reports on the activities and success of that project.

2. OVERVIEW OF THE PROJECT

One principal objective of the Ada Prototype Project was to investigate whether Ada would serve DLA as a systems programming language, and especially whether or not Ada would support an open systems architecture. The vehicle for this objective was a prototype programming project that would demonstrate both Ada's specific language features and its software engineering capabilities. In addition, to demonstrate Ada's immediate usefulness to DLA, the programming project needed to avoid being a self-contained prototype, or one which was not compatible with other existing software at DLA. While the prototype itself was a goal of the project, the major deliverable was to be the recommendation of the project personnel concerning future use of Ada at DLA. The project, therefore, contained the following component tasks:

- Analysis of the Ada and APSE (Ada Programming Support Environment) needs peculiar to DLA

- Development of a group of highly trained Ada programmers

- Creation of prototype software demonstrating Ada's viability for DLA systems needs

- Eventual integration of the project's outcome with other technology projects related to the LSMP

- Reuse of significant portions of the prototype project in future projects

The first of these tasks was begun by IDA as a preliminary assessment of need. This task was an ongoing one that underwent change as the project matured. The second task was the heart of the project. This was essentially a training phase, two intensive courses of study staffed by TeleSoft. It was specifically intended that the DLA personnel who participated in the project would then form the basis of a self-perpetuating cadre of Ada trainers and programmers. The third task consisted of the implementation in Ada of systems software to be usable throughout the Agency. In addition, it was to be engineered so that major portions would be reusable in future systems projects. At the end of the project, the developed implementation was to be demonstrated as a functional component of the DLA systems software. The fourth task, integration of the prototype with other components of the LSMP, has so far not been accomplished. This is at least partly due to a reassessment of the LSMP itself. The fifth task, reuse of portions of the prototype in other projects, is currently under way.

2.1 Hardware and Software Environment

The DLA computer facilities in Columbus consisted of a three-tier environment, comprising an IBM 3083, several Gould PowerNode 9050s, and numerous Zenith Z248 PCs. The Ada compiler for both the IBM and the Gould was developed by TeleSoft, and the compiler for the Zenith was developed by Alsys, Inc. This three-tier environment is modeled on one that was envisioned as desirable for the entire DLA LSMP. The development host for the Ada Project was the Gould computer.

3. PRELIMINARY PHASE

One initial need that IDA immediately identified was a set of software tools to be used by the project members. The makeup of this toolset was flexible, and though it was referred to as an APSE, it was so only in a loose sense, since there was no intention to erect a highly integrated environment early in the project. There was a demonstrable need, however, for a collection of usable Ada tools, since the existing environment had none at all.

A candidate collection of tools, one that met most of the perceived needs of the project, was located in the public domain repository on the SIMTEL20 node of the Defense Data Network. Many of these tools were developed under contract from the Naval Oceans System Center (NOSC) and are commonly referred to as the NOSC tools. These tools included a PrettyPrinter, Compilation Order tool, Data Dictionary, Source Instrumenter, Requirements Tracer, and a Statement Profiler. While some of these tools, principally those intended for use on PC-sized machines, were installed at DLA, the majority of the them, particularly those originally written for a DEC VAX computer, were not portable enough to install them easily on the Gould. No attempt was made to install them on the IBM. This effort to locate a toolset for the project is documented in [Carney88].

One other tool that IDA identified as vital to the DLA project was a generalized Forms Management System. As part of the preliminary phase, IDA prepared a specification for such a system [Hook87]. This specification was later implemented by the DLA team as part of the coding phase of the project. Finally, since the prototype project would involve database accesses, IDA also provided DLA with an Ada/SQL interface [Brykczynski87].

4. TRAINING PHASE

The project membership originally consisted of eleven DLA programmers; experienced, and familiar with the types of data processing important to

DLA. Their programming backgrounds included Pascal, C, COBOL, and both systems and applications programming. None had received any prior Ada training.

4.1 Structure

The course structure of the training phase entailed alternate weeks of classroom instruction and independent work. The DLA programmers were occupied full-time during this phase: courses lasted eight hours, for five-day weeks, for a period of twelve weeks. The classroom instruction was presented in two segments, each lasting six weeks. The first segment covered syntactic elements of the language. The makeup of the training included both traditional lectures and hands-on training. Much of the latter was achieved through the use automated self-teaching modules that covered all of the basic features of Ada syntax. The second training segment stressed items such as design and software engineering. To demonstrate software engineering and design, a case study approach was chosen. This study examined a large application that made significant use of tasking, and examined the relative merits of each design decision of the application. The application was carefully chosen for DLA, since it made use of a client-server model that depended heavily on remote procedure calls. This model fit well with the DLA goal of an open system architecture.

4.2 Results

In the first training segment, the DLA personnel embraced Ada as a language fairly quickly. The most common sticking point in the coursework was not purely linguistic, but was related to the differing backgrounds of the teachers and students. The teachers were naturally conversant with notions of compiler development and related issues, but were sometimes less fluent in some concepts of data processing; the students' backgrounds were largely the reverse. And for most misunderstandings that arose on both sides, it was revealing that Ada *per se* was not the cause.

The case study method had mixed success. One good result was that the students were totally immersed in a long and fairly complex example of Ada real-time code. It was, however, pedagogically demanding for both teachers and students. Further, the students were at this point more interested in discussing design from a top-down point of view, and wished to discuss general notions of design principles. The chosen course of study was more bottom-up, with notions of design flowing from specific application problems.

At the end of the twelve week training period, however, the result was a group of programmers strongly grounded in data processing for large systems and equally well grounded in Ada. Because of personnel reassignments the number of programmers had shrunk to six, but since then there has been no further decrease in the size of the Ada prototype team.

5. IMPLEMENTATION OF THE PROTOTYPE PROJECT

This phase lasted approximately eight months. The first task was to choose the nature of the implementation. The decision, made by the members of the prototype team, was to implement a systems project that could be put to immediate use by other persons at the DLA installation. This decision was grounded in one of the stated goals of the project, e.g., to demonstrate Ada's practical value for the system programming needs of DLA.

5.1 Nature of the Prototype Project

The DLA installation in Columbus uses a large modular Management Information System (MIS). The DLA MIS was supported by a database management system (UNIFY) and a UNIX mail system. The command system is called DLA Integrated Management Information System (DIMIS). Since virtually all personnel at that particular DLA command made use of DIMIS, this was an excellent candidate for the Ada project. The particular area of DIMIS that was selected for an Ada module was the one that dealt with training requirements of DLA staff members. A module was needed that would automate all processing of information concerning personnel training plans, the results of personnel training sessions, and the like. DLA already had paper forms and procedures that covered these areas: individual training plans were required for each staff member of DLA, and request/approval forms for specific training/education courses (DoD Form 1556) were already mandatory at DLA. The Ada Prototype Project would automate all processing of these forms. Choosing this module to implement for the Ada prototype had several benefits:

- It had a self-contained, standalone aspect.

- It was a "real" project: if the Ada team had not implemented it, DLA would have requested it in some other language from some other DLA ADP group.

- It was complex enough to contain several subcomponents: forms manager, database interface, a component to perform the processing of the data; and a three-tier interface, including remote procedure calls.

- It contained enough related items, particularly the forms manager and the remote procedure calling mechanism, that would clearly be excellent demonstrations of reuse.

5.2 Design of the Prototype

A significant effort was spent in capturing the requirements for the Training Module before the design of the Training Module took place. In fact, however, design and requirements capture interacted continually throughout this portion of the project. Among the factors that influenced the design, perhaps the most critical one was the tight compartmentalization of the various software systems of DLA. For instance, the general DLA personnel database was vital to the Ada project: personnel records would need to be accessed and updated. The Ada/SQL interface provided by IDA was of considerable use here. Understandably, however, the personnel database was not accessible to members of the Ada team. The only solution to the problem was to channel the database updates, in UNIFY format, to the system's database manager, who then did the actual update. While this added an unforeseen overhead, it also ensured that the external interface of the the Ada module be well designed.

Other issues were more related to Agency policy than to specifically software domains. For instance, each directorate of DLA was currently using a different paper format for the training requests; this prevented the prototype team from designing a machine replacement that was acceptable to all probable clients of the machine version. Another example was the problem, never solved, of selecting which machine tier would host the final prototype software. Since the prototype was developed on the Gould, this was the *de facto* host when the prototype was demonstrated.

Such issues as these were far from insurmountable, but in the aggregate, the number of such problems made the design process a strenuous one. None of the restrictions encountered prevented the team from achieving a sound final design for the system. The design underwent two reviews, during which all design decisions were scrutinized carefully by both TeleSoft and IDA.

5.3 Coding of the Prototype

Because the subcomponents of the Training Module were starting from different points of departure, coding of some portions began almost immediately. One major component of the project was the portion that made remote procedure calls. Most of this code was taken intact from the TeleSoft Case Study, so work on this code began immediately. It was notable that where modification was needed, the DLA programmers had no difficulty in altering sophisticated systems code. Another major component, the Forms Manager, was generally based on the specification prepared by IDA. Since the specification IDA provided was an example of Object-Oriented Design (OOD), this gave additional pedagogical value to its coding. With the exception of the Ada/SQL interface also provided by

IDA, all other code was written by the DLA programmers.

The difficulties encountered were similar to those that would be found in any comparable project: for instance, slight differences in behaviors of packages Sequential_IO and Direct_IO among different machines and compilers. Another problem, one that had been anticipated, was verifying the data sent between the remote procedure calls. Other than problems such as these, however, the implementation was straightforward. The completed project was an excellent exemplar of software reuse: it had incorporated major portions of the TeleSoft case study, including the remote procedure call package as well as an extensive package that handled dynamic string creation. The screen manager was robust enough to be distributed by the DLA prototype team to DoD programmers working on the WIS project. The project was completed on schedule, and the Personnel Training Management system was successfully demonstrated.

The recommendation of the prototype team was highly favorable to Ada. The only concern expressed was about the database interface. Presuming that such issues were satisfactorily resolved, the prototype team was highly enthusiastic about Ada's use for DLA systems programming.

6. OUTCOME OF THE ADA PROTOTYPE PROJECT

The recommendation of the prototype team has led to a continued presence of Ada at DLA. Although the team was temporarily disbanded, it has been reformed and given a new and more complex project in systems software. Another major success lies in the enthusiasm of the team members in embracing Ada. The team is able to solve major systems problems in Ada. They are beginning to convince many people in a highly traditional data processing environment that Ada's engineering principles are indeed viable. And they have entirely digested some Ada notions, reuse in particular, that are still only conversation items even in the mainstream Ada world.

One further indicator of the success of the project lies in the transportability of prototype's code. The Forms Manager that the DLA team implemented on a Gould has been successfully ported to run on IDA's Sun computers with only minor modification. It is noteworthy that this modification was needed only in a submodule written in C accessed through pragma Interface; none of the Ada code had to be modified in any way.

The new systems project is a measure of DLA management's confidence in the Ada team. The project, the Logistics Information Exchange (LINX), is an ambitious one. It is envisioned as a central conduit for virtually all information queries concerning price quotation for contracts throughout the DLA system. It reuses the forms management system and the remote procedure modules from the prototype. It also includes a module written in C that calls Ada modules, thus reversing the more common direction of Ada's pragma Interface to C. The LINX system is expected to interact with virtually all other data processing components throughout the Defense Logistics Agency. The LINX system has currently undergone both Preliminary Design Review and Critical Design Review, and is currently being implemented. The DLA programmers estimate that the final system will again reuse significant portions of the prototype project's code. The current guess is that 75% of the old code will be reused.

7. CONCLUSIONS

It should be mentioned at this point that the LSMP, the modernization program that engendered the Ada Prototype Project, is currently being reexamined. While the DLA will doubtless promote modernization of many of its systems, it is not clear at this time that the all-encompassing program of the LSMP will be fully implemented. But there can be little doubt that the Ada project has proven to be a highly successful component of the LSMP. And based on the decision to continue with the Ada team, regardless of the future direction of the LSMP, there can be little doubt that the use of Ada as a systems software language at DLA will continue to grow.

Ada has been resisted by many program directors for various reasons. Managers of large data processing installations have tended to show a bias toward COBOL, for example; or Ada is regarded as too difficult to be used by a widespread programming community. The Ada Prototype Project demonstrates the viability of Ada in a systems-oriented, non-embedded context. It also demonstrates that Ada is equally valid in a data processing context. And finally, it shows that a well-planned pedagogical effort can result in highly capable Ada practitioners in a relatively short time.

REFERENCES

Brykczynski, Bill et al. *Example Level 1 Ada/SQL System Software.* September 1987, IDA Memorandum Report M-361, Institute for Defense Analyses, Alexandria, VA. DTIC Accession number AD-A196 632.

Carney, David J. *Compiling and Porting the NOSC Tools for Use by the Defense Logistics Agency.* May, 1988, IDA Memorandum Report M-387, Institute for Defense Analyses, Alexandria, VA. DTIC Accession number AD-A199 007.

Hook, Audrey et al. *Defense Logistics Agency Data System Center Forms Management System (FMS).* September 1987, IDA Memorandum Report M-366, Institute for Defense Analyses, Alexandria, VA. DTIC Accession number AD-A196 633.

Management and Quality Aspects in the Realization of a Real Time Simulator in Ada

C. LAVEST   Software development Department
                   Project Manager

3IP
104, rue Castagnary
75015 PARIS
FRANCE
Tel : (33) 1 48 56 23 33   Fax: (33) 1 48 56 23 44

1. INTRODUCTION

1.1. Software Requirements

The project presented here was developed for AUTOMOBILES CITROEN. The aim of the project was to specify and to realize a Simulator of Manufacturing Machines Controlled by Industrial Programmable Controllers. This paper addresses only the realization part.

Manufacturing machines are usually divided into two parts:
- the controlling system: programmable controllers, control desks...
- the controlled system : engines, jacks, sensors...

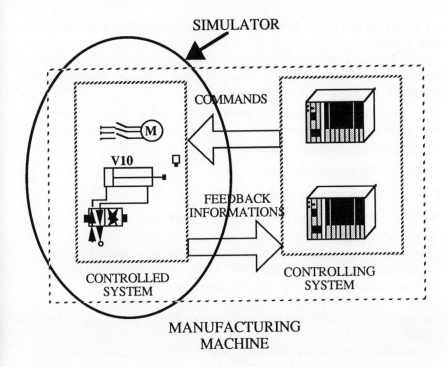

SIMULATOR

COMMANDS

V10

FEEDBACK
INFORMATIONS

CONTROLLED
SYSTEM

CONTROLLING
SYSTEM

MANUFACTURING
MACHINE

The aim of this software is to test the industrial programmable controllers (IPC) programs by simulating the behaviour of the controlled system in response to the controllers commands.

This system also automatically simulates failures from controlled system and analyses how the IPC program reacts to them.

The test of a machine is realized in three main steps:
- controlled system description: the user describes the operative equipment on a description station with WYSIWYG editors,
- simulation: the user specifies the tests and executes them on a simulation configuration,
- results exploitation: the user brings back the simulation results on the description station and processes them with a specific tool.

1.2. Technical Constraints

The main technical constraints we had were performance constraints:
- the system ability to simulate a machine including up to three IPC and 1200 logical I/O data (the number of logical I/O is proportional to the size of the machine),

- a cycle time of 150 ms, to be able to simulate fast mechanical movements (at least 600 ms),
- a maximum of three days effort to describe a regulary sized machine; this is possible only with very efficient description tools with high level duplication functions.

There was a hardware constraint on the description station. It has to be based on a widely used computer in order to use existing micro-computers of the factories.

The simulation configuration had to be DEC based.

Let's now detail these configurations.

1.3. Hardware Configuration

A personal computer, running MS-DOS, was chosen as a description station.

The second configuration (see scheme on annex) consists of :
- a personal computer, running MS-DOS, for the simulation user interface,
- a personal computer, running MS-DOS, for the control desks simulation,
- a VAX Station, running VMS, for code generation,
- a RTVAX, running VAXELN, as real time machine,
- an industrial local area network LAC2 from COMPEX for the logical I/O data capture,
- an industrial local area network LAC1 from COMPEX for console data capture,
- the real manufacturing machine programmable controllers.

The PC(s), VAX station and the RTVAX are connected via DECNet DOS,

2. CHOICE OF ADA

Various kinds of software are involved in this development:
- WYSIWYG editors,
- real time software,
- communication software..

We tried to find one language which could be used for all of them, to reduce the cost of formation, software developement and maintenance. Ada covers all these kinds of developments.

The hardware configuration shows that there are many environments to interface to. So we needed a language which makes it easy to exchange data, that is to say a language which allows data size and shape management and with a high portability. The Ada language features allowed us to manage data representation.

The user interface had to be user friendly because the users were supposed to be non computer specialists. So we decided to use a graphic windowing system. But this kind of software uses a lot of memory among the 640 KO allowed by MS-

DOS and leaves little room for the application program. At the time of the project, only the ALSYS Ada compilation system allowed us to get rid of this limit.

Last but not least, as nine people were involved in the development and as the realization time was short (less than two years), we needed a highly reliable language.

That is why we chose Ada as programming language.

We had to face three objections from our customer:
- the lack of Ada projects already developed in the company, and therefore the lack of people with an experience in Ada,
- the youth of the language, we were in 1987,
- the cost of Ada tools compared to other languages.

We convinced him that Ada was the best candidate in terms of reliability, portability and maintenability and then that using Ada was then the best way to secure their investment.

3. DEVELOPMENT CONTEXT

When we decided to use Ada as the programming language in this project, our company experience in Ada proceeded from the development of:
- standard software components,
- a Pascal Ada translator.

This experience helped us to define a method for the development of Ada projects. This method covers all the software life cycle. Three of this life cycle steps are mainly impacted by Ada:
- the preliminary design step, based on a standard design document using MASCOT formalism. The aim is to clearly define the interfaces of the different subsystems and modules designed,
- the detailled design step based on Ada PDL,
- the programming step, based on recommandations on Ada use.

We used this method on this project.

The development team was structured as follows:
- a project manager,
- a technical manager,
- three analysts,
- four programmers.

The team members experience in Ada at the beginning of the project resulted only from a one week course.

The development environment was composed of :

- 6 personal computers, running MS-DOS, with a 4 MO RAM, and connected to a VAX cluster via DECNet DOS, with the ALSYS Ada environment,
- a VAX STATION running VMS, with the DEC Ada environment and the VAXELN environment,
- a RTVAX running under VAXELN.

All the common units of the description part, the company standard software components and the ALSYS environment were located on a VAX hard disk.

The personal computers were used both as development and tests machines.

4. PROJECT PRESENTATION

4.1. Quantitative Aspects

As we can see from the software requirements, this software is divided in two main parts:
- a part on a personal computer, mainly composed of WYSIWYG editors and that we will name the description part,
- a part on the RTVAX which will be the real time part.

As they belong to different kinds of software, we will give separate data on each of them.

First of all , let's have a look at the size of the project in terms of lines with the table below:

		NSL	NASL	NI	NC	NP	AV NA
PC	App.	121 400	58 100	37 900	44 200	418	139
	Comm.	98 200	45 300	24 600	37 100	216	210
RTVAX	Appl.	44 800	21 200	14 500	12 500	80	266
TOTAL		264 400	124 600	77 000	93 800	714	

- The column "NSL" shows the number of lines of the source files, package interface and body. It doesn't take in account of the test programs,
- The column "NASL" shows the number of lines including Ada code (and declarations),
- The column "NI" shows the number of Ada instructions,
- The columm "NC" shows the number of comment lines,
- The columm "NP" shows the number of packages,
- The column "AVNA" shows the average number of Ada source lines per package.

In the PC part, we distinguished the units used only in one application from the one used in different applications we called "Common Units".

First of all it is important to notice that in our recommandations about Ada we recommand a size of 200 lines for packages. It explains that 200 is the average value of the average number of lines. We could say that, at least, the programmers followed our recommandations! But it shows principally that Ada has a big impact on software modularity

The common units represent about 45 % of the whole software on the PC. So Ada is of a great help as regards software reuse too.

Most of the common units are generic units. We have distinguished two kinds of reused components:

Company standard software components:
- a set management component with 2 instantiations,
- a FIFO management component with 5 instantiations,
- 2 kinds of lists storage components with a total of 27 instantiations,
- 4 kinds of lists management components with a total of 107 instantiations.

Some generic components, developed for the project needs:
- a screen redraw management component : 7 instantiations,
- a graphic on-line help component: 9 instantiations,
- 6 different dialog box components: 91 instantiations.

The Ada generic features improve modularity and software reuse tremendously.

4.2. Management Aspects

Apart from the requirements step which is programming language independent, we have noticed changes in the ratios between the different life cycle steps.

The table below shows the predicted ratios and what did really occur. We still distinguish the description part from the real time part.

	Description part			Real time part		
	predict.	realised	ratios	predict.	realised	ratios
Prel. Design	15 %	16 %	14 %	11 %	9 %	8 %
Detailled Design	20 %	20 %	17 %	22 %	22 %	19 %
Coding	30 %	41 %	36 %	34 %	47 %	41 %
Tests	20 %	17 %	15 %	22 %	21 %	18 %
Integration	15 %	21 %	18 %	11 %	16 %	14 %
TOTAL	100 %	115 %	100 %	100 %	115 %	100 %

- The "predicted" column shows estimations of effort for each step relative to the estimated total effort at the beginning of the realization part,
- The "realised" column shows the ratio between the actual effort for each step and the estimated total effort,
- The "ratios" column shows the ratios between actual effort for each step for a total of 100 %.

Remarks:

This data does not include:
- project management
- meetings
- Reference Manual and User's Guide composition.

Predictions were based mainly on Pascal experience.

We must distinguish between the main trends due to Ada and what comes from the project particularities.

The three main points are:
- The difference between estimated and actual data for coding steps is due, for one part, to an overall under estimation of the technical difficulties of the project. This under estimation was hidden during design steps but existed already and was cumulated during the coding step,
- The other reason is the time consumed by the compilation system, because developement machines were not powerfull enough,
- During the integration step, the power problem of development machines appeared worse than during coding and test steps. (the time consumed by compilation system is about 50 % of the integration time). We also had problems with IPC programs and simulation components which are not part of the software. In spite all of that, the integration ratios are quite correct. That is a clear benefit of Ada.

Our basic ratios are now:

Preliminary Design	Detailled Design	Coding	Tests	Integration
15 %	25 %	30 %	20 %	10 %

But of course they have to be adaped to each project particularities:
- kind of software
- quality constraints.

Even if the preliminary design step keeps to the same size, it becomes a fundamental step in an Ada developement. The design choices made by the analysts during this step have a big impact on the other steps of the life cycle: usage of private types, generic components, exception management may increase the effort for detailled design and coding steps. But it will also improve the quality of the software and will have a good impact on test, integration and maintenance steps.

That is why we have settled design reviews with experienced people and that we are doing the same on new projects.

Team training is fundamental too. Ada seems easy to learn but it takes a lot of time for new programmers to develop programs using the Ada features in the best way. This is the aim of our code reviews.

We saw on chapter 4.1. the importance of standard software components in the project. But people have to be trained to use these components. They need:
- good documentation
- some examples
- technical support.

That is the price to pay for the benefit of software components.

Software components ensure that the same problems will lead to the same solutions. So low level parts of the software look the same. It makes it easier for programmers to switch to different tasks (apart from very specific ones).

The last aspect of management to be taken in account is the development configuration. Ada needs:
- a powerfull CPU
- a large amount of hard disk space.

For example, a personal computer development configuration for Ada must be:
- 80386 based
- 80 Mo hard disk equiped or connected via a network to a host computer.

The next table shows the size of the libraries (only ADALIB.ADL) on the description part:

Company standard software components	Common units	Applications
7.1 Mo	30 Mo	31 Mo

It does not include the ALSYS environment (about 8 Mo), and some working librairies (2 Mo each).

4.3. Quality Aspects

We noticed a good impact of the language and of the design choices on most of factors which define software quality.

Ada is a high level language. With Ada, it is possible to define functions and objects close to those which appeared during the requirements step. For example :
- the different kinds of failures which may occur during the simulation have been implemented with an enumerated type
- every real re-initiating procedure after failure has it corresponding real time procedure.

It increases software traceability.

During the design step we used Ada as Programming Description Language (P.D.L.). It makes it very easy, to code a unit from its design. Ada improves software consistency too.

The data given in chapter 4.1 show that the Ada language features, and mainly generic units, increase software modularity and software reuse.

During the simulation step, as we explained in chapter 1.3., a personal computer runs the user interface and the RTVAX runs the simulation. So, during their execution, these applications have to exchange informations.

During the tests, result files are generated. At the end they have to be put back on a PC to be processed. These files have a complex structure based on lists of structured records.

The system programming features of Ada, such as representation clauses and enumeration clauses, allowed these data to be exchanged without any intermediate ASCII interface. Ada improves interoperability.

Project managers often worry about Ada code efficency. They always compare it to the C language efficiency. At the beginning of the project development, as the real time performance constraints were very critical, we decided to make a prototype. The same function, a basic machine simulation, was implemented using C and Ada and then executed under the same environment. The results were as follows:

C prototype	Ada prototype without optimization	Ada prototype with optimization
73.5 ms	130 ms	75 ms

The aim of this example is not to prove that Ada is always as efficient as other languages like C but that it can keep a good software efficiency level without having a bad impact on other software quality factors.

This software has been in use for 6 months since its delivery. Some problem reports have been issued. The next table shows the different kinds of problems which occured and the average time to correct them:

	Nb. of SPR.	Ratios	Av. correct time
Spec. mismatch	9	17 %	1h 20mn
error with excep.	19	36 %	1h 48mn
system error	8	15 %	1h 52mn
incorrect results	17	32 %	2h 14mn
TOTAL	53		

Four kinds of SPR(s) have been identified :
- specification mismatch : the sofware functions are not consistent with the specifications,
- error with exception : the execution of software is terminated with an exception trace back,
- System error : the execution of the software is terminated with a system error,
- incorrect results : the results produced by the software are erroneous but there is no interruption in execution.

The average time to correct a problem report is the time needed to locate the error, to define the modifications and to code them. It does not include compilation, bind and tests.

Several positive points have to be noted :
- the problem reports rate is quite low regarding on software size,

- the average time to locate and correct errors is very low,
- the exception management increases software reliability by preventing software from producing incorrect results without signal,
- the difference between the average time to correct an error when an exception is raised and when the system traps or incorrect results are produced outlines how exception management improves software maintenalibity too.

5. CONCLUSION

We have seen in the previous chapters all the things Ada can bring to software development:
- modularity,
- software components reuse,
- reliability,
- maintainability.

We have seen that an Ada project needs, to be cost-effective:
- good team member training,
- standard software components,
- design reviews,
- code reviews,
- the right sizing of the development environment.

Experienced people having already developed projects using Ada are key people to perform code and design reviews.

But the development of standard software components and team training cannot be assigned to a single project because it would dramatically increase its cost.

Generally, we think that Ada cannot be cost-effective on a single project and that the success and benefits of using Ada as programming language on a project depend on the Ada policy involving the whole department and/or company.

This Ada policy has to deal with:
- people training, as well for coding as for design,
- standard software components support,
- continuous standard software components definition and realization activity, from already developed packages and from projects needs.

It breaks the classical organization, where all the projects are independant, and leads people to exchange experiences as often as needed.

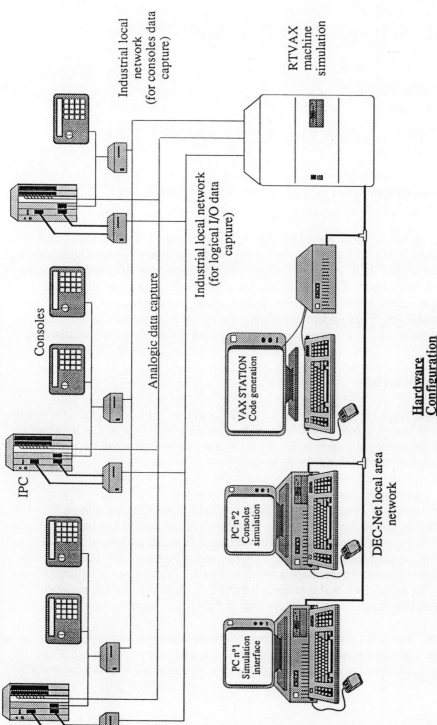

Industrial local network (for consoles data capture)

RTVAX machine simulation

Industrial local network (for logical I/O data capture)

Consoles

Analogic data capture

IPC

VAX STATION Code generation

PC n°2 Consoles simulation

PC n°1 Simulation interface

DEC-Net local area network

Hardware Configuration

An Ada Software Port Case Study

Tana P. Reagan
Gary J. Vecellio
William Battle, Annette M. Englehart, Ricardo H. Paris,
Norman Stewart

The MITRE Corporation, 7525 Colshire Drive, McLean, Virginia

Abstract. An Ada Software port of the U.S. Army's Maneuver Control System (MCS) has been performed. The MCS port consisted of moving the MCS Ada software, approximately 40,000 lines of code (LOC), from its development environment, an HP-based system, to a DEC-based environment. The focus of this port was to explore the portability of Ada software and lessons learned. This paper describes how the port was conducted, what was involved and acheived and presents the lessons learned. It is shown that the use of Ada, software standards and software engineering contributed to the effectiveness of this port.

1. INTRODUCTION

Software portability is defined as the capability of a program or component to be used, possibly with modifications, in host or target environments other than the one for which it was originally developed (Ausnit et al., 1985). As software costs continue to rise, considerable attention is being given to portability.

For a software program to be considered portable, it must be able to operate in a different environment without losing any of its original functionality and without incorporating additional functionality. Modifications to accommodate this may be minor so that the basic design and structure of the software module remain unchanged. For some modules, such as peripheral interface modules, however, differences between the environments may be so drastic that redesign is required. For any software port, modifications and changes to the software are probable due to variations in operating systems, compilers, input/output (I/O) devices, and system libraries and utilities available on each system.

Techniques have been identified to improve portability such as layering software to isolate host dependencies, and employing software standards and software engineering principles. In addition, the concept of language standardization and validation as given by the Ada language has been formulated to promote among other qualities, software portability. The focus of the port described here was to explore how Ada promotes portability and how a port should be conducted.

The software that was ported in this experiment was the Manuver Control System (MCS) developed by the Army. MCS is a message processing system that supports graphical and textual message composition and editing. MCS also supports data base management of message data through a menu- and prompt-driven system-operator interface, and it provides message reception, transmission, and relay functionality. The MCS software was chosen because its size is manageable, yet not trivial (i.e., approximately 40,000 Ada lines of code (LOC)); and it provides a significant porting challenge in that the software stresses data base, graphics, and communications functionality.

The target system for the port, a DEC Micro VAX II, provided the functionality necessary for MCS, yet the hardware architecture, the Ada compiler, and the COTS products are different from those of the MCS host system, an HP 330. These differences are summarized in Table 1.

Table 1
HP and VAX Environments

Host system Interfaces:	HP	VAX
Host Machine: Operating System: System services: Ada Compiler: Memory Size:	HP 330 HP-UX (Unix) Unix OS Services Irvine Ada Compiler 3mb + Virtual Mem	=> DEC micro VAX II => VMS => DEC OS services => DEC Ada Compiler => 9mb + Virtual Mem
Special Services		
DBMS: Graphics Interface: Windowing Interface: Graphics Device: Communications:	Informix RDBMS Starbase/Fast Alpha HP Windows Graphover PCIU LAN (Unix)	=> ORACLE RDBMS => VAX GKS => VAX GKS => VT 290 => PCIU => LAN (EXCELAN)

The success of the port was defined as the capability of providing the full MCS functionality on the target system. However, when this effort was initiated, the communications hardware (i.e., Programmable Communications Interface Unit (PCIU)) was not available on the target system. Consequently, message transmission was not performed as part of this exercise.

As part of the preparation for this activity, an early estimate of effort to complete the port was 16 staff-months. The actual effort consisted of 18 staff-months.

2.   MCS ARCHITECTURE

Statically, MCS consists of five separate executables (i.e., separately linked object code) (see Figure 1). The large box, labeled main MCS program, is one executable. This executable is where almost all the MCS functionality is contained. Below the main MCS program is a box labeled interprocess communication (IPC) and process management (PM) library. This box contains the IPC and PM executable library used by the main MCS program and the lower four boxes. Finally, below the IPC and PM library are four separate executables. These executables are referred to as driver programs. Each of these driver programs interfaces directly to either a COTS product or the PCIU. They handle requests from the main MCS program to access either the COTS products or the PCIU.

A requirement of the MCS application was that it must handle data base queries, transmit/receive messages, and perform graphics input/output (I/O) functions concurrently. Hence, asynchronous access is desired so that any activity performed via an external interface (i.e., DBMS or graphics COTS, or RS232 port) is nonblocking with respect to the application. This is difficult to ensure since most COTS products do not provide control over whether they are blocking or nonblocking.

The Ada language provides the task facility to express concurrent algorithms. However, depending on the Ada implementation, the capability to specify the access to the external interfaces (i.e., blocking or nonblocking) may be limited in the language. By performing I/O requests or interfacing with external devices, any task within the Ada program may place the entire program in a wait state until the outstanding request is satisfied. Therefore, in order to achieve concurrency in an application where there are potential blocking interfaces, subprocesses must be used for each blocking interface (i.e., COTS, system service, or device).

The MCS design used such an approach in that each subprocess is dedicated to an external interface. Therefore, the main MCS process does not block while the subprocess accesses the COTS or device interface. Only one Ada task blocks in the main process as the subprocess, in turn, blocks on the external interface. This design requires coordination between the Ada task scheduler and the system process scheduler. The IPC and PM library is used to achieve this coordination and is dependent on the compiler vendor's implementation.

Figure 1
Detailed MCS Architecture

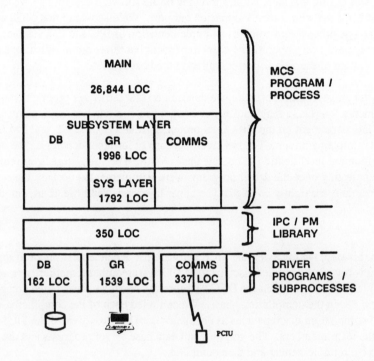

3.   PORTING APPROACH

The approach we took in porting MCS essentially divides into three major steps:

(1)   Determining the feasibility of a port. This step determines whether the port should be conducted by examining the complexity of the software, differences in machine environments, number of staff involved, and the amount of time to complete the port.

(2)   Conducting the port. This step identifies how to schedule the port, prepare the system and software, and document modifications made to the software in porting.

(3)   Testing the ported software.

STEP 1

It was during this step, while surveying of the software design, that we uncovered an aspect of MCS that significantly impacted our port. We discovered that MCS consists of more than one process and contains an implementation of IPC and PM services. This library is not only very operating system dependent but relies on modifications made to the runtime system of the Ada Irvine compiler on the host system.

After surveying the software, we determined that the driver programs required reimplementation (i.e., a major software change) because one was implemented in C and all were highly dependent on the HP COTS products. Likewise, the IPC and PM library required reimplementation. The sys layer, because of its dependencies on the operating system, required modification to operate under VMS. The subsystem layer required significant testing once the driver programs were reimplemented because the subsystem and driver programs are tightly coupled. The upper layer required little, if any, modification.

STEP 2

In this step, we reviewed the MCS software for dependencies on the Irvine compiler. The review revealed compiler discrepancies which were either temporarily removed, to be resolved later, or reworked in the DEC Ada format. Next, we determined compilation order, and began the compilation phase. We compiled each of the compilation units and resolved compilation discrepancies as encountered. Then, we divided the MCS software among the team members. The graphics and data base driver programs and the IPC and PM library were reimplemented and then compiled.

STEP 3

In testing the port, we first performed unit testing on each unit we modified in Step 2. Then, unlike unit testing, which directly tested our modifications, subsystem testing tested the software that relied on these modifications. Subsystem testing identified dependencies in the subsystem software or side effects no longer present in the reimplemented driver programs. Since subsystem testing tested the software that relied on the reimplemented driver programs, no other iterative testing was necessary. Hence, we moved to system testing. In our system level testing, we used the original developer's program performance tests (Ford, 1987). We chose a subset of these tests and used those tests to validate the port.

4. RESULTS

4.1 Compilation

Overall, the compilation phase was straightforward. The majority of the compilation discrepancies were due to the use of implementation-dependent language features as defined in the Ada Language Reference Manual (MIL-STD-1815A) (DOD, 1983).

Other compilation errors were encountered. For example, we discovered several instances where the DEC Ada compiler identified Ada language errors that the Irvine compiler had missed. This illustrates that the Ada Compiler Validation Capability (ACVC) tests are not exhaustive; a compiler can be validated and still incorrectly implement aspects of the Ada language. However, these discrepancies were few given the overall size of MCS. The entire compilation phase required only 17 staff-weeks, which included the time required to become familiar with MCS.

4.2 Data Base Subsystem

The MCS data base subsystem controls all data base activity within MCS. Once a request reaches the subsystem, it is translated into a Structured Query Language (SQL) statement processable by the COTS DBMS. The subsystem is structured so that the composition of the SQL statement is performed entirely within one Ada package, the Data Base Management (DBM) Package, which then forwards the SQL statement to the data base driver program. Once information pertaining to this request is returned by the data base driver program, it is received and processed by the DBM Package.

The data base driver program's main purpose is to interact with the COTS DBMS (i.e., INFORMIX on the HP, ORACLE on the VAX), instructing it to parse and execute the SQL statement. In addition, it fetches the data items requested by the SQL statement into their corresponding string or integer buffers. The data base driver program interacts with the DBMS through the DBMS language binding. On the HP, the C language binding to INFORMIX was used; therefore, on the HP the data base driver program was written in C.

In reviewing the subsystem, we identified two areas that were potentially DBMS-vendor dependent: the composition of SQL statements in the data base subsystem, and the data base driver program. The SQL statements were considered potentially DBMS-vendor dependent because of deficiencies in the SQL standard (American National Standards Institute: Data Base Language SQL, Document ANSI x3.135-1986). Specifically, it fails to support implementation-defined variations and extensions that should be defined as part of the standard. As a result, no two "standard" SQL implementations (e.g., INFORMIX SQL, ORACLE SQL) are identical. Similarly, the data base driver program was considered

DBMS-vendor dependent because of its host language ("C") embedded data base commands (e.g., OPEN, EXECUTE).

Initially, we reviewed the INFORMIX and ORACLE documents and compared the formats of SQL statements. The SQL statements used by MCS were identified and tested interactively using ORACLE. As a result, we found only a small number of variations between the two SQL implementations. Therefore, the SQL implementation concern was not as critical as we originally believed. The port effort was decreased because of the SQL standardization. Next, we examined the data base driver program in terms of its functional flow and embedded commands. We determined that the data base driver program would have to be modified since the embedded ORACLE commands did not correspond exactly to those of INFORMIX. Since modification was necessary, we chose to reimplement the data base driver program in Ada using the ORACLE Ada language binding.

4.3   Graphics and Text Handling Subsystem

The graphics subsystem implements textual and graphics requirements of MCS, including operator input. On the HP, graphics and text handling were accomplished through "C" interfaces to the HP COTS products. These were replaced by DEC's implementation of GKS.

After analyzing the MCS design, we determined that the interface between the graphics subsystem and the main application could be retained and most, if not all, of the code modifications could be isolated to the graphics driver program. Further examination of the driver program revealed that references to the HP COTS support products mapped well into GKS. However, we found that GKS does not offer the same level of sophisticated or specialized text-handling functions as does the combination of HP COTS products which were used by MCS on the HP. For example, two of those COTS products were specifically for text handling, whereas GKS does not directly support many text handling specific functions such as inverse text. To achieve these capabilities with GKS, we had to build up the functionality from more primitive services. For example, to achieve inverse text, the screen coordinates of the proposed text string location were obtained, the appropriate color was written to that rectangle, and finally the text string was inserted. The price of GKS standardization is a comparatively primitive level of functionality, although ultimately adequate for MCS needs. This is not to say the functionality could not be augmented with other COTS products, although their integration with GKS could add complexity.

4.4   Process Management and Interprocess Communication Subsystem

In porting the MCS software architecture from the HP to the VAX, the IPC and PM services originally used by MCS were not available. Therefore, we developed a library to emulate the semantic interface of the services on the HP, while mapping the functionality to equivalent services under VMS. This approach minimized the changes required in the MCS software, but it also required additional software to achieve the equivalent level of functionality.

Interprocess communications. The MCS processes communicate through an IPC link, which on the HP is called a pipe. Standard Unix file I/O services (e.g., read and write calls) are used when communicating via a pipe and the operating system resolves the necessary buffering and synchronization.

The VMS mailbox facility was selected as the IPC service for MCS under VMS. It is a virtual device that supports message transfer between processes. As used in MCS, a mailbox transfer occurs by using the DEC Ada interface to the VMS QIOW service. The mailbox provides capabilities similar to the Unix pipe service. The mailbox also provides the flexibility to support a unique requirement of the graphics interface. The Immediate I/O option of the QIOW service allows the process to examine the mailbox to determine if data is available, and it also returns data if it is present.

Process coordination. For the MCS application to perform, for example, a data base query or display graphical text, several steps are required: (1) An Ada task in the main process must send a request, via IPC, to the respective driver program, and the task must block while the request is performed; (2) the driver program must perform the necessary function through the external interface (e.g., COTS DBMS) and notify the main process of completion; and (3) the main process, in turn, must activate the correct Ada task to complete the subsequent processing required by the request.

The goal here, is to achieve concurrent processing of the various requests throughout the MCS system. As such, there are two requirements in the above scenario that are significant issues for porting:

- A mechanism is necessary to suspend an Ada task, not the process containing the task, pending the completion of a system service. This mechanism involves a complex interaction between the compiler vendor's run-time and the host operating system and is currently outside the scope of the language definition.

- A mechanism must exist to alert asynchronously a system process of a condition such as the completion of a request. This capability is accessible from the Ada language, but it is host dependent.

Satisfying these requirements on the HP entailed several complex modifications. First, the Ada run-time support system was modified by the compiler vendor to couple Unix

IPC services with Ada tasking services. This provides the capability to suspend an Ada task that sends a request, via IPC, to a driver program. Secondly, a common pipe and system interrupts (i.e., Unix signals) are used to synchronize the main process and the driver programs. The common pipe is accessible by every process in the MCS application. Therefore, once a driver program completes a request, it places identification data in the common pipe and sends an interrupt signal to the main process. The main process, in turn, identifies the driver program from the data in the common pipe and schedules the appropriate Ada task to complete processing of the request.

Building blocks exist on the VAX computer environment to satisfy the process coordination requirements stated above. First, there is an Ada package named TASKING_SERVICES that satisfies the initial requirement. Through this package, Ada tasks can access VMS system services synchronously. For example, our approach uses this package to access VMS mailboxes (i.e., IPC links). As an Ada task accesses an IPC link on the VAX only the Ada task is suspended while the MCS main process continues executing.

In satisfying the requirement for asynchronous signaling on the VAX, system-level interrupts were not necessary. Instead, this requirement was satisfied by implementing a Request/Response protocol over the same IPC link. Therefore, once a task sends a request to a driver program, the Ada task immediately waits (i.e., the task suspends) for the response from the IPC link. The TASKING_SERVICES package unblocks the Ada task when the driver program sends the response.

The process coordination issue has an important implication for porting as well as for the Ada language. Utilities for software architectures that require concurrent processing of external interfaces (e.g., COTS software and hardware devices) cannot be represented using the facilities provided by Ada alone. As discussed in this section, such provisioning can involve a complex interaction between the compiler vendors runtime and the host operating system. For both the DEC and the Irvine compilers, host dependent services are required. However, in the case of DEC, it provides a mechanism to simplify the access to these services. This increases the software portability because most of the complex services (e.g., interrupts) are handled by the run-time system instead of the application software.

5.   LESSONS LEARNED

The objective of this section is to abstract lessons learned from the porting exercise: the high-level results pertaining to conducting future ports and to writing more portable software. This section presents the lessons learned at four levels: general, compilation, operating system, and COTS specific.

5.1   General Lessons Learned

Layering beneficial. Although the following has been the central theme of this document, it is included here for completeness. It is sufficient to simply state that a layered design where host dependencies are concentrated at the lowest levels will significantly enhance porting feasibility and ease the porting effort. A design that incorporates software engineering principles such as abstraction, modularity, and effective exception handling will ease the porting effort because the software will be far more readable, understandable, and modifiable.

Error analysis time consuming. We concluded that time involved in identifying the cause of an encountered problem (e.g., attributable to some type of host dependency) was generally far greater than the time involved in resolving it once it was identified. This implies that tools related to debugging and understanding software packaging and data flow are of significant importance to a port where programmers are expected to quickly become familiar with large amounts of software.

COTS integration an issue. Although we only encountered one problem that dealt with COTS integration, it took approximately one staff-week to resolve, and the vendor could not offer any assistance. Resolution of this problem required a very detailed knowledge of the interaction of the operating system and the COTS products.

Establishing the execution environment required trial and error. Establishing the appropriate environment (e.g., disk quota, process limit) for the ported application occurred through trial and error because no documentation was available that described the original environment. This is an area of system development that is often overlooked and almost never documented. Yet numerous hours were spent chasing problems in the code that later were attributed to an environment variable inadequately specified.

Subsystem testing preparation very involved. Subsystem testing was far more involved than just identifying what needed to be tested and where. Unlike system testing, there were no Program Performance Tests. Once we identified the interface that was to be tested, we had to develop an understanding of the meaning of the parameters of the interface. The documentation at this level is usually very minimal, generally explaining just the general functionality. For example, several of our tests failed initially because we were not aware that certain subprograms were required to initialize data objects. Designing the software so that subsystems can be tested once ported is an area of software engineering that warrants further study.

Minimal knowledge of MCS functionality necessary. Although, as previously stated, the porting team was expected to quickly become familiar with a large amount of documentation, we successfully ported the MCS system without having a prior knowledge of the MCS functionality and without developing an intimate knowledge of the MCS functionality while porting. We were able to concentrate our efforts at the software level, abstracting the details of MCS functionality out of the exercise. Instead of exploring the functionality of MCS ourselves, testing the functionality of MCS relied on the use of the developers' Program Performance Test. This places significance on the developers' test plan.

5.2   Lessons Learned and Ada Compilation

Compilation was a lower order issue. We found compilation relatively straightforward. It was not as time consuming as the other areas of the port, and the compilation errors encountered were fairly easy to understand and correct. This can be attributed to Ada validation and standardization.

Real-time Ada services immature. As was discussed previously, MCS requires near-real-time performance whereby a user can continue to obtain keyboard response while the application is processing incoming messages. To date, achievement of such performance is not straightforward due to the required interaction between the compiler run-time system and the operating system. The Irvine compiler on the HP required explicit modification in order for MCS to provide this capability. Fortunately for the porting effort, the DEC compiler provided the necessary services for this capability. Compiler vendors are not required at this time to provide these services for validation. Furthermore, although DEC and eventually Irvine did provide the necessary capabilities, they were not achieved entirely in Ada but required several operating system services (i.e., subprocesses and mailboxes or pipes). Ultimately, this will have to be addressed by the Ada community and a standard model for achieving real-time performance accepted. Until then, however, this will continue to be a porting and implementation issue handled best by isolating these aspects of the design, if possible, and providing an explanation of the underlying model used.

5.3   Lessons Learned and Operating Systems

Operating system dependencies easily overlooked at implementation. Although MCS possesses a layer of software where operating system dependencies were to be localized, several operating system dependencies were found throughout the application. Unlike COTS dependencies, the operating system dependencies were not well isolated. This can be attributed to the fact that operating system dependencies are usually very subtle and often go undetected at design and implementation. Of course, once the software is ported to a new operating system, an exception or some indication of a problem will occur and the dependency will be identified. Hence, tools and guidelines to enhance portability are especially important to operating system dependencies.

5.4   Lessons Learned and COTS Products

SQL standardization eased porting effort. Certainly it is acknowledged that the use of a standard will improve portability (Nissan and Wallace, 1984). The use of Ada (MIL-STD-1815A, 1983) is an example. However, the effectiveness of the SQL standard is currently under debate. The SQL standard (American National Standards Institute: Data Base Language SQL, Document ANSI x3.135-1986) employed by both INFORMIX and ORACLE minimized the porting effort. For example, the MCS application builds the appropriate SQL command at run-time. If the SQL commands used by the two data base products had been different, a significant amount of software would have required modification. As a result of the standard, only two small changes were made to the SQL statements, and the need for these changes was identified by consulting the documentation of each data base product.

6.   CONCLUSIONS

The objectives of the MCS porting task were met. We found that portable Ada software can be developed. Data has been collected which can be used in future ports. We have shown that the procedures we defined are valid. Finally, we have completed an actual port exercise and have identified aspects of MCS that were host dependent and suggested alternatives that would minimize these dependencies.

7.   REFERENCES

American National Standards Institute (1986).
   ANSI: For Information Systems - Database Language - SQL, ANSI x3.135-1986, NY, 1986.

Ausnit et al. (1985).
   Ada Reusability Guidelines, Waltham, MA: Softech, Inc., 1985.

Booch, G., (1983).
   Software Engineering With Ada, Reading, MA: Benjamin/Cummings Publishing Company, 1983.

Date, C. J., (1987).
   A Guide to the SQL Standard, Reading, MA: Addison-Wesley Publishing Co., 1987.

Ford Aerospace and Communications Corporation, (1987).
Computer Program Product Specification for the Tactical Computer Processor (TCP) Maneuver Control Program (MCP) for Segment 10 of the Maneuver Control System (MCS), Type C5, Colorado Springs, CO, 1987.

Ford Aerospace and Communications Corporation, (1987).
Computer Program Product Specification for the Tactical Computer Processor (TCP) Maneuver Control Program (MCP) for Segment 10 of the Maneuver Control System (MCS), Colorado Springs, CO, 1987.

Ford Aerospace and Communications Corporation, (1985).
Computer Program Test Procedure for Segment 10 of the Maneuver Control System Program Performance Test Volume II, Ft. Monmouth, NJ, 1985.

International Standards Organization, (1984).
Computer Graphics-Graphics Kernel System (GKS), February 1984.

International Standards Organization, (1984).
OSI/Basic Reference Model, 1984.

Melton, J., (1989).
ISO-ANSI (working draft) Database Language SQL2 and SQL3, ANSI X3H2-89-110, February 1989.

Nissen, J. et al., (1984).
Portability and Style in Ada, Cambridge, England: Commission of the European Communities Cambridge University Press, 1984.

U.S. Department of Defense, (1989).
Ada 9X Project Plan, 1989.

U.S. Department of Defense, (1983).
Reference Manual for the Ada Programming Language, ANSI/MIL-STD-1815A-1983, 1983.

LIST OF AUTHORS

L.A. Ambrose

J.A. Anderson

P. Andribet

C.J. Antonelli

J. Arnol

W. Battle

H. Bonnaud

O.P. Brereton

A.L. Brintzenhoff

D.J. Carney

F. Cassinari

S.R. Chandler

K.J. Cogan

A. Crespo

C. Dahlke

H. Doscher

A.G. Duncan

A.M. Englehart

A.B. Gargaro

M. Gauthier

R. Di Giovanni

S.J. Goldsack

A.J. van de Goor

I. Häggström

A.T. Jazaa

D. Johnston

M.A. Juan

J. van Katwijk

M. Lai

C. Lavest

A. M. Levy

J-M. Lippens

A. Di Maio

H.A. Neumann

K. Nielsen

I. Ögren

R.H. Paris

R.H. Pierce

T.P. Reagan

K.L. Rogers

J-P. Rousselot

D. Schefström

K. Shumate

O. Sørensen

M.C. Springman

N. Stewart

G.J. Vecellio

L. Vedani

R. Vivo

R.A. Volz

J.T. Webb

A.J. Wellings

B.A. Wichmann

LIST OF REFEREES

A. Alvarez

J. Avramopoulos (and colleagues)

J. Bamberger

J.G.P. Barnes

R. de Benito

S. Björnsson

J. Bundgaard

A. Burns

F. Clarke

P. Connolly

G. Green

S. Heilbrunner

R.S. Hurst

T. Käer

R. Klebe

H-J. Kugler

F. Long

M. Nagl (and colleagues)

D. O'Neill

A. Pèrez-Riesco

J.A. de la Puente

I.C. Pyle

K. Ripken

J-P. Rosen

O. Roubine

R. Van Scoy

K. De Vlaminck

P.J.L. Wallis

I.C. Wand

A.J. Wellings

G. Winterstein (and colleagues)